PRAISE FOR *THE SOUL OF TH...*

"This memoir is an exceptional document by an extraordinary person. Éva Fahidi does an excellent job depicting the life of upper middle-class Jews from outside Budapest prior to the Holocaust, a subject that – tragically – could never be covered sufficiently. With its poignant reflections on questions of universal relevance, *The Soul of Things* has the potential to be included in the essential canon of Holocaust-related literature."

– Ferenc Laczó, Maastricht University

"The Holocaust is the demarcation line in Éva Fahidi's long, remarkably robust life. But by allowing us to connect experiences from the good and bad parts of her past, she also reaches forward to the future. Fahidi is speaking here to a new generation. Her book is, perhaps, the strongest endorsement for physical education, learning languages, and gaining empathy by embracing the past."

– Alice Freifeld, University of Florida

"Éva Fahidi was the only member of her large family to survive Auschwitz and slave labour in Germany. Her memoir is not only about her survival as a girl of eighteen, but it is also an intimate portrait of a provincial bourgeois Jewish family's life in interwar Hungary, recounted with unflinching honesty and self-reflection. Fahidi's personal story at the same time closely reflects the tragic history of Hungary in the twentieth century."

– Louise O. Vasvári, Stony Brook University

"A narrative so compelling and engrossing it made me want to hear what Éva Fahidi had to say about her life, her experiences, and her understanding of her own history. A female version of Primo Levi, Fahidi has produced a memoir that is beautifully written and informative in ways that go beyond a scholarly article or textbook."

– Hilary Earl, Nipissing University

the
soul
of
things

memoir of a
youth
interrupted

Éva Fahidi

Edited by Judith Szapor
Translated by Susan Sullivan

UNIVERSITY OF TORONTO PRESS
Toronto Buffalo London

Toronto Buffalo London
utorontopress.com
Printed in the U.S.A.

ISBN 978-1-4875-0744-2 (cloth)   ISBN 978-1-4875-3626-8 (EPUB)
ISBN 978-1-4875-2512-5 (paper)   ISBN 978-1-4875-3625-1 (PDF)

Library and Archives Canada Cataloguing in Publication

Title: The soul of things : memoir of a youth interrupted / Éva Fahidi;
    edited by Judith Szapor ; translated by Susan Sullivan.
Other titles: Anima rerum. English
Names: Fahidi, Éva, author. | Szapor, Judith, editor. | Sullivan, Susan
    (Translator), translator.
Description: Translation of: Anima rerum.
Identifiers: Canadiana (print) 20200295829 | Canadiana (ebook) 20200295837 |
    ISBN 9781487507442 (cloth) | ISBN 9781487525125 (paper) | ISBN
    9781487536268 (EPUB) | ISBN 9781487536251 (PDF)
Subjects: LCSH: Fahidi, Éva. | LCSH: Jews, Hungarian – Biography. |
    LCSH: Jews – Hungary – Biography. | LCSH: Holocaust, Jewish
    (1939–1945) – Personal narratives. | LCSH: Birkenau (Concentration
    camp) | LCSH: Allendorf (Concentration camp) | LCGFT:
    Autobiographies. | LCGFT: Personal narratives.
Classification: LCC DS135.H93 F3413 2020 | DDC 940.53/18092 – dc23

This book has been published with the help of a grant from the Federation
for the Humanities and Social Sciences, through the Awards to Scholarly
Publications Program, using funds provided by the Social Sciences and
Humanities Research Council of Canada.

University of Toronto Press acknowledges the financial assistance to its
publishing program of the Canada Council for the Arts and the Ontario Arts
Council, an agency of the Government of Ontario.

 Canada Council   Conseil des Arts
for the Arts   du Canada

 ONTARIO ARTS COUNCIL
CONSEIL DES ARTS DE L'ONTARIO
an Ontario government agency
un organisme du gouvernement de l'Ontario

Funded by the   Financé par le
Government   gouvernement
of Canada   du Canada
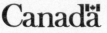

*For my grandchildren, Marci, Zsófi, and the twins,
Misi and Luca,
so they should never forget where they belong.*

Contents

The Storyteller of the Shoah: Éva Fahidi and *Anima Rerum*

ÉVA KOVÁCS and JUDITH SZAPOR

There you stand, A HUMAN BEING, on the Appelplatz, naked as the day you were born, with nothing on Earth to call your own. For what do you have? The impression of your personality and your dignity sheltered in your sub-conscious mind, and in your conscious mind the hope that what you are now going through will soon be over, that you will get five more spoonfuls of inedible slop, and that they will motion you to the right side.

...

Neighbours come with photographs ...

Before long you, A HUMAN BEING, begin your feverish search for anything, anything at all that might serve as tangible proof of your memories, your childhood years, vanished into thin air, your pre-Auschwitz life that was perhaps never really your own to begin with.

Objects accumulate around you. Their value cannot be appraised. Once, a long time ago, my father, my mother, my little sister had touched them.

Every object speaks volumes about the unrecoverable past.

Every object has a soul. They speak to us.

The opening lines of Éva Fahidi's memoir, from the bold allusion to Primo Levi to her characteristic tone, shifting between the nostalgic and the wry, summarize the traditions in which she grounded her own book. At once speaking to the personal and universal Holocaust experience, demarcating the before and after, and conjuring up the minutiae of her childhood, the memoir fits into multiple European and Hungarian strands of egodocuments and, more specifically, Holocaust memoirs. By frequently shifting in its tone and perspective between the confessional, the observational, and the analytical, it captures the author's unique voice. The end of the second quote helps explain the book's somewhat enigmatic original title: *Anima Rerum*, in this edition presented as "the soul of things." What could be the significance of the few possessions, salvaged from a lost upper-middle-class household, upon the author's unlikely survival and return? (The usually futile attempt to recover one's property and possessions is a common trope of Holocaust survivor memoirs.) It is certainly not their material value but what these randomly preserved objects represent: the everyday domestic rituals, traditions of hospitality, a life of authenticity and integrity, and the author's lifelong effort to keep the memory of her murdered family alive.

Anima Rerum: The Soul of Things, a chronicle of life before and during the Holocaust, was published in Hungarian in 2005;[1] it became an unexpected bestseller, reaching an unusually wide readership – and in the process made the author an important public figure. A survivor of Auschwitz and Nazi slave labour camps, Éva Fahidi is a veritable phenomenon: a Holocaust educator, a bestselling memoirist, a media personality, and a frequent participant in the Hungarian cultural scene. Since 2005 the memoir has sold out three printings and is into the fourth; and the German edition sold approximately eight thousand copies in Germany, Austria, and Switzerland.[2] (It is a reflection of Fahidi's stature as a public figure in Germany that the 2011 German edition's cover has her photo in front of an Auschwitz barrack.) An Italian edition appeared in early 2020.

Since the publication of the memoir, Éva Fahidi has become a regular speaker at major events of Holocaust commemoration, such as the anniversaries of the liberation of Auschwitz and Buchenwald. At the former's seventieth anniversary in January 2015, she was the guest of honour of then German President Joachim Gauck. She is a member of the International Auschwitz Committee and the recipient of Hungarian and international awards for her community work against racism and for an authentic memory culture. For the last decade and a half, in addition to her regular media appearances and interviews in Hungarian and German, she has held four to five talks yearly in both Hungarian and German high schools and has made at least two appearances a year in Hungarian Roma organizations, commemorating the genocide of the Roma during the Second World War. A widely known and beloved public figure in Hungary, she has become revered in Germany, and has appeared at events and been featured in countless newspaper and TV interviews and portraits in Austria, Switzerland, Serbia, and the United States as well.[3]

Every Shoah survivor's story is unique, and this is also true for every testimony. Part of the uniqueness of Fahidi's writings comes from their delayed arrival in the German and Hungarian Holocaust literature. Initially, she seemed to join the line of single-book Holocaust survivors who record their memories late in life, to pass them on to their own family's next generations – yet she is unique in that she has continued to write and has just completed her second autobiographical book, about her life in the postwar decades. Titled *The Subject and Object of Love*, it chronicles the author's faith, then disillusionment, in Marxism and her decades of living an ordinary working life after the Shoah, all the while obeying the unwritten social consensus of keeping silent.[4]

In 2015, at an age when most people would be long retired or resting on their laurels, Éva Fahidi embarked on a new adventure: she joined the Budapest dance company "Symptoms" to create a unique performance titled *Sea Lavender or The Euphoria of Being*.[5] In this play, through a combination of dance and texts, ninety-year old Fahidi and her young professional dancer partner, Emese Cuhorka, who personifies a young Éva, developed yet another language to convey her life story to the audience: the language of the body. Originally planned as a one-off, to be performed as a characteristically unconventional celebration of Éva Fahidi's ninetieth birthday, the play became a sellout success. Since 2015, *Sea Lavender* has been regularly mounted at Vígszínház, one of the most renowned theatres in Budapest, as well as at many other theatres and dance festivals in Europe. At last count, it was performed seventy-seven times, including in venues in Berlin and other German cities, in Vienna, and in Serbia, in front of audiences totalling an estimated ten thousand. At the writing of this Introduction, in late January 2019, Fahidi is attending and speaking at a series of commemorations in Germany, returning to Budapest in time for the premiere of a new documentary film on her life with the title *The Euphoria of Being*.[6]

Her path from retiree to full-time witness, author, and performer has also been unique: as she describes in the introductory chapter of the memoir, it began in 1989 with an invitation from the municipal council of Stadtallendorf, the German town in the province of Hessen and Thüringia (then in West Germany) that grew up in place of the village of Allendorf and the neighbouring former concentration camp, Münchmühle. The following year, the town hosted Éva Fahidi and her fellow former inmates and asked for their forgiveness. This first visit was followed by many more, resulting in close personal connections with local leaders and high-school students, as well as a short memoir, at the request of the Documentation and Information Centre opened at the site of the former camp.[7] This much shorter text, all of eighty-four pages, was Fahidi's first attempt to articulate her memories in writing. It is highly meaningful that it was written in German, the language of Fahidi's captivity but also of her childhood, which she learned from an Austrian governess and still speaks with native fluency. The positive reaction and success, for an inexpensively produced little book, eventually led to the writing of the fuller, Hungarian version of the memoir.

The other impetus came from Fahidi's first – and this time voluntary – return visit to Auschwitz-Birkenau in 2003, after fifty-nine years. Once there, her fruitless attempt to find her former barrack prompted the overwhelming feeling that the physical site of the camp was vastly inadequate as a place of commemoration, that "nobody else but she knows the truth," and that it was her obligation to "shout it as loudly as possible for everyone to hear."[8]

Importantly, the first commemorative event in 1990, initiated by a German community atoning for crimes in which it had no part – as Fahidi carefully notes, "our hosts were not even born there, were themselves newcomers, and had nothing to do with what had happened to us" – represented her first encounter with the (West) German memory culture, an unexpected surprise in the best possible sense. The yearly return visits to Stadtallendorf led to invitations to talk to other German local and school communities, resulting, in the last fifteen years, in a total of approximately fifty "Zeitzeugengespräche" – roughly translated as "conversations with witnesses," held with groups of high-school and university students. Fahidi's flawless spoken and written German and expert delivery made her a frequent, favourite speaker at German Holocaust memorial sites and events – one of her proudest moments, posted on her Facebook page, was sitting next to German Chancellor Angela Merkel in Berlin at the opening of the seventieth-anniversary commemoration of the liberation of Auschwitz.[9]

Keen on introducing this format into the Hungarian context, Éva Fahidi has also become an observer and commentator on the halting and largely unfinished process in Hungary of dealing with the memory of the Shoah, including the responsibility of the Hungarian authorities, perpetrators, and bystanders. In the Preface to her memoir, she briefly reflects on the decades of state socialism during which "it was, to put it mildly, not 'polite' to mention the deportations." Writing in 2004, she laments that the fourteen years following the regime change were not sufficient to produce a permanent exhibition about the Holocaust in Hungary. The Holocaust Memorial Centre in Budapest's ninth district opened its doors later in that year, 2004, with a temporary photo exhibition of the so-called Auschwitz album, and mounted a permanent exhibition on the Holocaust in Hungary two years later.[10]

In her countless interviews and in private conversation, Fahidi has expressed special pride over her visits to virtually every leading high school in Hungary, including, prominently, those operated by the churches. Frequently, she hosts smaller groups of students at her home and – as is the wont of the professional storyteller – she is always ready to share her stories with anyone who will listen. Yet a recurring theme of her interviews is the sharp difference between Germany and Hungary when it comes to memory culture, and she is highly critical of the reluctance, at times even refusal, of Hungarian political and religious leaders to acknowledge, let alone atone for, the crimes of the past.

The two authors of this Introduction are long-time admirers of Éva Fahidi, the Holocaust witness and activist, but also have personal connections to her: Éva Kovács facilitated Fahidi's introduction to Austrian audiences and arranged for performances of the play *Sea Lavender* to be mounted at Vienna's famed Volkstheater. Judith Szapor is the mother of two of the young adults to whom Fahidi dedicated her book, "so that they should never forget where they belong." Thus she knew Fahidi before she became an author and activist, and watched with awe how she forged, post-retirement, an entirely new career. But with our respective personal connections to Éva Fahidi, we are not all that different from her other readers, listeners, and admirers. For much of her appeal comes from her irresistible personality. She has an almost regal bearing, owing to a lifelong habit of daily exercise, impeccable manners, an absolute lack of prejudice, and a rare common touch and ability to make connections with people from all nationalities and walks of life. Her manner of speaking Hungarian is a vanishing art: rich in idioms that reflect her roots in the Southeastern Plains and Debrecen, enriched by a deep knowledge of Hungarian and world literature. Her ability with languages contributed to the ease with which she moved between countries during her decades as an export-import agent of a state-owned trading company, selling socialist Hungary's steel products abroad – and in interviews she never fails to mention this glorious part of her life, tongue firmly in cheek.

In order to assess the book's significance, we should briefly survey the Hungarian literature on the Holocaust – both the existing body of testimonies and the relevant scholarly literature. The commemoration and narration of the horrific experience of the Shoah and the remembrance of its victims had created their own practices from the beginning – at times requiring superhuman efforts on the part of those remembering. Suffice it to mention such examples as the documents collected, preserved, and hidden in the Warsaw Ghetto by the group known under the code name *Oyneg Shabbos*, today known as the Ringelblum Archives, or the hidden and surviving writings of Załmen Gradowski, published under the title *From the Heart of Hell: Manuscripts of a Sonderkommando Prisoner, Found in Auschwitz*, a shattering testimony of the extermination of Jews at Auschwitz. The surviving Hungarian Jewry also established a remarkable, massive collection of testimonies, recorded immediately after liberation, as well as a number of often self-published, individual testimonies.[11] Of these, the memoir of Miklós Nyiszli, the Hungarian Jewish physician who as an inmate worked under Mengele at Auschwitz, was self-published in 1946 after his return to Nagyvárad/Oradea in Romania and consequently has become one of the earliest standard primary sources of Holocaust scholarship outside of Hungary.[12] We are aware of commemorative events held by the surviving religious communities;[13] as well, historians have benefited immensely from the documents of postwar war-crime trials and the committees charged with vetting public servants in Hungary. These documentary collections contain testimonies of many survivors describing both the atrocities suffered and the occasional assistance rendered.[14] The early wave of memoirs included those of a number of female survivors who published their experiences shortly after the war but whose memoirs have not become known to the broader public either in Hungary or abroad.[15]

By the 1950s, however, this first wave of personal recollections and testimonies had come to an end. It would be an exaggeration to say that the survivors had completely retreated into silence, as references to the Holocaust in Hungary have kept appearing, mainly in coded form and in traces, in film and television.[16] Nevertheless, we can state with certainty that women's testimonies have not earned their rightful place in the mainstream of either the historical scholarship of the Holocaust or the memoir literature and literature at large – at least not until the second half of the 1970s.[17] To explain this phenomenon in greater detail would go beyond the scope of this Introduction – suffice it to say that the post-1945 trajectory of Éva Fahidi, described at the beginning of her book, illustrates the decades historians today often call the "decades of silence." During these years, between the early 1950s and the mid- to late 1970s, the personal memory of the Shoah, as of a stream running underground, remained confined to private and familial spheres.[18]

The exceptions,[19] the books on the Holocaust in Hungary whose publication or reissue (in cases of an already existing, earlier postwar edition) can be grouped around the mid- to late 1970s, a period known for its capricious cultural politics, also represent some of the peaks of the genre in Hungary. Their authors were leading popular writers and journalists whose books in some cases germinated during decades of silence. It is indicative of the winding path of Holocaust memory in Hungary that the writers who published their books immediately after the war were clear about their documentary nature. In contrast, the writers whose books were published for the first time in the 1970s invariably designated them as novels and used fictive names instead of their own, thus blurring the line between memoir and fiction. According to the period's practice, the print run was not indicated, and we can only guess these books' impact. But it is safe to assume that the number of copies remained in the low hundreds – considered very low at the time but frequently assigned to publications considered to fall into the tolerated, as opposed to the supported, category; and we can presume that their readers consisted mainly of fellow survivors and their families. All this resulted in the books' failure to make a significant impact on mainstream public discourse.

In the aftermath of the 1989–90 regime change in Hungary, along with books on previously suppressed political and historical subjects, a slew of Holocaust testimonies was published.[20] Éva Fahidi's book was published in 2005, at the tail end of this memoir production when interest in the topic was already on the wane. But despite its author's status as a newly minted writer, the book was more firmly grounded in the pre-1989 strands of fictionalized testimony and literary memoir, criss-crossing the lines between the two genres with ease. What distinguished the book among the rich memoir production of the post-1989 period was the close attention it paid to the period before the Shoah, covering it on half of its pages. When describing its wide appeal, readers often mention the vivid description of the author's close-knit, extended family, scattered among the far corners of the former Austro-Hungarian Monarchy, from Northern Hungary to the Great Plains. A richly textured family history, it depicts the local social and household customs, with their rituals of hosting friends, exchanging favours and produce with neighbours, practising charity, and making preserves. It pays tender tribute to the author's extended family, whose over fifty members, with the exception of two cousins, were all killed. As such, it offers a rare description of the way of life of upper-middle-class Hungarian Jews of the countryside, a world destroyed almost without a trace, as a result of the deportation to Auschwitz-Birkenau and the murder of Hungarian Jews, affecting disproportionally those outside of the capital.

Over the last few decades, Holocaust memoirs have come to occupy a significant place in North American university curricula. Outstanding examples of the genre, such as the works of Primo Levi and Elie Wiesel, regularly figure on the reading lists of specialized courses on the history of anti-Semitism and the Holocaust, but also on those of general courses on Eastern, East Central European, and European history in the twentieth century, or the history of modern Germany and Nazism. Lately, memoirs have gained an even more significant role, owing to the growing interest of historians in oral history and testimonies and the need to offer new cohorts of students material that they can relate to on an intellectual but also on an emotional level. A prime example is the exquisitely written 1985 memoir of Heda Margolius Kovály, a Czech-Jewish survivor of Auschwitz and Bergen-Belsen.[21] A popular addition to courses on the twentieth-century history of East Central Europe, this first memoir was recently followed by *Hitler, Stalin and I, An Oral History.*[22] The latter is a transcript of a conversation with Margolius and, in contrast with the first memoir, a much more detailed account of her life during the Holocaust. Her clear-eyed perspective is especially revelatory on the specific female experience, such as the significance for survival of family-like ties between inmates. The book, in many ways reminiscent of

Fahidi's, has proven to be a great success with students in modern European and women's history courses – and it well illustrates the potential, in higher education, of oral histories and memoirs, and their ability to resonate on both an intellectual and emotional level with young readers. Judging from the reactions of readers of all ages to Fahidi's book in its German and Hungarian editions, we are confident that it will reach and touch a similarly wide readership in English.

For, it seems, the need to remind people of the Holocaust, by the very people who were its victims and witnesses, has never been greater. On January 27, 2019, designated as the date of Holocaust Memorial Day, a British poll found that one in twenty British adults do not believe the Holocaust happened.[23] These findings are far from being unique to Great Britain: another recent poll conducted to gauge anti-Semitism and awareness of the Holocaust in seven European countries found not only a stubborn persistence of anti-Semitic prejudices but also that the memory of the Holocaust is fading.[24] To counter these trends, the leading American organizations of Holocaust research and commemoration with vast holdings, the United States Holocaust Memorial Museum, the Fortunoff Video Archive for Holocaust Testimonies, and the USC Shoah Foundation Visual History Archive, as well as the Centropa Foundation, based in Central Europe, have all been increasingly posting testimonies recorded with survivors on their web sites.[25] Among other efforts, these organizations have recently begun to develop teaching materials for college- and university-level courses. One of the units the United States Holocaust Memorial Museum offers to instructors highlights the previously neglected perspectives of gender and sexuality and more generally the gendered experience of the Holocaust.[26] The prominent place of testimonies recorded with women survivors helps fill out a previously missing dimension of the memory of the Holocaust;[27] and the interview subjects' warm and frank discussion of their own experiences seems to create a special bond with the viewers – albeit one that, increasingly, is possible only in digital form.

We close on a personal note, citing the words of the grandson of Éva Fahidi. They illustrate the power of the written and oral testimony of an authentic personality and a now inevitably passing generation – and demonstrate their tremendous potential to build a lasting connection with the following generations. We believe it requires no commentary.

"At the sixtieth anniversary of the liberation of the Buchenwald concentration camp in 2005, the great Spanish writer Jorge Semprun gave a keynote address in Weimar's national theatre. When he began lamenting how there likely would not be any survivors there for the seventieth anniversary, a woman's arm shot up to interrupt him. 'I will!' she cried out. It was my grandmother. She told me this story a few years ago, sitting at her kitchen table in Budapest, and we decided that I would join her when the date arrived. I never doubted her. This weekend, as one of the keynote speakers at the commemorative events of the seventieth anniversary, she related that story to loud applause in the same theatre in Weimar. In the afternoon, we stood together on the grounds of Buchenwald, under a warm spring sun and giant beech trees, beneath a watchtower whose clock is frozen now at 3:15 pm, the moment of liberation. In several languages, the attendees reaffirmed a Buchenwald oath written by the camp's survivors in the days after the liberation in April 1945. Among its final lines, it proclaims that 'the building of a new world of peace and freedom is our goal.' And how much work there is still to be done, one survivor remarked that afternoon."[28]

NOTES

1 Éva Fahidi, *Anima Rerum; A Dolgok Lelke* (Budapest: Tudomány, 2005).
2 Éva Fahidi-Pusztai, *Die Seele der Dinge*, transl. Doris Fischer (Berlin: Herausgegeben im Auftrag des Internationalen Auschwitz Komitees und der Gedenkstätte Deutscher Widerstand, 2011).
3 Among others, Alison Smale, "A Holocaust Survivor Tells of Auschwitz at 18 and, Again, at 90," *New York Times*, March 13, 2015. https://www.nytimes.com/2015/03/14/world/europe/a-holocaust -survivor-tells-of-auschwitz-at-18-and-again-at-90.html?login=email&auth =login-email, accessed January 25, 2019; "Auschwitz Survivor Eva Fahidi Captivates Audiences with Her Life Story in Dance," Euronews, January 27, 2016.

https://www.euronews.com/2016/01/27/90-year-old-auschwitz
-survivor-eva-fahidi-captivates-audiences-with-her-life, accessed January
25, 2019; https://www.dw.com/en/92-year-old-holocaust-survivor-eva
-fahidi-dances-for-remembrance/a-41311829, accessed January 25, 2019.
4 *A szerelem alanya és tárgya* (Budapest: Ariel International, 2019).
5 The performance has been widely reviewed. See, among others,
"Auschwitz Survivor Eva Fahidi Captivates Audiences with Her Life Story
in Dance." The "sea lavender" of the title is a reference to a childhood
memory, described in the memoir.
6 *A létezés eufóriája*, directed by Réka Szabó, 2019. https://www.youtube
.com/watch?v=OYe7of4FFcg
7 Éva Fahidi, *Anima rerum, meine Münchmühle in Allendorf und meine wahren
Geschichten* (Stadtallendorf: Magistrat der Stadt Stadtallendorf, 2004).
8 Personal communication of Éva Fahidi, January 2019.
9 "Assignment for the Future." https://www.auschwitz.info/en
/commemoration/commemoration-2015/70th-anniversary-of-the
-liberation-of-auschwitz-2015.html, accessed January 29, 2019.
10 For more information, see the web page of the Holocaust Memorial
Centre of Budapest, available only in Hungarian: http://hdke.hu
/rolunk/tenyek-adatok. See also Regina Fritz, *Nach Krieg und Judenmord:
Ungarns Geschichtspolitik seit 1944* (Göttingen: Wallstein 2012).
11 Rita Horváth, "Jews in Hungary after the Holocaust: The National Relief
Committee for Deportees, 1945–1950," *Journal of Israeli History* 19.2 (1998):
69–91.
12 In English: Miklós Nyiszli, *Auschwitz: A Doctor's Eyewitness Account* (New
York: Arcade Publishing, 2011).
13 Judit Kónya, "Pusztulás és gyász: vallásjogi problémák (1945–1949)"
[Destruction and Mourning: Problems of Religious Law (1945–1949)],
REGIO 24.2 (2016): 7–21.
14 László Karsai, "The Hungarian Holocaust As Reflected in the People's
Court Trials in Budapest," *Yad Vashem Studies* 32 (2004): 59–96 and "The
People's Courts and Revolutionary Justice in Hungary," in István Deák,
Jan Gross, and Tony Judt, eds., *The Politics of Retribution in Europe: World
War II and Its Aftermath 1939–1948* (Princeton: Princeton University Press,
2000), 137–51.
15 Erzsébet Frank, *365 nap. Versben írt vallomás a poklok tüzéből* [365 Days.
Testimony in Verse from the Fire of Hells] (Miskolc: Munkaszolgálatosok
Szövetségének Felsőmagyarországi Csoportja, 1946); Teri Gács, *A
mélységből kiáltunk hozzád* [De Profundis], (Budapest: Tábor Kiadás, 1946);
Teréz Rudnoy, *Szabaduló asszonyok. A szabadság első 24 órája* [Liberated

Women. The First 24 Hours of Freedom] (Budapest: Dante Kiadó 1947);
Gisella Perl, *I Was a Doctor in Auschwitz* (New York: International
Universities Press, 1948).

16 András Lénárt, "Perek: A holokauszt tematizálásának példái a hatvanas
évek magyarországi nyilvánosságában" [Trials: Examples of the
Holocaust in Public Discourses of 1960s Hungary], in Tibor Bónus,
Csongor Lőrincz, and Péter Szirák, eds., *A forradalom ígérete? Történelmi
és nyelvi események kereszteződései* [The Promise of Revolution? Crossings
of Historical and Linguistic Events] (Budapest: Ráció, 2014), 511–37; Vera
Surányi, ed., *Minarik, Sonnenschein és a többiek: Zsidó sorsok magyar filmen*
[Minarik, Sonnenschein, and the Others: Jewish Fates in Hungarian
Films] (Budapest: MZSKE/Szombat, 2001).

17 The handful of exceptions include Edith Bruck, *Ki téged úgy szeret* [She
Who Loves You So] (Budapest: Európa, 1964) – first published in Italy,
where the author moved after the war, the book's Hungarian publication
was considered a minor miracle; Ágnes Gergely, *Ajtófélfámon jel vagy* [You
Are a Marking on My Door Frame] (Budapest: Magvető, 1963); Magda
Székely, *Kőtábla* [The tablets] (Budapest: Magvető 1962).

18 Ferenc Erős, Éva Kovács, and Júlia Vajda, "Intergenerational Responses
to Social and Political Changes: Transformation of Jewish Identity in
Hungary," in Yael Danieli, ed., *International Handbook of Multigenerational
Legacies of Trauma* (New York and London: Plenum, 1998), 315–24.

19 Mária Ember, *Hajtűkanyar* [Hairpin Bend] (Budapest: Szépirodalmi, 1974);
Ernő Szép, *Emberszag* (Budapest: Keresztes, 1945, and Szépirodalmi,
1984), in English: *The Smell of Humans: A Memoir of the Holocaust in
Hungary*, transl. John Bátki, introduction Dezső Tandori (Budapest and
New York: Central European University Press, 1994); Béla Zsolt, *Kilenc
koffer* (*Haladás*, in instalments, 1946, and Budapest: Magvető, 1980), in
English: *Nine Suitcases*, transl. Ladislaus Löb (London: Jonathan Cape,
2004); György Moldova, *A Szent Imre induló* [The March of St Emerich]
(Budapest: Magvető, 1975). Despite their tremendous deprivations,
neither of these authors was deported to Auschwitz. They survived,
respectively, forced labour service (Szép), the Budapest (Moldova) and
Oradea/Nagyvárad (Zsolt) ghettos, and, in Ember's case, a so-called
family camp in Vienna.

20 For a more complete bibliography, see Louise O. Vasvári, "Lefordított
traumák, lefordított életek" [Translated Traumas, Translated Lives],
Múlt és Jövő 1 (2009): 35–62. Katalin Pécsi, ed., *Sós kávé; Elmeséletlen női
történetek* [Salty Coffee: Untold Stories by Jewish Women] (Budapest:
Novella, 2007) is an anthology of short memoirs. A late, valuable addition

to the genre, Judith Magyar Isaacson, *Seed of Sarah: Memoirs of a Girlhood* (Urbana and Chicago: University of Illinois Press, 1990), was published in the United States.

21 Heda Margolius Kovály, *Under a Cruel Star – A Life in Prague 1941–1968* (New York: Holmes & Meier, 1986).

22 Heda Margolius Kovály and Helena Třeštíková, *Hitler, Stalin and I: An Oral History* (Los Angeles: Doppel House Press, 2018).

23 Harriet Sherwood, "One in 20 Britons Does Not Believe Holocaust Took Place, Poll Finds," *Guardian online*, January 27, 2019. https://www. theguardian.com/world/2019/jan/27/one-in-20-britons-does-not-believe -holocaust-happened, accessed January 29, 2019.

24 Richard Allan Greene, "A Shadow over Europe," CNN, November 2019, http://edition.cnn.com/interactive/2018/11/europe/antisemitism-poll -2018-intl/, accessed January 29, 2019.

25 https://www.ushmm.org/online/oral-history/; https://sfi.usc.edu/vha; http://www.centropa.org/, all accessed January 30, 2019.

26 https://perspectives.ushmm.org/collection/gender-sexuality-and-the -holocaust, accessed January 29, 2019.

27 For Hungarian women's testimonies, see Louise O. Vasvári, "En-gendering Memory through Holocaust Alimentary Life Writing," *Comparative Literature and Culture* 17.3 (2015): https://doi.org/10.7771 /1481-4374.2721; "Hungarian Women's Holocaust Life Writing in the Context of the Nation's Divided Social Memory, 1944–2014," *Hungarian Cultural Studies, e-Journal of the American Hungarian Educators Association* 7 (2014): http://ahea.pitt.edu DOI: 10.5195/ahea.2014.139. For a general discussion of women, gender, and the Holocaust, see, among others, Dalia Ofer and Lenore J. Weitzman, eds., *Women in the Holocaust* (New Haven: Yale University Press, 1998); Carol Rittner and John Roth, eds., *Different Voices: Women and the Holocaust*, Mazal Holocaust Collection (New York: Paragon House, 1993); Zoe Waxman, *Women in the Holocaust: A Feminist History* (Oxford: Oxford University Press, 2017).

28 Personal communication of Martin Lukacs.

... Because We Cannot Go On Otherwise

GYÖRGY GÁBOR

I am a human being, I am European, I am Hungarian, I am a Jew, I am a philosopher. Each one of the most important components of my identity will explain why I have read so many books about the Shoah – works by historians, works by writers, as well as memoirs. But I have never read a book anything like this. It is said to be impossible to write about the inconceivable, the indefinable, the indescribable, the irrational.

It is said to be.

For Éva Fahidi does not describe, she does not tell a story, and she does not initiate us. Instead, by presenting her own never-ending story, she makes public something that is our own basic story regardless of whether we were alive at the time or were born only after it. Éva Fahidi has given me the most that a writer can give a reader – by conjuring up my own past from before the time I was born, I have come to know myself in new ways and in greater depth. The author has repopulated my family and has resurrected my dead, those who left us then and those who left us afterwards, those I know and those I never met, and maybe even those who are waiting to be born. Éva Fahidi's book is a family saga, the shared saga of all people, Europeans and non-Europeans, Hungarians, Germans, Chileans, and Australians, Jews and non-Jews.

But can the community of humans have a family saga in common? Do we really belong to one family, though not in the Darwinian sense and not in the sense of *imago Dei*? Do we share memories in common, and if we don't, is that bad, and does it give cause for sadness or resignation? Do we need snippets of the memory that unites every descendant of *Homo sapiens* in a common chain of tradition? And if so, can we be sure that it is a good thing and a noble thing? Can we be sure that this experience of belonging is indispensable and elemental? Is it an experience at all? And if so, as long as I am capable of pronouncing the word "I," then I (and always just this I), wouldn't I attempt till my dying day, if need be, to free myself of all bonds, of all superfluous things outside of myself that bring me news of belonging and togetherness through the loose texture of those bonds, if that, and in no other way?

A chain for its own sake.

I always believed that one could not survive Auschwitz. Engaging in a discussion about whether poetry is possible after Auschwitz is a vain, obdurate, and ridiculous cliché. There is no getting free of Auschwitz and the maw of the death factories. Some people did go free, but not because it was possible. In this respect this word loses its meaning and import, because in Auschwitz nothing was possible. Not even as a negative particle. The substantive verb has no form to indicate that some people came out of there nonetheless. The very use of the substantive verb makes us blush, and its weight crushes us.

Éva Fahidi made it home. She did not survive anything, because there was nothing to survive, nothing, because everything and everyone became as dust and died or, put another way, the everything and everyone that became as dust and died made it impossible for anything or anyone to survive. This was the terrible *danse macabre* of not-being, the terrible vicious circle of not-being.

Éva Fahidi made it home not as a survivor but as a witness, which makes her perish again and again, day after day. Her clear thinking, unequivocal views, and amazing irony, her way with words, her brains and experiences, her twenty-year-old self, have remained. She made it home not because it was possible, but because that's how it happened. And because that's how it happened, she, from whom they took everything, received from herself, and only from herself, the thing that we are capable of giving ourselves only if we experience frenzied pain and only if we are among the best – bereft of her humanity, she herself, and no one but herself, gave herself back to herself. Not those she lost, for there is no mercy shown in the other direction, only deaf and senseless emptiness.

Éva Fahidi could not remain a human being under those inhuman circumstances, since then and there whatever was human was annihilated by the inhuman with no recourse to humanity and no recourse to pathos. She, along with everyone else, was continually and steadily bombarded by decrees enacted into law, the latest technology of the age, its logistics, neighbours eager to get their hands on rugs and chandeliers that were not their own, and by the manifestations of the triumph of murderous instincts backed by ideology – a concerted effort so that she should end up in the gas chamber not as a human being but an animal, the way we tend to treat rats. First they murdered human dignity, and only afterward its tenement of clay, as a necessary evil.

This is the place from which Éva Fahidi made it back home, her tenement of clay in ruins, but with her dignity intact. This is what we should – indeed, what we must – learn to read out of her shocking testimony. It is high time that we did so, whether we are Christians or Buddhists, Hungarians or non-Hungarians, but not so that we should see history clearly, not so that we should understand the past at long last, and, through the intricate net of the past, understand ourselves. That's not why.

We must learn from this book because we, Jews and non-Jews, Hungarians and non-Hungarians, cannot go on otherwise.

Cover of the 2004 German edition of the author's book.

Preface to the German Edition (2011)

GÖTZ ALY

Nearly eighty years old, Éva Fahidi lives in downtown Budapest. Her memory is crystal clear, her manner of expression sharp as a razor. She had just past her eighteenth birthday when on June 27, 1944 she was crowded into a cattle car in her native Debrecen in Eastern Hungary and was deported to Auschwitz. Of her immediate family she was the only survivor. If we count her uncles, aunts, and cousins, about fifty of her relatives became victims of the Holocaust.

"Anyone who has been in Auschwitz has two lives," she writes in her characteristic, wry style, "a life before Auschwitz and a life after it." This is what makes this book special. The author does not treat this, considering its length, brief period of her life – a period that was defined only by persecution and which, apart from small, vital moments, became the object of German racial policy – as separate from the rest of her life's journey. The feeling of safety and normalcy, taken for granted, is the "before," everything else is "after." Éva Fahidi does not tell her story chronologically. The force and emphatic nature of her "true stories" lie in the fact that at first sight and in a formal sense she does not speak systematically, but, depending on the subject, she jumps around and keeps drawing parallels. To give you an example, Éva Fahidi describes the reality of Auschwitz from the perspective of July 1, 2004, when she visited today's memorial. She arrived in Birkenau on the same day fifty-nine years earlier. She asks, puzzled, "What has become of 'our' Birkenau, where we were crowded together, where we could not move, because we bumped into each other at every step? What has become of the air heavy with the stench of burning bodies? What has become of the cease-less screaming of the Aufseherins, the commandos, the transports, the constant coming and going of the trucks?"

Anyone who visits the Auschwitz Museum today and walks around the area of Birkenau will be shocked to see human bones scattered here and there that the rain still washes out of the ground. Still, today's visitor cannot get a realistic picture of what was once there – the humiliation, the starvation, the thirst, the latrines, and the unrelenting presence of death. Éva Fahidi has the following to say about this: "The place where not a single blade of grass could survive between the Lagerstrasse, and the Appelplatz, today nature is everywhere."

Gilike (Ágnes), the author's eleven-year-old little sister, was killed upon arrival in a gas chamber, and her body, like hundreds of thousands of other bodies from the so-called Hungarian trans-ports, was incinerated the same day. Her mother, the thirty-nine-year-old Irma, suffered the same fate. The momentary hesitation that she shouldn't leave her child alone was enough for the SS doctors responsible for the selection to decide that the possible consequences of the pain over being separated from her child jus-tified sending her to her death instantly, rather than having her do forced labour. The forty-nine-year-old father, the lumber merchant Dezső Fahídi, became a victim of "annihilation through labour." He could only endure the suffering for a couple of weeks.

This is how the middle-class Fahidi family disappeared from Debrecen. They were Jews who spoke German at home but who were proud Hungarians. The family's love of their homeland has survived in the passage where the author speaks about the terrible injustice of the Treaty of Trianon. The Fahidi girls attended a con-vent school, learned to play the piano, and enjoyed playing tennis. Granted that the semi-parliamentarian, semi-dictatorial Hungarian government had passed a number of stringent anti-Jewish laws from 1938 on, most of the Jews living in Hungary – including the author's own family – felt that they were living "on an island of peace and security, and not in a country soon to fall under German occupation." Theirs was a respected family, while the girls were attending a school where the steadily growing Jewish persecution was not mentioned, but was "elegantly glossed over."

After a six-week stay in Auschwitz, Éva Fahidi was deported along with a thousand other Hungarian Jewish women to one of the outlying Buchenwald camps, the Münchmühle work camp located in Allendorf, Hessen province. The change in camps played a vital role in her survival, even though the women were forced to work with highly toxic materials in the munitions industry and were no better than slaves toiling without benefit of safety equipment or protective clothing. Some of the German guards demonstrated their sympathy, or at least were not sadistic. Although the imprisonment and the forced labour in Münchmühle were terrible, the chances for survival were still better there than in the death camp of Auschwitz. Survival also required luck, and Éva Fahidi and her fellow inmates were lucky because they retained their human dignity against all odds. They observed the rules of personal hygiene, recited poems, and when the need was greatest, they evidenced true solidarity and helped each other as best they could. "We refused to be demoralized." But all this would not have sufficed if the American army had not liberated the camp on March 31, 1945.

Éva Fahidi writes about the unparalleled genocide, the Holocaust, in a manner that no historian would be able to do. The historian provides a dry, objective account of the innumerable anonymous victims of the state-directed annihilation machinery. Thanks to the author's stories, the world whose annihilation was the objective of the "final solution" of the Third Reich comes to life once again. Éva Fahidi portrays individuals who died because they were Jews with sympathy and understanding, and she does so while describing their weaknesses and strengths, their customs and amiable qualities. In the camp Éva Fahidi was still dreaming of reuniting with her parents and younger sister. But after her liberation she had to face the fact that she could never accept – the "cruel truth."

THE SOUL OF THINGS

I have learned the most magnificent of all things,
what it is like to be a human being.
It is the most that anyone can hope for.

Sándor Márai

The Soul of Things

Can you imagine not owning anything? There you stand, A HUMAN BEING, on the Appelplatz, naked as the day you were born, with nothing on earth to call your own. For what do you have? The impression of your personality and your dignity sheltered in your subconscious mind, and in your conscious mind the hope that what you are now going through will soon be over, that you will get five more spoonfuls of inedible slop, and that they will motion you to the right side.

And then one day you, A HUMAN BEING, find yourself back in the town from which you were dragged off, the house where you were born, the house that is your father's and your mother's, and therefore your own. You get thrown out of your own house because it now belongs to strangers. There is nothing left of your former self of nineteen months ago, the pampered and carefree child of this house, nothing but the memory in your soul.

You, A HUMAN BEING, ring the bell on the main gate of your gardener's house. The gardener's entire family comes running. The wife hugs you as she wipes the tears from her eyes with the edge of her apron. "Where are the others?" she asks. Her daughter, the same age as your younger sister, used to inherit her outgrown clothes. She brings me some of my little sister's blouses and night shifts. "Maybe Gilike will come back, too. She may need them."

Next, the amiable maid we'd brought up to town from a farm shows up. When she married we made her a present of enough lumber to make furniture for a whole room. She also cries as she

The silver anniversary of my maternal grandparents, Ógyalla
(Czechoslovakia), 1929. Front row centre: my maternal grandparents
Ernesztína Gross and Alfréd Weisz; front row left: my parents, Irma Weisz
and Dezső Fahidi; front row right: my aunt and her husband, Hédi Weisz
and Dr Géza Weil; back row: my grandparents' as yet unmarried children
Pál, Miklós, Natália, Imre, and Sándor Weisz; sitting on the floor: me at the
age of four and Gerti Weil aged a year and a half.

embraces me. She brings with her the cookbook she wrote while
she was in our service with entries like this: "The recipe calls for
15 tbs. of sugar, but we use only 10." "We," because she always felt
that she was one of the family.

Neighbours come with photographs ...

Before long you, A HUMAN BEING, begin your feverish search
for anything, anything at all that might serve as tangible proof
of your memories, your childhood years, vanished into thin air,

your pre-Auschwitz life that was perhaps never really your own to begin with.

Objects accumulate around you. Their value cannot be appraised. Once, a long time ago, my father, my mother, my little sister had touched them.

Every object speaks volumes about the unrecoverable past.

Every object has a soul. They speak to us. In accordance with our family's tradition, they tell "true stories."

The author in 2005.

Preface

In 1989, city council officials from Stadtallendorf looked me and my fellow former Häftlings[1] up because at one time we and a thousand others were forced labourers at one of the largest munitions factories of the Third Reich, hidden inside the Herrenwald, a forest near the village of Allendorf.[2] Why?

The second generation of Germans born after the war began asking questions and trying to make sense of the things that their parents and grandparents, the builders and supporters of Nazi Germany – or simply those who lived with and under it – tried to hide from them. In the three or four decades following the war, Allendorf grew into the town of Stadtallendorf, and in the 1960s, the cows began to die. During the search for the reason behind the mysterious deaths, it was discovered that the cows were ingesting poisoned grass. Next they found the toxic pasture itself, where the grass was growing over the ruins of the outdoor trinitro-toluol storage of the defunct munitions plant. For their part, school children came upon documents to prove not only that there had been a munitions plant there but that the plant had used tens of thousands of forced labourers, who were quartered in the nearby camps.

All notes, unless indicated otherwise, are by the editor.

1 Häftling: Inmate (German).

2 The article by Fritz Brinkmann-Frisch at the end of the book (Appendix A) provides a short history of the factory, including details of its geographical location, organization, and significance in the Nazi war industry. Also included (as Appendix B) is the list of the one thousand female forced labourers, the author's cohort, transferred from Auschwitz to Allendorf on August 13, 1944.

In 1990 the city extended an invitation to us and apologized, even though between August 1944 and March 1945, when we were there, the village had only fifteen hundred inhabitants, and our hosts were not even born there, were themselves newcomers, and had nothing to do with what had happened to us.

We couldn't believe the changes we saw in Germany. During our weeklong stay our hosts outdid themselves. Young volunteers were at our beck and call. We were taken to the location of our former camp and the munitions plant. We met prominent representatives of the city and the province, as well as various social organizations who spoke with us and apologized, while the children put on a show for our benefit. We will never forget that week as long as we live.

The contrast, namely, that back home it was, to put it mildly, not "polite" to mention the deportations, was now more glaring than ever. Of course, I understood the reasons all along. As the Hungarian saying goes, it is the height of bad manners to mention a rope in the house of a hanged man. There is no comparing Auschwitz to anything; it cannot be likened to anything or measured by any other standard. Still, I can't help thinking of Siberia. They had no need for ovens, of course. They had the cold. But in either case, it is the end result that counts.

It is still not too late to acknowledge the omissions of the socialist years when everything unpleasant was swept under the carpet. But when will that acknowledgment come? Hopefully it won't take twenty-six years, which, according to a recent economic prognosis, is how long Hungary will need to catch up to the European Union.

In 1992, two years after the Stadtallendorf meeting, the city opened a Documentation and Information Centre dedicated to the documents and other reminders of our life in the camp and as forced labourers that we, the former Häftlings, had kept – pieces of clothing, milk coupons, personal ID, photographs. We gave the Centre everything we possibly could, because we felt that that's where these items belonged. Among ourselves we call it "our" museum, because it is safeguarding the mementoes of our suffering for all posterity. It is mandatory for German school children, soldiers, fire fighters, etc., to visit it. "Our" museum is a living body. Hundreds of people visit it every year. The director of the Centre sends each of us an annual report on the Centre's activities.

I mention this only for the sake of the truth and will try to stick to the facts and be as objective as I can when I say that, in Hungary, where they dragged off six hundred thousand Hungarian Jews, we had to wait fifty-nine years for the Hungarian prime minister to declare that they, too, were Hungarians. This is how long it took for a Holocaust Memorial Centre to open its doors to the public, a centre where they still haven't compiled a list of the victims, and where there hasn't been a single, if ever so humble, exhibition about the Hungarian Holocaust.[3] The facts speak for themselves.

In the early 1990s, the director of the Documentation Centre of Stadtallendorf asked me to write my memoirs. But back then I wasn't up to it. Another decade passed, and, succumbing to gentle pressure, in 2005 I finally wrote a brief sketch of sorts in German, thinking that there couldn't possibly be anything new left for me to write about. After all, the libraries are full of books on the subject. To my great surprise, the first edition was sold out by the end of the year and a second edition was in the works. I gave several readings in Germany. Since I am as vain as the next person, I would like to brag about my greatest success: when I held a press conference in Berlin, six copies of my books were stolen! My friends and relatives pestered me until I wrote these couple of pages in Hungarian as well. But please don't think that this makes me feel like I am a writer. On the contrary. I hereby apologize to those who are "the real thing" for my humble, dilettantish efforts. I hope they will consider my age. Not that it's a merit in itself. On the contrary. With time, it becomes decidedly unpleasant.

An old woman likes to remember her childhood years and her youth, when she was still in full possession of her faculties, when she had parents who thought she was the bee's knees and who watched over her, and when she was beautiful and innocent,

---

3 A year after the publication of this Preface, the Holocaust Memorial Centre in Budapest unveiled a permanent exhibition on the Holocaust in Hungary. The Centre also has been compiling a complete list of victims. More information about the permanent and temporary exhibitions and collections of the Centre can be accessed at http://hdke.hu/en/, last accessed on July 12, 2019.

because youth is always beautiful, for we are born with a clean slate, each and every one of us.

Despite what life held in store for me, I feel like Fortune's darling, because for eighteen years and six months I had a home, a father, a mother, a little sister, grandparents, nearly twenty cousins, and countless other relatives. I led an active and exciting life full of adventure and discoveries in music, literature, and sports. I lived in the city and I lived on the farm, I lived on the plains and by the edge of the marshlands. I lived among all kinds of animals, domesticated and wild, and there were always people around me who gave me a lot of love. At the time, this was the most natural thing in the world.

My youth came to an abrupt end on the 1st of July 1944 on the ramp of Birkenau. The life I have described above was gone in the split second it takes to wave a hand – Mengele's motion that ordered me into one line and the rest of my family into the other.

My youthful years were enriched by an impressive congregation of storytellers who had seen life and who had seen war. Everyone around me told me stories, my maternal grandfather, my uncles, even the servants on the farm. After a while, what they'd seen came pouring out of them in the shape of stories, and so I had a chance to observe that if the stories were personal and involved the venues of the First World War – *the* Battle of Isonzo, *the* battle of Doberdo, like this, with the definite article emphasized – the stories would be more complete, and would end with a punchline, the heroic actions of the storyteller. So I learned to suspect stories that turned into stereotypes.

My story is just one of many. It is, to a degree, typical, which is one reason why I have decided to write it down. The other is that, as I have already mentioned, so many different people have encouraged me to do so, even though I wondered what I could possibly say that was new sixty years after the fact. And would anyone care?

An old man thinks back on his life the way a wanderer on a mountain top looks back down on the landscape lying below his feet. He takes everything in at once, what is near as well as what is far. But because he sees everything at once, events in time do not line up in chronological order, but dovetail one with the other. Though the law of physics would seem to counter-indicate it, it *is* possible to be in several places at the same time. It doesn't even take much imagination. After all, a person has gone through so many things and their opposites as well. All you have to do is to remember.

And now I will gather my fistful of courage, and humbly, yet with full conviction, would like to tell Freud and Jung and Fromm and all their predecessors and successors, disciples and detractors, all the vulgar psychologists of our age, that growing up in a happy, well-balanced family is nothing to be ashamed of. On the contrary. It is the best thing in the world.

My childhood, lost in a haze of purple clouds, so ideal that it cannot be idealized enough if I'm to render its true atmosphere, has been my faithful companion throughout a lifetime. I have clung to those eighteen and a half years with my soul. It is those eighteen and a half years that have given me the support, strength, and compassion that will now surely hold out for as long as I need them.

Auschwitz-Birkenau, July 1, 2003.

The Twenty-Third Hour. Is Anyone Left to Remember?

Anyone who has been in Auschwitz has two lives, a life before Auschwitz and a life after it. In your life after Auschwitz, be it ever so long, in every moment of that life and in every recess of your body and in every hidden corner of your soul, it is there whether you like it or not, whether you try to suppress it or choose to talk about it. Auschwitz is there lurking in the background.

After decades of deliberation, hesitation, and anxiety-filled preparations, on July 1, 2003, fifty-nine years to the day after I arrived in Auschwitz-Birkenau in the early morning of July 1, 1944, I finally took the plunge. I wanted to confront my memories alone, without company. I could almost say that I returned home to Birkenau. If members of certain primitive tribes take the bones of their ancestors with them when they move camp because they say that their home is where the mortal remains of their ancestors repose, if one's roots are where one's dear departed lie in the earth, then I should never have left Birkenau to begin with. The ashes of my immediate family were dumped in the nearby swamps, and so were the ashes of my extended family, and if I say they are fifty in number, I am not far off the mark. I can't help thinking that I have deserted them, and that my place should be with them, one more handful of dust in the swamps of Birkenau.

I dreaded this reunion, the reunion with the all too familiar landscape, the swamp, the long rows of barracks, the fences topped with barbed wire and charged with electricity, the watch towers that encircled the camp, from where the guards kept an eye on us day and night, the dreary, desolate surroundings, where nothing, not even a blade of grass, could survive, because tens of thousands of feet trampled over it day in and day out.

I dreaded having to experience yet again the atmosphere, filled with tension, bursting at the seams with cries, cruelty, filth, and the stench of overcrowded humanity, the hunger, the thirst, and the constant humiliation that was relentlessly doled out to us, the unaccountable bad feeling that the loss of control over one's fate, the uncertainty, the sense of futility bring out in a person, because this is what Birkenau had meant to me, and more.

But I was in for a shock. What I saw left me unimpressed. Auschwitz had become a tourist destination, accompanied by an incredibly bad Russian film that did more to hide what had taken place there than to reveal it.

In Birkenau the air was refreshing and pleasant, the landscape transformed beyond recognition, the meadow covered in a thick carpet of undulating green grass imparting a sense of calm, the wildflowers nodding their heads at me from among the grass. Peace and tranquillity all around. My eyes wandered in search of grazing sheep and the shepherd boy with his penny whistle, for nothing could have suited the idyllic landscape more. Instead they found a strange forest of chimneys and the remnants of the heating system that stretched along the former barracks and ended in the chimneys. At one end of the landscape, like a baroque garden, ruins – the tumbledown remains of the demolished crematorium. But where was the Lagerstrasse,[1] and where the Appelplatz?[2]

I had never been in this place before.

And I couldn't refrain from thinking that if this place says nothing to me, who had experienced things here that have influenced the rest of my life and will weigh on my soul like a nightmare as long as I live, if what I see here has so little effect on me, what could it possibly say to an "outsider"? Is there a way to relate, to explain, to pass on what had happened in Auschwitz and Birkenau sixty years before?

---

1 Lagerstrasse (German): the main road between lines of barracks in the camp.
2 Appelplatz (German): a large central square, the site of the notorious twice-daily roll calls.

The fact that there is no Hungarian-language slate in front of the demolished crematoria to tell the world that, in a record-breaking fifty-one days starting in April 1944 (according to the latest data), three hundred and forty thousand Hungarian Jews were cremated in this camp with no regard for age or gender – this made me think. Still, better late than never. I hope to see the day when this plaque, too, will be unveiled to stand in the company of all the others.

How many of the survivors are left to remember?

Hundreds of us die every day. Even the youngest of us is past seventy, but most of us are in our eighties and nineties.

Though I tried to relegate them to the deepest recesses of my subconscious mind (if, indeed, there are several recesses of the subconscious), my memories, like the memories of us all, are indelible.

Is anyone left to remember with me the almost tangible, persistent tension in the air in which there was no knowing what catastrophe might strike at any moment? Is anyone left to remember the constant screaming ringing in our ears? Because in Auschwitz, nobody spoke. The Kapos,[3] the Blockältestes,[4] the Stubendienstes,[5] the SS, the guards, even the truck drivers knew only one way of making themselves known to us – by screaming at the top of their lungs.

Is anyone left to remember the crowded conditions under which you couldn't walk a yard's length without bumping into someone? Or the everlasting Appels[6] early every morning and every night, the Lagerstrasse paved with sharp, pointed basalt rock on which we're forced to kneel with arms stretched towards the sky whenever the Appel doesn't tally, and we can't move until the "culprit" is found, maybe a woman who has heard that her daughter or mother is in the other camp and has gone to find them, only

---

3 Kapo (German): Often notoriously sadistic overseers of the inmates' work details, usually chosen from the criminals within their ranks. Also used to describe any concentration camp inmate put in charge of other inmates by the SS.
4 Blockälteste (German): Literally "elders of the block," inmates put in charge of a single barrack.
5 Studendienste: Inmates responsible for domestic chores, such as delivering the daily food rations.
6 Appel (German): Roll call, held twice daily for long periods during which inmates were forced to stand.

to be brought back, and the two of them beaten to death in front of our eyes?

Is anyone left to recall the swamp as the only available source of water, whose only purpose is to add to our suffering because it is filthy and it stinks and it is contaminated, and you can't drink from it? Can anyone explain how we could restrain ourselves from drinking from it under the scorching sun of July and August, when we were made to sit outside all day long, because the barracks were only for sleeping?

Is anyone left who remembers the water barrow and the driver who filled it up? Way back when our camp, number BIIc, was built, they set up a water tank meant to serve a hundred people at most. This tank was refilled every day. But by the time I was taken to the camp, we numbered in the tens of thousands. We had no water, and the driver who brought the water beat the thirsty crowd with a whip when we stormed the water barrow like a herd of wild animals. His favourite pastime was to knock the water out of the hand of anyone who, by some miracle, was able to dip her cup into the barrow.

Is anyone left to remember the air, always laden, the smoking chimneys not far from our block, and can they remember that when we asked our Kapos where the rest of our family were, they laughed, pointed to the rising smoke, and said: There! We didn't believe them. Why are they so mean, we asked, why do they say such horrible things to us? Why do the Kapos want to add to our suffering?

I still remember our Blockälteste Sosanka, who was brought to Auschwitz from Czechoslovakia along with her five siblings in the winter of 1942 when there was nothing but snow and more snow in place of the future barracks. They were among those who started building the camp. They were surrounded by dogs, with the SS barracks at a distance. They toiled in the snow, for months they washed themselves with snow, with no place to huddle up for warmth. Of the six siblings she was the only one to survive. Today I know why she kept pointing to the smoking chimneys. Could anyone who had spent even one day in Auschwitz keep their humanity intact? And what is to be said of a person who buried her five siblings and survived at the price of unendurable physical hardship, humiliation, and evil acts that weighed on her soul for the rest of her life? For in order to survive in Auschwitz for years, you had to trample the living, and the dead, too, underfoot. You could survive, but you could not remain a human being.

Is anyone left who remembers the Blockälteste who stood in the door of her barrack all day long and screamed, demented, "I am a political prisoner! I am a political prisoner!" thus trying to distance herself from the miserable wretches around her, whereas even by non-Auschwitz standards she was as fat as a pig, because she gobbled up the rations of her fellows? She didn't seem to mind, apparently.

Is anyone left to remember the Revier[7] that was two blocks away from my own block, and where they took the corpses wrapped in blankets after every Appel? One day I was happy to discover that Auntie Kató Horváth, our paediatrician from Debrecen, was working in the Revier. We loved Auntie Kató very much. She was a sweet, kind lady. When we were ill, she treated us children as if we were grown-ups. She would explain to us what the matter was and what we could do to make it better. If she had to give us a shot, she always told us in advance that it would hurt a little, but it was going to make us better. Knowing that Aunt Kató was just two blocks down from me made me feel safe. But when the infectious dysentery caught up with me and I ran to her in the Revier, she screamed at me and threw me out, and even when I was outside, she still kept screaming, "You better not show your face here again, or I'll slap you!" I thought she'd gone crazy, whereas she was just trying to save me.

Is anyone left to recall the food portioning and the bowls that had been taken from the belongings of the deportees? Five of us ate out of one bowl, others out of a pot, a pan, a cup, but needless to say without utensils or a chance to rinse them. Small piles of chloride of lime were scattered throughout the camp, which we used for cleaning the bowls, because there was no water around. To this day, when I smell chlorine – and I smell it every time the water from the tub flows down the drain – I am back in Auschwitz.

Is anyone left to remember the unparalleled Auschwitz cuisine? In the morning they gave us some sort of liquid in our shared

---

7 Revier (German): the sick barrack.

bowl. They said it was coffee (who were they kidding?), and we drank it in the following manner: each of us took two sips, and then maybe two more the second time around, and if anything of the nondescript liquid was still left at the bottom, each of us could have one last sip. We were not yet familiar with the dog-eat-dog rule of Auschwitz. We still counted the sips to make sure that each of us received an equal share.

Anyone who has been to Auschwitz remembers the Auschwitz recipe for Dörrgemüse. Under normal circumstances, Dörrgemüse is a tasty vegetable dish made from dried ingredients. In Auschwitz there was no knowing what was in the cauldron from which we were given an inedible mixture of grass, wood, twigs, leaves, and other ingredients of unascertainable origin. But we kept on telling each other that we must stay strong and healthy, until we actually managed to force ourselves to eat the contents of our communal bowl. There was one dish, however, that I couldn't swallow no matter what – the sweet porridge. I have never been able to guess how and from what it was made. It was so cloyingly sweet that a single bite turned my stomach, so no matter how hungry I was, I couldn't swallow it.

Anyone who has been to Auschwitz also remembers the slop-pail, which became a reliable means of humiliating us. Thanks to the over-eager Hungarian authorities, in just under two months, four hundred and thirty thousand Hungarians were taken to Auschwitz, a veritable flood of newcomers that the camp was ill prepared to receive. Though I did not have a chance to study the original blueprints, I speak from experience when I say that in order to function at an optimum, the carefully planned death camp would have been ideally suited to a tenth of its inmates. There were at least ten times as many of us, alas, and consequently, there were ten times fewer latrines than were needed.

This is where the slop-pail came into the picture.

The slop-pail was a sort of ante-latrine, which is one way of putting it. The other is that every full slop-pail had to reach the latrine. Except, because of the above-mentioned state of over-crowdedness, there weren't enough slop-pails either, and so the overflowing slop-pail also became part and parcel of the Auschwitz "landscape."

In order to use it, it had to be emptied out, which meant that it had to be picked up, and owing to the law of gravity, even with the greatest of care this entailed the spilling of its contents all over our hands, feet, and clothes. Then once we reached the latrine, the pail had to be slightly tipped so its contents could be dumped where they belonged, which invariably meant yet another close encounter with them over our hands, feet, and clothes. Water, soap, and towels were not part of the amenities of Auschwitz.

The suffering and humiliation cannot be forgotten, nor do I want to forget – neither I, nor my former fellow inmates. But how can "our" Auschwitz, or "my" Birkenau, be handed down even to our closest relatives and loved ones, if they weren't there with us in a place then? The place where not a single blade of grass survived, where sharp grey stones lined the Lagerstrasse, where we stood for Appel until we fainted, and where today nature holds sway?

Our memories of the real Auschwitz and the real Birkenau have been overgrown by grass, now and for all time to come.

Adolf (Ábrahám) Fahídy, my paternal grandfather, at the age of seventy-seven, Kassa, 1937.

The Fahídy/Fahídies. What Is a Fahidi Like?

In 1939, our family asked my uncle Miklós Fahidi, the district physician of Kassa, to obtain documents related to our ancestry. During the war some of these documents were lost, some survived thanks to my uncle Miklós's circumspection. When, with the end of the war in the mid-1940s, we wanted to replace the missing documents, it turned out that during the German occupation of Hungary and after, the family records kept by the Jewish congregations had been destroyed.

Beginning with 1939, the authorities asked for the originals of the documents to be presented to prove that we, the Fahídy/Fahídies, had been living in Hungary since before 1848, and that we were Hungarian citizens. The documents also proved that we were always called Fahídy, sometimes with a *y*, sometimes with an *i*, but we were never Feigenbaum or Fuchs. We didn't Magyarize our name, like so many other Jews. It also turned out that all the Fahídies known to me hailed from Fehérgyarmat and its vicinity. Regardless of where fate took them, everyone by this name hails from the same branch and they are all related.

At the time we didn't know about Kamen'ets-Podolsk.[1]

---

1 Kamen'ets-Podolsk (today Kam'ianets-Podil'skyy in Ukraine), in Soviet Ukraine, territory then occupied by the German army, was the location of the mass murder of approximately twenty-three thousand Jews. Eighteen thousand of them were Jews from Hungary, expelled and handed over to the SS by the Hungarian authorities because they did not have the documents to prove their Hungarian citizenship. For more details and the massacre's place in the Holocaust, see the entry in the Holocaust Encyclopedia of the United States Holocaust Memorial Museum, last accessed July 3, 2019, https://encyclopedia.ushmm.org/content/en/article/kamenets-podolsk.

Születési anyakönyvi kivonat.

21 szám.

Kelt: *Fehérgyarmaton*

1*899* (ezer *nyolczszázkilenczvenkilencz*) évi

Februái hó *21* (*huszonegy*) napján.

Megjelent az alulírott anyakönyvvezető _____ előtt

Fahídy Ábrahám ,

akinek állása (foglalkozása): *Szabómester.*

lakóhelye: *Fehérgyarmat*

s aki *alulírott anyakönyvvezető*

személy *eseu isme*

és bejelentette a következő születést:

családi és utóneve: *Fahídy Ábraham*

A törvényes atya

vallása: *izraelita*

állása (foglalkozása): *Szabómester*

lakóhelye: *Fehérgyarmat 460 Luiszaiu*

születéshelye: *Mező Tarpa* *Tarpa*

életkora: *37* (*harminczhét*) éves,

családi és utóneve: *Fahídy Ábrahámné –*

Született Reteh Fáni

vallása: *izraelita*

állása (foglalkozása): *háztartásbeli*

Az anya

lakóhelye: *Fehérgyarmat*

születéshelye: *Fehérgyarmat*

életkora: *31* (*harminczegy*) éves,

(Above and opposite) Birth certificate of Herman, Adolf Fahídy's son, February 14, 1889.

A születés helye: *Fehérgyarmat*

ideje: 1899 (ezer *nyolczszáztilenczvenkilencz*)

évi *februári* hó 14 (*tizennégy*)

napjának délután 4 (*négy*) órája.

A gyermek neme: *fiú*; vallása *izraelita*

utóneve: *Herman*

Megjegyzés:

Felolvastatván

helybenhagyatott és *aláíratott*

anyakönyvvezető.   bejelentő.

Bizonyitom, hogy ez a kivonat a *Fehérgyarmat* i anyakönyvi kerület születési anyakönyvével *szószerint* megegyez.

Kelt *Fehérgyarmat*

anyakönyvvezető.

Kiállítási díj

We like to tell the world about the contributions Hungary made to European culture and history. Throughout the centuries, we can always find something we can be proud of. On the other hand, historians have not yet explained why the prelude to so many shameful events was also played out here. For instance, as one of his "good deeds," our overzealous Prime Minister Pál Teleki[2] pushed through Parliament the first anti-Jewish law of the twentieth century, not that he had to twist anyone's arm. Our "Chief Scout," as he was known, thus served as a model for Hitler, who, politically speaking, was still in diapers at the time. As a prelude to the Holocaust in Hungary, we also deported and killed over twenty three thousand Jews in Kamen'ets-Podolsk in August 1941.

A couple of years ago when I translated approximately three thousand personal histories for the Claims Conference, I was horrified to read the testaments of some of the survivors. Without exception, they were all Hungarian citizens, and women.

After the German occupation of Poland in 1939, the Hungarian government allowed Polish military troops to seek asylum here, and along with them came Polish Jews fleeing the Germans. For a while the Hungarian authorities looked the other way. Some of the newcomers married into Hungarian Jewish families, including families like ours. The newcomers, along with many other Jews who could not provide proof of citizenship simply because they had never bothered to acquire the necessary documents, were considered as so much chaff. A family might have lived here for a hundred years or more; if they didn't have papers to prove it, they were considered "aliens."

Because of the responsibility of Hungarian state authorities, the massacre has been the subject of ongoing controversy. In 2014 the director of the government-funded Veritas Historical Institute characterized the massacre as not part of the Holocaust and merely an "administrative measure" to deal with foreign citizens.

2 Count Pál Teleki (1879–1941), a prominent geographer, was prime minister of Hungary 1920–1 and 1939–41. Under his government, in September 1920, Parliament enacted the notorious numerus clausus law, the first anti-Semitic act of legislation in interwar Europe. He committed suicide over Hungary's breach of the Yugoslav-Hungarian treaty of friendship in April 1941. He was honorary chief of the Hungarian Scouts.

I like to slip inside other people's skin and see the world through their eyes. It is only possible to understand someone if you have shared experiences. I know what it is like to wander about in the world without roots like a piece of windswept straw, with nothing to hold on to. I know what it is like when there is no one in the big wide world to make you feel that you are needed. I know what it is like when you know that if you were to disappear, no one would notice. This is how those unfortunate Polish Jews must have felt who managed to flee the occupying German forces, probably at the cost of incredible difficulties, and who found a community to welcome them in Hungary. They joined Hungarian families and perhaps even found themselves loving wives. But they were not Hungarian citizens, and they did not become Hungarian citizens by virtue of becoming members of families who had put down roots in Hungary a hundred, a hundred and fifty years previously.

Not by a long shot.

They had to register with the KEOKH.[3] How was it decided when they would be forced to leave the country? The day when the authorities came for them (mostly in August 1941) – some remember policemen, others soldiers – and dragged them off, together with their wives, children, in-laws, and all their relatives who lived in the same house, with no regard to the fact that these family members were Hungarian citizens of long standing. And while they were at it, the Hungarian authorities also dragged off those Hungarian Jewish families who had been living here for decades but didn't have papers to prove it. They were taken to Kamen'ets-Podolsk in German-occupied Ukraine, where German firing squads were waiting for them, and where, with inconceivable cruelty, they made the fathers watch as they beat their children to death, and the children, as they killed their fathers. I came in contact only with the testimonies of women whose lives were saved by Hungarian soldiers who helped them sneak back to Hungary.

---

3 KEOKH: the Hungarian acronym of the Central National Authority for the Control of Foreigners, a branch of the Ministry of the Interior between 1931 and 1944.

Jegyzőkönyv.

        Készült Tarpa községben 1939 évi május hó 2o-án Dr.
Fahidi Miklós kassai lakos kérelmére Blau Izráel?Simon József
és Rácz József tarpai lakosok kihallgatása alkalmával.
        Jelen vannak alulirottak.
        Mely alkalommal fentnevezettek megjelentek a közsé-
gi elöljáróság előtt és a következő nyilatkozatot tették:
        Blau Izráel 82 éves tarpai lakos a következőket ad-
ja elő.Tarpán születtem 1857.évben és határozottan visszaemlék-
szem,hogy Fahidi József,akit a zsidók között Mózesnek is hivtak
tarpai lakos volt,fuvarozással foglalkozott és tudomásom sze-
rint - hallásból tudom anyámtól aki 1831-ben született - hogy
tarpai születésű volt.Édesanyámtól hallottam,hogy Fahidi József
Mózes 1825 körül születhetett itt Tarpa községben.Tudomásom van
arról,hogy Fahidi József Mózesné szül.Paul Katalin 1873-ban halt
el Tarpa községben és akkor a legidősebb leánya 21 éves volt,
aki itt tarpán született.
        Simon József 84 éves és Rácz József 80 éves,mindket-
ten tarpai lakosok a fenti ügyre vonatkozoan előadják a követ-
kezőket már gyermekkorunkból határozottan visszaemlékszünk Fahidi Józsefre,akit köznyelven Orás Józsefnek hivtak,emlékszünk
arra is,hogy fuvarozással foglalkozott.
        Blau Izráel előadja még a következőket:
        Fahidi József Mózest azért hivta a köznép Orás Jó-
zsefnek,mert gyermekkorába árván maradt és nagybátyja Fahidi
Izsák nevelte,akinek a foglalkozása orás volt igy maradt ő reá
is az Orás elnevezés.
        Jegyzőköny a felek által aldiratott.

                Kmf.

                                    Rácz József
                                    Simon József
                                    Blau Izráel

1253/1939 k.i.sz.

        Tarpa község elöljárósága hivatalosan igazolja,hogy
a fenti jegyzőkönyvet fentnevezettek a községi elöljáróság előtt
sajátkezüleg irták alá és nyilatkozatuk megtétele előtt a hamis-
tanuzás büntettére figyelmeztetve lettek.

                Tarpa,1939 évi május hó 2o-án.

            Reinár   Filep Zsigmond
            jegyző   TARPA   biró

Evidence given by Izráél Blau, József Simon, and József Rácz at Tarpa,
May 20, 1939 (translation opposite).

Recorded in the township of Tarpa on the 20th day of the month of May in the year 1939 upon the request of Dr Miklós Fahidi, resident of Kassa, on the occasion of the questioning of Izráél Blau, József Simon, and József Rácz, residents of Tarpa.

Made in the presence of the undersigned.

On which occasion the above-mentioned appeared in front of the town prefecture and made the following attestation:

Izráél Blau, 82, of Tarpa attests as follows: I was born in Tarpa in the year 1857, and I remember perfectly that József, whom the Jews also called Mózes, was also a resident of Tarpa and was a carter by trade, and as far as I know – I heard it from my mother, who was born in 1831 – he was born in Tarpa. I heard from my mother that József Mózes Fahidi must have been born around 1825 here in Tarpa township. I also know that Mrs József Mózes Fahidi, née Katalin Paul, passed away in 1873 in the township of Tarpa and her eldest daughter was 21 years old at the time, and she was also born here in Tarpa.

József Simon, 84, and József Rácz, 80, both residents of Tarpa, further attest to the following with regard to the matter at hand: We remember József Fahidi perfectly from our childhood, who was popularly called József the Watchmaker, and they called him that because having been orphaned as a child, his uncle Izsák Fahidi brought him up, who was a watchmaker by trade. That's how he also became to be known as the Watchmaker.

Affidavit as signed by the participants,

József Rácz
József Simon
Izráél Blau

Case no. 1253/1939

The prefecture of Tarpa township officially attests that the above affidavit was signed by the above-named in their own hand in front of the prefecture and that they were were cautioned about the crime of bearing false witness before making their attestation.

Tarpa, 1939, 20th of May.

(Signatures: Notary and Magistrate)

So then, in 1939 we Fahídy/Fahídies were able to prove that our ancestor, a haulier by the name of József/Mózes, came into the world most probably in 1825 (exactly a hundred years before me) in Magyartarpa, and that he was the nephew of Izsák Fahídi, born at least twenty-five years previously, who made an honest living from watch-making and took in our József/Mózes when he was orphaned. This is why our ancestor József/Mózes Fahídi received the nickname Joseph the Watchman. In retrospect, the document acquires a certain *je ne sais quoi* by dint of the fact that the information came from Izráél Blau, an eighty-six-year-old man from Tarpa, whose words the esteemed Hungarian authorities accepted as an official statement in the turbulent years just before the war.

My grandfather Ábrahám/Adolf Fahídy was the oldest Fahídy I knew. I never liked him very much, and I was afraid of him. He never stroked my hair, he never sat me on his lap or told me stories. I didn't like him, and he never had a chance, because I kept comparing him to my maternal grandfather, Alfréd Weisz, whom I adored. For me, his granddaughter, he was one of the most attractive and most interesting people in the world!

By the time I became acquainted with Ábrahám Fahídy, he had already changed his name to Adolf. Let it be said to his credit that when in the early 1900s he abandoned the to me beautiful but too Jewish-sounding biblical name of Ábrahám for Adolf, he had no way of knowing what a shameful career his newly adopted name would enjoy. He was a well-known master tailor in Kassa by then, but he began practising his trade in Fehérgyarmat, where he married my grandmother, Fáni Retek, and where he fathered eight boys and two girls in the following order:

1887	Móric
188?	Henrik
1890	Antal
1893	Zoltán
1895	Dezső
1899	Herman
1901	Miklós
1904	Sándor

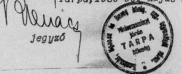
From the prefecture of Tarpa township
No. 1285/1939

Town Certificate

The Prefecture of Tarpa township hereby certifies that by the late 1840s
József (Mózes) Fahidi was a permanent resident of Tarpa township and
owned real estate at the time and paid taxes on it.

The authentication of the above is based on the writ of ownership
presented to us by the person in question, appended for the archives
by József Fahidi, according to which during the time mentioned above
the attachment designated him as the owner.

Tarpa, in the year 1939, on the 22nd day of the month of May.

(Signatures: Notary and Magistrate)

Certificate issued by the town of Tarpa (top) and the translation of the
certificate.

| 1906 | Gizi |
| 1908 | Emma |

Adolf Fahídy reminded me of an ascetic rather than a tailor. His grey, deep-set eyes looked out at the world with an expression of surprise and severity. I mention only by way of an aside that, as far as I was concerned, a real tailor was more like Jóska Molnár, first of Debrecen, then of Pest. He made me my first grown-up coat when I was eighteen, and he continued to make me very happy with countless suits and coats until he was eighty-five years old. He was a true artist. When I went for a fitting and he found something on a shoulder or collar that needed fixing, he got up on a small stool so he could reach me. Adolf Fahídy was thin-boned and tall. I inherited his hands and his deep-set grey eyes along with love and respect for the sewing needle and, indeed, all work done by hand.

Adolf was profoundly and deeply religious. He visited us once a year. Before his arrival, the household went into a frenzy. We slaughtered several pigs every year and sinned right and left because of the treif[4] kitchen we kept, so our kitchen could not provide so much as a morsel for my grandfather's kosher gullet. We needed to get Grandfather's strictly kosher food from a strictly kosher place. But it did not stop here: strictly kosher cooking called for two sets of pots and pans, one for dairy and one for meat, and the two kinds of dishes had to be stored and washed in two different wash basins, and the two places for storing meat and dairy had to be made kosher every year to the accompaniment of my mother's malicious comments, which, let it be said to her credit, were not delivered in my father's presence.

Anyway, it was early summer, and the time for Grandfather's visit was fast approaching. Out in the garden the arbour of lilacs bloomed in their full magnificence so that Grandfather could conduct his memorable morning prayers under it. I felt uncomfortable with the accoutrements of this ritual, and the way he went about his prayers scared me.

---

4 Treif or trayf (Yiddish): Food that is not kosher, not handled according to the rules of the Kashrut, the Jewish dietary rules, and as such is forbidden to Orthodox Jews.

Group photograph of the older Fahídy boys.

Later, when I was a little older and discovered that as soon as my grandfather finished davening he lost no time in gulping down a shot of our best homemade strawberry schnapps, which was conveniently near at hand, I thought sacrilegiously that perhaps that was why Grandfather had to hurry so much with his prayers, and this warmed my heart towards him a touch.

Even later, when I was a grown-up, I thought back on Adolf's prayers with humble respect, because by then I knew that anyone who has faith goes through life on a path strewn with roses. He has an explanation for everything that happens to him, all his sufferings have a purpose, and throughout a lifetime, and even beyond, he is compensated for all his losses by his FAITH. Someone who has faith is happy and is to be envied.

I also didn't like Adolf very much because every time he came, he made disparaging remarks about my favourite tree, which shaded the window of my room, insisting that we should cut it down. Wanting to play it safe, Uncle Janatka, our neighbour and

Imperial and Royal gardener,[5] had grafted two buds onto the seed-ling, cherry on one side and sour cherry on the other. This became apparent for all concerned only when the small tree planted under my window grew big enough to burst into bloom, and it produced an abundant yield. What a magnificent tree it was! I was the only person around who had a tree that could yield cherries and sour cherries at the same time! Also, it offered its branches to my feet so invitingly that I kept climbing up, and I built a treehouse among its branches. It was a fabulous place for reading. Yet grandfather Adolf wanted this tree to be felled because his God knew only one kind of tree, and that tree yielded only one kind of fruit, and if a tree didn't conform, it went against nature and had to be got rid of. To think how many people and things have been annihilated on this earth in the name of God!

Ábrahám/Adolf Fahídy was otherwise a modern man who welcomed new things. He changed his name, too, to show his willingness to assimilate. He was proud of the fact that his workshop was the first in Kassa to have electric light installed, and that his apprentices and assistants didn't need to work by the pale glow of a candle or petroleum lamp. On the other hand, like so many things on this earth, his striving to be modern also had its limits. When in 1936 his beloved fifth son, my father Dezső, decided to go one better and continue his father's striving for assimilation by abandoning the faith of his ancestors in favour of Roman Catholicism, Adolf went into mourning. As far as he was concerned, his son's decision had trespassed the permissible limits of assimilation. In keeping with ancient custom, he rent his clothes, sprinkled ashes on his head, in his heart buried, mourned, and disowned us, and never forgave us.

Many years had to pass before I dared to subject my father's actions to scrutiny. The "List of questions I never asked him" is headed by the belated question, why did he do it? Or, more to the point, how could he, with all his brains, be so naïve as to put his

5 Imperial and Royal: from the German "Kaiserliche und Königliche," in abbreviated form K. und K., was part of the official name of the institutions of the Austro-Hungarian Monarchy.

hopes in the conversion? I know that he did it to save us from harm. I know how difficult it is for someone to defend his actions in his own eyes when everyone around him thinks that they are indefensible. But a human being is always what he is – he is himself, a fact that he must accept, regardless of the circumstances.

From the age of eleven, I was brought up as a pious Catholic, which confused me, to say the least. We had never been observant Jews, and suddenly, when we turned Catholic, I found myself face to face with dogmas. Up until then I was taught that if I didn't understand something, I should keep asking questions until I found an explanation. But dogmas cannot be questioned, whereas I can believe only in something I understand. And so, although I'm not a religious Jew, I am a highly aware Jew. Of course, what else could I be with Auschwitz behind me?

I wonder what my grandmother Fáni Retek was like. I never met her. Her name is like music to my ears.[6] All I know about her is that she was the daughter of the master tailor of Fehérgyarmat who initiated Ábrahám/Adolf into the mysteries of tailoring. I also know that, in contrast to Adolf, she must have been a thick-boned, long-limbed young woman, which is why some of her sons wouldn't stop growing until they reached at least 180 centimetres in height – her legacy to them. This legacy was also passed on to my father and my uncles Antal and Herman, who represented the Fahídy/Fahidi spirit in my eyes. I was brought up in the same spirit and was taught to be proud of it.

When I think of Fáni, I think of the old Jewish joke according to which a woman is either expecting or nursing, and if she is neither then she is sick. She brought eleven children into the world, and, what was a rarity at the time, only one died in childhood. For all I know, I may have inherited my mania for cleanliness from her. Fáni gave birth to her children, for a time looked after them, and then, like one who had done her duty here on earth, she gave her soul back to her Maker.

Adolf mourned Fáni as he should and then, in accordance with the divine dictate to be fruitful and multiply, he married again.

---

6 The last name, Retek, translates as "radish."

(Besides, he had a bunch of unruly children at home.) With the waning of his procreative powers, he had to be satisfied this time with siring two beautiful girls, Rózsika and Szerénke, who ended up in the gas chambers of Auschwitz.

Independently of historical circumstances and the facts that continue to be treated from various perspectives and judged and explained in line with a variety of considerations, I would like the world to take note of the following:

For our family, Trianon was a personal disaster.[7]

Both on my father's and my mother's side, the newly established frontiers separated members of our family, and we never stopped talking about our grievances. For one thing, in order to see each other we now had to apply for a passport, and for another, the existence of the new frontiers, whose legitimacy we refused to acknowledge, prevented us from seeing each other as often as we would have liked. We tried as best we could to retaliate, to get back at the ridiculous situation by cheating at customs and also cheating when it came to exchanging currencies. For instance, we could take flowers and presents across the border now only after we'd paid customs duty, a circumstance that we used for revenge, as you will later hear. The frontier that yesterday was not there but now formed a very real obstacle was not something we could accept or even comprehend. As far as we were concerned, Hungary lay on both sides of the border.

All at once, Fahídy Adolf became Adolf Fahidy, and his daughters were now called Fahidiová, which we couldn't even pronounce without hurting our tongue, even though we spoke Slovak.[8] Furthermore, without ever leaving his home in Kassa,

---

7 The Trianon Treaty, signed in June 1920, annexed over two-thirds of Hungary's pre-war territory and over 60 per cent of its pre-war population to Romania and the new states of Czechoslovakia, Yugoslavia, and Austria. The dominant right-wing, nationalistic rhetoric of the interwar period blamed the disaster of Trianon on Hungary's two postwar revolutions, said to be orchestrated and led by Jews. According to the same rhetoric, Jews could not possibly share in the national trauma.

8 In the original, the author uses the familiar and sometimes derogatory "Tót" for Slovak.

which remained in the same place, on the same street and at the same address, one fine morning my grandfather woke up in Czechoslovakia, whereas he'd got used to the fact that for him, the sun rose in Hungary and set in Hungary. He received a summons to town hall, and when he showed up, he was told that he'd do wise to change his dangerous-sounding Hungarian name to Fučik or something similar that sounded Czech. Adolf Fahídy lost his cool and said:

"I was born a Hungarian, I will die a Hungarian, and as for my name, I will not change it."

In this way he became a dangerous Hungarian element, and for a long time had to make a weekly, then monthly, visit to the police headquarters of Kassa. But he refused to relinquish the name Fahídy. For their part, the authorities refused to grant him a passport for some time to come.

What could life have been like at the home of Ábraham/Adolf and Fáni? Their oldest and youngest children were separated by twenty-one years. The eight oldest children had already flown the coop when, having crossed the threshold of adulthood at the age of thirteen upon their bar mitzvah, my grandfather sent them on their way. They all made something of themselves. Some finished middle school, two had a high-school diploma, one became a doctor, and one a high-school teacher. Others became merchants, bank clerks, and entrepreneurs. None of the boys continued in his father's footsteps or became an artisan, though. Only the two girls learned to sew.

This family, like so many other families, was divided into rich and poor branches. The wealthy branch of the family were very close and were business partners. They signed mutual contracts as if they were total strangers, and they honoured these contracts to the letter, because the family stood at the top of the pyramid of values. Such a trivial thing as money could not harm the most important thing, the unity of the family. If they lent money to each other, they repaid it on time to the last penny. Naturally, they did not charge each other interest. As for the poorer branch of the family, the wealthy branch made sure to assist them with money, clothing, invitations, and the like.

Though they may not have finished the six grades of elementary school, Adolf and Fáni knew a thing or two about bringing up children. I would bet that they were responsible for the rules that the family followed after them, and which made us capable of telling right from wrong, and what traits the family should be proud to own. There were a number of guidelines or slogans, though that's not what we called them back then, that were repeated to us until they became second nature.

We were not allowed to lie, not because, as the saying goes, a mendacious man is caught quicker than a lame dog, but because telling lies is below a Fahídi's dignity. Besides, it would be discovered, and then we'd have to hang our heads in shame. And also, the best lie is the truth. It doesn't call for complicated stories. From time to time, though, the family stooped to threats. "I'll rip your tongue out through your back if you lie," my mother said, since she was prone to sanguinary outbursts that we considered theatrical and humorous rather than deadly serious. I even imagined Mother holding a gigantic pair of tweezers, and looking for my tongue in the middle of my back and not finding it. No wonder. The end result was that no matter what mischief we were up to, we weren't afraid to own up to it. We knew that we'd be punished, but it was a relief to talk it out.

It took me many years to learn the advantage of telling a white lie. I hate to think of the consequences of telling the truth regardless of the circumstances. For instance, upon meeting them, I would say to my beloved old classmates: "You look absolutely wonderful!" Can you imagine me saying to them, instead: "What an old bag you've become since I last saw you. You look absolutely terrible!"

The world has changed beyond recognition since then. Nowadays the saying goes: Speak the truth and you get your head cracked.

We were proud of being the way we were – that our grandfather is a tailor, that my aunt is a seamstress, that we're a big family, that we work hard, that we love and help each other, and everyone else as well.

It's been a source of amusement to me that since the regime change in 1989, when searching for one's roots began enjoying a renaissance, no one seems poor enough not to have found at least an unassuming Polish duchess among their ancestors. Among my circle of acquaintances, from the dermatologist of humble gifts through a former colleague in foreign trade with a string of decent, down-to-earth Slovak ancestors in Pilisszentkereszt to her credit, suddenly everyone has a Polish duchess among his ancestors, or else a Transylvanian nobleman. We Fahídy/Fahidies always had plebeian tastes. We didn't look down on our ancestors who made a decent living with their own two hands. Luckily, our mother, who'd come from a very different environment, felt the same way.

There was one other thing we had to keep in mind at all times. We had to honour our given word, which included always being on time. Even today I feel a surge of shame if I am running late. It took me a while to realize that I'm sometimes late these days because, whereas in the past it took me twenty minutes to reach a place with ease, it now takes me forty at a slow crawl. Now I know.

The sanctity of the given word, honour, reliability, and "gentlemanly" conduct are concepts long gone.

I was taught that when I give my word, it weighs more heavily in the balance than any written document. As soon as I understood the full meaning of this teaching, I had my doubts, even if I couldn't put them into words, and I began to form some idea of what they call hypocrisy. This is how it came about.

Day after day, I was compelled to promise something that all of us – my parents, who made me promise, as well as I and my governess Ruth, and Grandfather and Grandmother, and every dog and cat in the yard as well as every horse in the stable and every hog in the sty and every sheep in the meadow and crane on the rooftop – knew that I would never keep, not today, not tomorrow, not ever, because I would never but never eat my soup, whereas I had to promise at every meal that the following day I would eat it.

The ritual around that soup was degraded into a monotonous daily chore, but we suffered through it all the same. Ours was a proper provincial household. We slaughtered at least two pigs each season, and God only knows how many more on the farm, since a side of bacon was part of the seasonal labourers' pay. We also cooked in the provincial style, rich, with lots of lard, so the soup had gleaming circles of fat floating on top and it was thickened with lots of roux. Maybe I knew back then that years later both lard and roux would be exiled from health-conscious households!

The soup was brought in, it was placed on the table, I smelt that typical fatty and roux smell, and my hunger vanished without recall. Everyone had finished lunch, the grown-ups had drunk their coffee, my soup had been taken away at least three times, warmed up, and placed in front of me, but the smell remained, and I couldn't eat it. And then my father or my mother would come and say:

"You're a bad, naughty girl, not eating that nice soup when so many poor children would gladly eat it, if only they could, so promise to eat your soup tomorrow!"

When my parents talked this way, all I could think of was that grown-ups are so silly. Why must we repeat this scene day after day when we all know perfectly well that it won't do any good?

From July 1944 I learned more about what lay behind this sentence. Anyone who has never gone without food doesn't know what hunger is like. In Allendorf, where our labour camp was located, we got soup made with roux every morning or, to be more exact, we got some nondescript lukewarm liquid with the consistency of water that had something that looked like little bits of congealed roux swimming at the bottom of a cauldron. Depending on whether you were very hungry or even hungrier, you stood at the head or the back of the line. Up front, you got your thin slop quickly. Standing in the back meant that you could cling to the hope that luck might smile on you and that a bit of roux might land in your plate in the shape of a small ball. Heaven itself! That's when I remembered the soup I wouldn't eat at home. I remembered every plate of soup I refused to eat.

I think that the earnestness with which we set about our chores was Adolf and Fáni's heritage. Whatever we did we did not only with the best of intentions, but with the solid resolve that whatever we were engaged in doing – today I'd say what we create – we engaged in to the best of our ability and were not satisfied with work half-done. As I remember it, every member of my family was driven by an inordinate amount of determination to do things. And truth to tell, whatever they did, they brought the maximum out of it.

At the beginning of the twentieth century, we still knew the meaning of honour, and I do not mean the rowdy, senseless circus that ends up with a duel between empty-headed fools. Back then people lived off of their honour, from the shoemaker and the carpenter through the bank president, though in the case of the latter, this concept was open to interpretation. But the majority of people were definitely honourable.

In the summer of 1943, the last I spent on the farm with Grand-father, I lost my wristwatch. It was a catastrophe because it was a graduation present, a Schaffhausen that my parents said I should have received only when I'd come of age, which at the time was twenty-one. My parents were happy if they could make me happy, so they gave me the watch early, and I lost it! Needless to say, I was afraid to tell them. I was anxious the whole day, worried that one of the grown-ups would discover that I was not wearing the watch. The next morning I was loitering in what we called the small kitchen when Uncle Móré, who was in charge of the oxen, came in with the watch.

"Young lady, Mari (the two oxen were called Misi and Mari) nearly stepped on it. A good thing I noticed," he said, and he handed me the watch. Uncle Móré could have easily kept it. He could have taken it to Miskolc to sell, or given it away. He could have done lots of things with it and no one would have been the wiser. But Uncle Móré gave me back the watch, because he had a sense of honour, even though he lived in a servant's quarters in ter-rible poverty. He could have spent the money he got for the watch in a thousand ways. But Uncle Móré gave me back that watch, because he was an honourable man.

The Fahídi Brothers Lumberyard Joint Stock Co. that my father and his brother founded in 1924 lived off of people's honour. The petty clerks, the tradesmen, especially the carpenters, the peasants – in short, just about everyone – bought the lumber for their houses and furniture on credit, and the credit was often for years, even a decade. Though they were insured, they and the lumberyard were taking a risk. But back then, the people extending credit were willing to take the risk because they knew that their creditors would not cheat them, because people held their honour in high regard and did not want to lose it. Today it would be a miracle for a painter to say that he will come at six on Monday morning to start working on the house, and to show up on time. Back then, if he promised to finish by the following Wednesday, he did finish. Because he had a sense of honour.

We learned to tell the difference between good and bad mainly from my mother. The greatest bad is what is bad for me. It must not be tolerated. But the bad that I do unto others is just as bad, even if it wasn't intended. Could it be that the secret of happiness is never having to do anything that is bad for me, but always being able to do what is good for me? Oh, how often I thought about this in Auschwitz and Allendorf! Does anyone actually live like that?

I was always a head taller than my contemporaries, and regardless of how scrawny I was – they used to call me titmouse and dried mosquito – because of all the exercise and sports, I was also nimbler and more adroit than they. I liked to show off, and still do, god forbid. I was taught to use my gifts to help those who were not like me. A weaker person than you should be protected and not beaten up, a person not as brainy as you should be instructed and not laughed at.

I was always surprised that in my father's eyes as well as my uncles' and my aunts', Adolf Fahídy enjoyed a special cachet that I simply could not understand. They respected him. They even said they loved him. Sometime during the 1970s, when Hungary still had a steel industry and Libya was swimming in money – after Kuwait, it was in Libya that the pittance of a per diem we got in forints was worth something – the unsold steel stocks of the Metalimpex Foreign Trade Company sent me to Tripoli. Life was a bowl of cherries there, the sidewalks were paved with gold, at the Arab market, the souk, the merchandise was piled from floor to ceiling, customs duty was non-existent, and sales tax was non-existent, so everything was actually cheaper than where it was made. The building boom was at its height. They needed the steel, and they bought it. They bought it from me, too. The merchants were doing well. Some of them spoke Italian or English, so we managed to communicate. To my great surprise, the head of the family, the merchant's father, was usually present at our discussions. He didn't speak any other languages, he couldn't read or write, but he had the last word. Whether he understood what was going on or not, if he nodded, the deal was struck, if he didn't, then not. He was the head of the family, the oracle, the Semitic ancestor whose word was law, just like Adolf Fahídy's word in his family. But then, we're descended from the same Semitic stock.

The words "value system" or "intellectual sensitivity" never passed our lips. We just lived by them.

Ernesztína Gross and Alfréd Weisz. Photograph taken at Nagytanya in the 1930s.

My Maternal Grandparents, Alfréd Weisz and Ernesztína Gross

There was no couple anywhere more mismatched than they.

Of course, I learned about this only much later, when their ashes had long since been absorbed by the swamps of Birkenau and I revisited my childhood with the throbbing pain you feel when you beat your fist against the wall of the irretrievable, knowing full well that it is in vain. For me they were the proverbial grandparents, and for them I was their first grandchild, the Liebling, the favourite, the Goldinko, the Golden One.

Grandfather was, above all, impressive. He was tall, corpulent, with hair that began to thin out at an early age. He was witty, even boisterous, a bullying god in the flesh issuing orders – an omnipotent authority. But you knew not to ask him for anything, because he'd give you the shirt off his back. We were always in awe of him, and he was like a benevolent lion. When he was in high spirits – which was luckily quite often – you could do anything you liked with him. But suddenly, often quite suddenly, he'd growl.

Oh, how he loved to growl!

When he was a young man, he loved letting his tenor loose on the world until the walls shook to their foundations. Also, when he cursed he had a formidable vocabulary. His curses knocked like sleet against a windowpane. They invariably started like this: "Herrgott, Sakrament," followed by a deluge from which, it must be said to his credit, all the unambiguous expressions used today to describe the classical manner of procreation and all its tools and variations were utterly missing, and which always ended with, "I'm no two-penny marlot." Actually, you learned to fear only the first round of curses, because by the time Grandfather launched into the second round, you realized that for him curses were just a way of letting off steam when he was close to the bursting point, and before long you'd hear, as a last echo, the familiar "two-penny marlot," and Grandfather would be all smiles again.

The most exciting thing about Grandfather was the special horse smell that issued from him. He didn't smell of horses because he was constantly with them; after all, the carriage drivers also smelled of horses, and so did the horses. My grandfather smelled of horses from the inside, because horses were his god, his one true love, his purpose in life, his pride, his everything. But right after his horses came I, his Goldinko.

Preoccupied with his horses as he was, Grandfather hardly noticed that he'd sired seven children with Ernesztína, especially since the first three were girls and so they didn't count. They were followed by four boys, but by that time the whole thing had become a bore – on home ground, at least – and especially where raising his children was concerned. Fortunately, he had his Lipizzaners to keep him occupied.

I'm not entirely fair to Alfréd. I understand perfectly well that in a proper Jewish family the firstborn has to be a boy, and that, in his case, something had gone terribly amiss. Being a practical man, however, he decided to treat his firstborn, the girl by the name of Irma who later became my mother, as if she were a boy. And because he loved her so much, he shaped her into his own image. This is how he compensated himself for his loss.

When she was of marriageable age, Grandfather watched his daughter like a hawk. He sent all of his three daughters to a girls' finishing school in Trencsénteplic, where their morals were strictly monitored, and where they were taken on their daily constitutionals only as far as the goose pasture. (Anna Kéthly[1] and Margit

---

1 Anna Kéthly (1889–1976) was the second woman elected to Parliament in 1922. She represented the Social Democratic Party until 1944. After the Second World War, between 1945 and 1948 she was deputy president of Parliament. During the Stalinist period she was arrested and spent four years in prison without trial, liberated in 1953. During the 1956 revolution she was named minister of state in the Imre Nagy government. After November 1956 she lived in exile.

Schlachta[2] were also students there.) Alfréd liked those months best when his two younger daughters were at the boarding school and his beloved Irma was at Ógyalla with him. Alas, such months were all too few and far between!

Irma couldn't wait to be married. She got meticulously dressed every morning, as if she were expecting an important visitor, because there was no telling who might show up on her doorstep, and show up he did.

The neighbour of our farm was a respectable matron of the Konkoly-Thege family,[3] an old countess who always wore black, and who, poor soul, was probably left behind in Ógyalla by way of safe deposit when most of the Konkoly family moved to Hungary in the wake of Trianon. She used the formal mode of address with her dogs, but reverted to the informal mode when talking to her servants. We, on the other hand, abided by plebeian morals and used the informal mode of address with all creatures of God. Also, the kissing of hands was out. I don't want to make us seem better than we were; the interdiction about the kissing of hands was probably for hygienic reasons. (Not so for the countess.)

My grandfather was born to run an estate and could not look on without comment when her servants, and especially her steward, led the poor countess by the nose. He soon became her confidant, discreetly guiding her in the right direction.

Visits from members of the populous Konkoly-Thege family were few and far between. Still, by some miracle a distant great-nephew landed on the old countess's doorstep. Though his name has not been recorded in the family annals, his story was.

Alfréd Weisz had no doubt that Irma would make a good match. For one thing, she was his daughter; for another, she looked like

---

2 Margit Schlachta (1884–1974), Conservative Catholic activist and the first woman representative elected to Parliament between 1920 and 1922. As founder and head of the religious order Catholic Social Sisters, between 1940 and 1945 she defended, rescued, and hid persecuted Jews. She went into exile in 1949.

3 Miklós Konkoly-Thege (1842–1916), astronomer, physicist, member of Parliament, and descendant of an old noble family, built the first observatory of international standards at his family estate in Ógyalla. After the Trianon Treaty, the core equipment of the observatory was moved to Budapest.

him. And last but not least, she was generally known to be expecting a handsome dowry. Also, Alfréd Weisz was no dope. He saw that his daughter was sitting on pins and needles, looking after her toilette more than usual ever since the countess's nephew had discovered his beloved daughter's charms and started paying daily visits to the estate. But he also knew that the Konkoly-Theges would consider a match with Irma a *mésalliance*, and clearly, that would not do. On the other hand, he couldn't very well fling the young courtier out by the seat of his pants. And so, Alfréd Weisz waited like a spider in the corner of its web, ready to spring into action. He didn't have to wait long.

There's no knowing when a member of the gentry might have stepped on Grandfather's toe, but we do know that as far as he was concerned, yellow riding boots were the embodiment *par excellence* of the gentry he so disparaged. We never had anything but black riding boots ourselves. Anyway, one fine day early in the morning it transpired that after an ample rain had thoroughly soaked the land, Irma's beau showed up in a pair of yellow riding boots. Through the glassed-in veranda of our house, girded round with Harzer canary cages, one could clearly make out a shape getting off a horse and a pair of yellow riding boots making for the house as their owner gingerly avoided the numerous puddles. That's all Alfréd Weisz needed! A red cape to the bull. He yanked the veranda door open and started shouting in his best tenor, "I dare you to enter my house in yellow riding boots! Who do you think I am? Gentry? I'm just a stinking Jew! So get lost!" Poor beau, he was so nonplussed that he backed away towards his horse and tripped and, I'm sorry to say, fell into a puddle, with his two yellow booted legs sawing the air.

In the years that followed, we thought less and less of the old countess, until one day something curious happened. In our house in Debrecen, all household duties had an appointed time and place. As far as Mother was concerned, Friday afternoons, for instance, were expressly created so that the silver could be polished. When she got married, my mother received a very handsome tray with legs, a so-called Aufsatz, from the countess, who must have been inordinately relieved that her family was now out of danger. Since it was made of silver, it too had to be polished when its turn came. (The polishing was done with a mixture of talcum and rubbing alcohol and applied with deerskin, and, around the ornaments, with a soft toothbrush.) And then one fateful Friday, quite unexpectedly, a suspicious-looking yellow hue came to dominate the Aufsatz. Incredible! The Aufsatz was made of brass gilt with silver! That wasn't very nice of the countess.

I learned from my mother's birth certificate that when she, the first of their children, was born, Alfréd was twenty-eight and Ernesztína twenty-six years of age, which at the time of their marriage the previous year made Grandfather a veritable bachelor and Grandmother dangerously close to being an old maid.

When I returned from the camp in 1945, a kind-hearted neighbour returned some photographs to me, including a picture of Alfréd and Ernesztína. I studied that picture for a long time. Alfréd was exactly as I had remembered him, but the Wicked Witch of the West was gazing back at me where Ernesztína should have been. Still, I will always see her as beautiful as I did back then, even though she left me not only her beaked nose but her hump as well. But from her, even that is a welcome gift.

How did Alfréd and Ernesztína end up in the bonds of holy matrimony?

I can't quite picture Grandfather riding up to Ernesztína's balcony on a white horse (he bred Lipizzaners), flinging a silken ladder up to her window, and Ernesztína climbing down to join him in the saddle. "Gidde'up," Alfréd shouts, "gidde'up!" and, driven by yearning, off he rides with her in the saddle to his castle in the clouds, to live happily ever after, and all this because he has heard of Ernesztína's legendary beauty. As I have said, Nature did not shower her bounty on Ernesztína. She gave her a hump on the back and a double-sized nose up front. On the other hand, Nature made Alfréd incredibly handsome. Alfréd knew this and acted as if the world was his oyster, which didn't make him have any more money than he already had, alas. He didn't have as much as a wooden farthing to his name, as the Hungarian saying goes. He was as poor as a church mouse. A charmer and a beggar.

Ernesztína's father, on the other hand, had more than one homely daughter, but he also had loads of money against despair. He had enough money to ensure that his ugly duckling daughters got the best education available at the time. They spoke French (plus Hungarian, German, and Slovak from the time they were toddlers); they played the piano and sang; they knew how to sew and embroider, and how to manage a big household. I need say no more to make you understand the happy end to Alfréd and Ernesztína's story.

Was Ernesztína in love with Alfréd? She must have been. I know I would have fallen head over heels in love with him at first sight. As for Alfréd, I'm afraid that – in the beginning, at any rate – he must have thought that Ernesztína's dowry would help him close his eyes. He couldn't have known then that my grandmother Ernesztína was the wisest and best woman in the whole wide world – and because of this, the most beautiful, too, in my eyes, at any rate. Of the things she saw or heard, she allowed only those things to penetrate her conscious mind that were not bad for her, that's how wise she was. And if anything was bad for her, she elegantly let it pass. She treated Alfred with kid gloves, pampered and calmed him, nursed him and served him if he was ill, overlooked his faults, and forgave his indiscretions even before they were committed. She put up with his shouting with a knowing smile, and satisfied his smallest whim. In short, she adored him. She grew up in the city, but she left the city, her girl-friends and relations, the concerts and the theatres, for Alfréd's sake, and once on the farm, she learned how to tend to the animals, how to grow and gather fruits, vegetables, and medicinal herbs – in short, how to be a farmer.

There was a picture of Emperor Joe[4] on Grandfather's desk. Not of Francis Joseph, mind you, but of Joe, they were on such intimate terms as far as Grandfather was concerned. He took it for granted that if Emperor Joe were to come face to face with him in front of the row of stables at Ógyalla, he'd greet him and say, "Servus,

---

4 The popular Hungarian name of the Austrian emperor, "Ferenc Jóska," with the diminutive of Josef, loosely translates as Joe.

humillimus,"[5] because they'd be using the familiar form of address. As far as Grandfather was concerned, Emperor Joe was one of the family, after the Compromise,[6] at any rate. Like so many of the Habsburgs, he may have been an anti-Semite deep down, but after the Compromise he helped the Jews in many ways. They were free to prosper, to attend college and make decent lives for themselves.

Take Grandfather's brother, Uncle Shami (for Shámuel), for instance. He was a *rashe khol*, president of the congregation of Nagyszombat. When the Jewish New Year came around, he would take a huge roast duck on a silver platter to the Burg in Vienna for Emperor Joe; this is what his His Majesty's grateful subjects, the members of the Jewish congregation, called him. He might as well be reminded once a year what real roast duck tastes like!

Alfréd was a first-rate farmer. He knew everything there was to know about horses, he was a good organizer, and he made sure that everything that transpired on the estate was recorded in a big ledger. This ledger was in the office, the first door to the left along the hall. The office was home to very important things – the Wertheim safe, the guns (Winchesters), the telephone, and the writing desk (not the one with Emperor Joe). The hall was laid with big, red square tiles. Who would have thought that the basement of the former palace-like apartment building that is now the Central European University on the corner of Zrínyi and Nádor streets in Budapest was covered with the same red floor tiles as the hall of our small country house? You could see the basement from the upper floors of that building, and when I worked there – at the time it was still the headquarters of my alma mater, the unforgettable Metalimpex Export-Import Company – the sight of these tiles warmed my heart every day.

Alfréd liked to boast that on his farm there wasn't a square metre that wasn't liberally sprinkled with manure every year. It was all there in the ledger, he could prove it. If a new foal or new calf was

---

5 A joking version of "servus," the familiar greeting used to this day in Austria and until recently in Hungary, referring to the word's Latin origin.

6 The Compromise or Ausgleich of 1867 established the constitutional framework of the Austro-Hungarian Monarchy as a personal union of two equal parts, for the rest of its existence.

born, the event was recorded in the ledger along with their names. Lambs, piglets, geese, ducks, and chickens were recorded only by number. When an animal died, that too was put in the ledger, and also what grew in each field and in what quantity; and the date of the beginning and end of the harvest was likewise recorded. The ledger also recorded how much money was received yearly for the produce and the animals, along with what was taken to the market at Miskolc once or twice a week for sale. That big book was like the Bible. Everything was recorded therein. I'd give half my kingdom for it.

What was life like on the farm? No one described it better that Gyula Illyés in his *People of the Puszta*.[7] The Spanish Courts didn't observe etiquette with more care than the hierarchy of the farm. People did not have dots of various colours in the middle of their forehead, yet it took a veritable miracle for them to move from one caste to another. Life was wretched in all the castes. In one it was next to impossible to put bread on the table, in another it was nigh impossible, that was the sole difference.

Those who prided themselves with being at the top of the hierarchy lived on a separate lane, in separate houses. Such a man was Uncle Vígh, the mechanic, a veritable wizard of the Kühle & Nagel steam engine, the thrashing machine, the lift, and the Hoffher & Schrantz tractor. He was the person responsible for machine maintenance, the lord and master of the locksmith's shop. He had a shotgun like ours, loaded with lead, unlike the field guards, who had salt stuffed into the barrels of their guns. Still, it couldn't have been pleasant if they got the backside of a rascal on the prowl for illegal game; he'd have to sit in a barrel full of water for days.

Uncle Vígh also owned a house in a nearby village, and he played a major role in keeping us well fed in winter. He'd dispatch a goose liver, a pheasant, or a rabbit every week, for Easter a young lamb, and for New Year's Eve a suckling pig. Since we valued only the

---

7 Gyula Illyés (1902–1983), poet, writer. His masterful study of rural labourers, published in 1936, is an outstanding example of literary sociology or anthropology, a unique genre of the so-called "populist" literary and political movement in Hungary during the interwar period.

liver and not the goose, Uncle Vígh wrapped it between two flat-tened Modiano cartons, in which they sold the cigarette paper in which to roll loose tobacco. Uncle Vígh tied a string round the neck of the pheasant, hare, lamb, or piglet, from which hung a small piece of cardboard with our Debrecen address. He sent it one day, and we had it the next, even though it was sent through the Hungarian Post Office. But back then, it was still functioning properly!

Jánosi, the shepherd, was the other person on the farm who had everyone's respect. He earned this respect because his father had also been a shepherd, and so had *his* father, and his father before him, and so on. In short, he was the descendant of a dynasty of shep-herds. He was straggling and tall as a poplar. We rarely saw him, because he spent most of his time in the pastures with the sheep, even spending the night in a makeshift hut patched together out of corn stalk or reed. His wife had eyes the colour of cornflowers, and her apron was always starched to a crisp. The house of the shepherd and his wife was at the far end of the estate, adjacent to the place where the sheep's-milk cheese and the cottage cheese were made.

I don't mind sharing my food recipes. On the contrary, I'm proud of the fact that my friends like to use them. I never leave anything out, ever, in case someone should go into a rage thinking that they can't make something that I can. I will therefore write down the recipe for making sheep's-milk cheese. Here it is. Take at least a thousand sheep, milk them, and pour the milk thus col-lected into thirty-litre copper kettles. Reach up to the small shelf and take down the inoculator. Pour ten drops into each kettle. Wait a bit. Before long the inoculated milk will curdle. Roll up your shirtsleeves, scrub your hands until they are spotless, get down to the kettles, and knead the curdled milk. In no time at all the whey will separate out. Reach up to the small shelf again, and take down the kitchen towels that previously have been boiled clean and placed there in readiness, then ladle as much of the whey into each as you need to make a nice-sized sheep's-milk cheese. Tie the four corners of the kitchen towels together and hang each bundle on a hook, but make sure to place a tub under each hook first. What will drip through the towel is the whey. Transfer it to a pot and put the pot on the stove to cook on a low flame. What will rise to the surface is the sweet whey. What you're left with after all the extra liquid has dripped into the tubs is the sheep's-milk cheese. Mark each cheese with the date and place it on a shelf outside in neat rows. Let each cheese dry. Once it has hardened, scrub it with hot water, because the flies have landed on it, then mark each with the AW (Alfréd Weisz) brand mark, and take it to the market at Mis-kolc to sell. The most important thing is the brand mark, because that's what people are looking for at the market. Then, if they have extra time on their hands, or Irma (my mother) feels like it, they grate the sheep's-milk cheese, knead it with a bit of salt, place it in pretty little wooden barrels made by the cartwright especially for this purpose, and either take it down to the ice cellar waiting for one of us to take it upstairs or else to cart it to Debrecen.

I might also mention that the brand mark AW was also put on every watermelon when it was no bigger than ten centimetres. The watermelon and brand mark matured in unison. Back then, a self-respecting watermelon weighed around ten kilos, and by the time the watermelon grew to full size, the brand mark also grew to about fifteen centimetres. It helped identify the product. But the AW logo would also find its way onto the backs of the bulls, oxen, cows, sheep, and so on, except in their case not as a brand name, but to identify the owner. It never occurred to anyone in the fam-ily that once something had become the property of Alfréd Weisz it could ever be the property of anyone else. My grandfather had no way of knowing back then that there would be a "Jewish law," more than one, in fact, followed by deportations, and that the live-stock branded with the AW monogram would be carried off in all four directions of the compass.

The blacksmith and the cartwright also fascinated me. I've for-gotten their names. The blacksmith was only an extra player in some sort of larger system. There was a smithy on the farm, but the blacksmith came in from a nearby village with his sons once or twice a month to shoe the horses and see to all the block-work. That's when I learned that one smith is no smith, two smiths are half a smith, and three smiths are one smith. The ringing sound that three blacksmiths produce when they forge horseshoes is unforgettable. I could listen to it all day.

The cartwright made barrels and wheels. He was also our joiner and carpenter and jack-of-all-trades for anything made of wood or lumber. He carved a beautiful little stool especially for me. Every part of it was worked with decoration, the two sides with curlicue tulips and trailers, the top with my name. When they herded us into the cattle cars headed for Auschwitz, my little sister Gilike sat on it. Who got my little stool when they flung it out of the wagon at Birkenau? Did it end up in a barracks, or was it trampled underfoot?

Uncle Pesta Hegyi, the farmer, used to come to the farm office in the early evening. He hailed from Szentistván, where he had a house. I never knew why the steward of the estate was called "the farmer," when my grandfather Alfréd was the farmer. Pesta Hegyi was told the chores for the following day, which he passed on to the carriage drivers, the farmhands, the seasonal labourers, the tobacco hands, and so on.

I feel sorry for today's city children who don't come in contact with nature except on special occasions. If they're lucky, they're taken on excursions once or twice a year. They may go skiing in winter and may attend summer school in the open, possibly next to a body of water. But most of their lives are spent walled in by the city. In Debrecen we had a house with a garden, and ever since I can remember I had my own little garden, too, which I tended myself. There were lots of animals around me as well. We spent only the month of August on the farm, but I always felt that the farm was my real home, and that we had to move up to Debrecen only because of school. Life on the farm was so rich and eventful, so many wonderful things happened to me, that it was enough to last me the rest of the year. I always had something to think back on.

The most wonderful of all was the plain.

When Petőfi[8] wrote in one of his poems that he had no need of the wild Carpathians, he spoke after my own heart, even though we were taken into the mountains once a year to counteract the dust of Debrecen. Regardless of where it is located, even if it is in

---

8 Sándor Petőfi (1823–1849), the leading Romantic poet of the nineteenth century. He came from a poor peasant background and died in battle during the Hungarian War of Independence.

the desert, there is nothing to compare in beauty to the plain. The feeling of elation that comes to you when you are standing in the middle of a flat field with nothing but the infinite freedom, the sky touching the earth and a tree or two in the distance that has been struck by lightning, the chirping of crickets and the cawing of kites – there is nothing to match it. Nowhere is a storm as spectacular as on the plain. There is a sudden, deadly hush, the animals fall silent; even the flies forget to buzz. Dark clouds roll overhead, the horizon turns the colour of ink, the lightning zigzags between heaven and earth. The animals huddle together, the dogs whine and rub up against their owner. The storm respects no boundaries and spares no one its whistling winds and torrential downpours. On the farm, though, we usually had no rain all in August, whereas the hoers (sugar beet, corn, etc.) needed it. You could almost feel the thirsty tablelands absorbing every blessed drop once it came. I love a sudden storm. I've seen lightning strike from up close three times. There's no fear left in me. There is no smell to compare with that of the land after a downpour. That is the main compensation for a heavy rain.

The other inexhaustible source of wonder for me was the swamp.

By the time we got there in August, it was on its best behaviour, offering us free passage over a trail that had been marked out beforehand. But those who lived on the farm all year round were familiar with all its faces, because it had several, and they told marvellous stories about it. In spring, when the Tisza overflowed its bounds, the swamp grew to great proportions. "Where we are standing now, in this meadow, the water came up *this high*," they said. "We herded the hogs into the water to stir it up, and we caught fish with our bare hands *that big!*" And the people showed us with their hands what size they meant. And after the flood retreated, the path that would lead across the swamp had to be marked out once again. They always used the same old horse for this purpose. As it passed they cut the reed, and that was the path, year after year. The winter, the snow, the flood washed it away every time.

The marshlands are incomparable not only because of the reeds – though this would suffice to make the marshes miraculous – but because of the other things in it, the water plants, the rushes, the bulrushes, the sedge and duckweed, and on the edges forget-me-nots, marigolds, mint, ground-nuts, clover, buttercups, and wild sorrel, which we ate raw, and lots of other things that are now protected or have already disappeared. And the concert provided by the frogs every night! Anyone who has never heard the incomparable whispering reeds, the insistent chorus of frogs, reads István Fekete[9] in vain, because reading about such wonders is one thing and experiencing them first hand is quite another.

Those marshes were a home to all the water birds upon earth, or so it seemed to me. Storks, herons, lapwings, water hen, the coot, the reed bunting, the lesser whitethroat, and God knows how many other kinds of birds were my daily companions. Flocks of wild geese and scoters passed me overhead. Storks were still literally nesting on every rooftop, and on the boughs of the trees, too, for they were plentiful. Come August, they flocked together by the hundreds on the fields to practise for their great migration in autumn.

One summer we accidentally wounded a stork's wing with a gun. Grandmother wasted no time in putting it in a splint, but the stork did not recover in time for the great migration, and could not take off with the flock. We called him Stevie the Stork. He spent the winter in the big family kitchen, huddled under Grandmother's protective wings. He was very sad all winter, even though he had raw meat to eat, and we feared for his life. When we called the farm, our first question was: How is Stevie Stork doing? and we were jubilant when Grandmother told us that as soon as the first stork appeared on the farm, they set Stevie Stork free, and he took off as if he'd never been there to begin with.

I blush to think of it, but in those days I was inordinately proud when I strolled along the promenade in Debrecen wearing a hat topped with an egret feather. No one else had a hat with an egret feather. It was a gift from Uncle Sanyi. Back then there was plenty of everything, including egrets. Today, all the birds of my childhood are protected, if they are indeed still around to enjoy it!

---

9 István Fekete (1900–1970), Hungarian writer, best known for his books for young readers depicting nature.

There was no electricity on the farm. We used oil lamps. We had oil lamps everywhere, in the stables, the small kitchen, the sties, the granary. Oil lamps were hanging everywhere. The shaded lamp stood inside a wide ring to which there was fixed on one side a metal sheet the size of a palm ending in a hook. The metal sheet functioned to disperse the heat. This type of lamp came in various sizes, depending on what it was used for.

The oil lamps meant for the rooms were a lot more intriguing. They were set on artistic, often valuable Alt-Wien or Rosenthal bases decorated with dancing women or mythological figures or else exotic animals (prancing about or baring their teeth), and they had interesting porcelain shades or unusual funnels. In the best of cases they were hung from the ceiling, and could be moved up and down with the help of a simple system of pulleys, and in the worst case, they were placed on the table. We had to be careful, because if anything tipped over on the table, it was sure to be the oil lamp.

In short, we had no electricity on the farm, but we did have a telephone! In those days, the accoutrements of a telephone were as follows:

- a small call box attached to the wall, with the mechanism inside
- on it a crank
- a hand-held earpiece on the side, and
- a headpiece.

Thus, talking on the phone acquired the status of a social event, not only because, thanks to the separate ear- and headpieces, two people could listen in – and they did – but because, whether she wanted it or not, the telephone operator who connected the two parties couldn't help but overhear the conversation.

Making a call happened in the following manner. The person wishing to speak on the phone stepped over to the wall of the farm office, unhooked the earpiece, and then vigorously yanked the crank a number of times. The operator who heard the sound in the village post office then picked up her own earpiece and said:

"Hello!"

"Hello!" Thus the riposte from the farm.

"Who may I connect?" Thus the operator.

When she heard the answer, the operator took the wire with the small split plug and attached it to the appropriate socket of the switchboard hanging on her wall. At least two minutes passed before the parties concerned could begin their conversation, but only if the young lady at the switchboard was in a rush. However, since the young lady at the switchboard was bound to overhear every word, she was rarely in a rush, and a good thing, too! Have you ever heard of a switchboard operator who wasn't curious? Of course, given the workings of the telephone, we might say that she was merely discharging her duty, and since we knew this, if we wanted some piece of news to spread through the village like wildfire but had no time to go in ourselves, all we had to do was pick up the phone and make a call.

The rifle case in which the Winchesters stood in a neat row with the butt-end pointing down was an important feature of the farm office. We were not allowed to play with the guns, and even if we made sure that a gun was not loaded, we were not allowed to point it at each other or at any of the farm animals. The first time I could hold one was preceded by a long and serious lecture. Regardless of the path we took back to the house, there was always a tree, a bush, or some other spot at which we had to empty the cartridge chamber. Pulling the trigger just for fun was out of the question. We pulled the trigger only with good reason; for instance, if we wanted to have rabbit, pheasant, quail, or partridge for dinner, and especially when we were expecting company – the lord lieutenant of the county, the town clerk, the constable, and so on, along with their entourage. When that happened, Grandfather sent a carriage to the station to pick them up, either a two- or a four-horse carriage, depending on the guest's rank. (In those days no one sped around in an automobile, not even those who came to visit, even though they were high officials indeed. Of course, the unpaved roads would have made a journey by car highly uncomfortable.) Jani Móré, the son of Uncle Móré, the keeper of the oxen, was also our liveried driver. He was a handsome lad and made a fine figure in his uniform and beribboned hat. I remember his hands as they held the reins. He had beautiful hands. They were strong, manly, adroit hands. The fingers were strong and perfectly proportionate. But his nails were the most beautiful of all. Their perfect white arches reached almost to the middle of each nail.

As for Alfréd, he rarely sat in a carriage himself. He surveyed his realm on a two-wheeled cart pulled by his old friend Sultan, now out of commission. Sultan refused to budge if anyone held the reins other than Alfréd. (I know this for a fact, since I tried it.) Alfréd had me sit by his side. It was pure heaven. He had no suspicion that in April 1944 they'd have him and Ernesztína sit in his elegant carriage to be driven to the ghetto at Mezőkeresztes, from where no one returned, not even they.

My Father, Dezső Fahidi

No picture has remained of my father that is true to life. So he lives in my heart just the way he was. No retouching can stain him.

The four Fahídy boys who came into the world before my father were robust and strong. They were respected by the local youth of Fehérgyarmat, because they could fight like nobody's business. When the local boys released pigeons inside the synagogue, the Fahídy brothers beat them out of there so effectively that they never thought of repeating their prank. (P.S. Still, they paid a visit to the Catholic church to give as good as they got.) Once, when two of the four Fahídy brothers were on the train, someone happened to make certain remarks about the Jews.

"Who was that?" one of the two brothers asked, raising his brow. Nobody volunteered.

"What do you say, brother? Shall we start?" the younger of the two brothers commented, whereupon they ejected all the passengers from the compartment. Why should those people who think Jews stink have to travel in the same space with them?

My father did not take after his brothers. Compared to them, he had delicate bones and was not much of a fighter. He preferred to meditate and to read. He wanted to soak up all the knowledge he could.

Dezső had two faces, though it wasn't as if one cried while the other laughed, no. One of the two Dezsős, Father, was for daytime use; the other, Daddy, was reserved for the evening.

Until I started going to school, I saw Father, who got up very early, only late in the morning, when my governess, Ruth, took me by the hand and we took Father's mid-morning meal to him at the lumberyard. At such times he didn't pay much attention to me and I was free to run around in the yard, to climb atop the wood piles and jump off, regardless of how high they were.

I loved it when Dezső wore his Father face, because it demanded such respect, even if it did scare me at times. Still, I was impressed that Father could be like that. Once, when a man from the village asked me at the lumberyard gate, "Whose daughter might the young lady be?" meaning my uncle Antal's or my father Dezső's, I pulled myself up to my full height, looked him in the eye, and proud as a peacock said, "I'm Father's daughter!"

Father founded the Fahídi Brothers' Lumber Yard Ltd. with his brother Antal in 1924 in Debrecen. My father was the "handsome" Fahídi, Antal the "heavy" Fahídi. But generally, and this included the workers, they were addressed as Mr Dezső and Mr Tóni.

Antal was like a tympanum stood on one of its pointed sides, the peak of which, now situated in the middle, was his paunch. He was decidedly tall and decidedly corpulent. He had curly blond hair, blue eyes, and padded hands. He liked to stand by the gate of the lumberyard and exchange a kind word or two with anyone who passed by. The out-of-town customers would deal only with him and would not buy anything except on Mr Tóni's recommendation.

He was clearly proud of his paunch. It didn't just protrude, it pricked! When he put me on his lap, it pricked as hard as any stone. He even decked it out, because it was adorned with a gold watch chain and a gold-encased Omega watch sunk in a pocket made especially to hold it. One would think that this would be sufficient for all the world to see how its owner valued that paunch. But the crowning glory was a pendant swinging from the middle of the chain somewhere between the button-hole to which the chain was attached and the watch pocket – a gold medal with the image, in enamel, of an ocean-blue butterfly caught in mid-flight. In my eyes, this butterfly was the embodiment of my uncle Tóni's love and patience for me. As I've said, he liked to snuggle me in his lap, while I liked playing with the medal on his watch chain.

Me at the age of thirteen months.

I used to say "beautifly." Tóni laughed and said "butterfly." "No," I said, "beautifly." At such times Tóni displayed a highly restricted vocabulary, because he said again, "butterfly." We would go on with this game for minutes on end, never tiring of it. But I always had the last word. I looked meaningfully into Tóni's blue eye and said, "beautifly!"

On June 26, 1944, the ocean-blue was gone from Tóni's eye, because before he was herded into the wagon, he was beaten beyond recognition by our valiant gendarmes, who wanted to thrash the hiding place of his gold stores out of him.

Part of my father's daytime face included the daily ritual at lunch, which at times ended like the Inquisition, with me being locked in the bathroom because I refused to eat so much as a morsel. The more they insisted, the more I refused. Then came *the bathroom*.

You will understand why the bathroom was repeatedly turned into a torture chamber if I reveal to you that its window gave out on the part of the garden where the sand box, the swing, the rings, the bar, the horizontal bar, and the parallel bars were in plain sight. The more you looked out the window the more miserable you were, and the more your state of imprisonment weighed on you. There you were, held under duress, kept from your favourite sand box, swing, rings, and so on, whereas it was so much better running around out there than wasting away in the bathroom. And to make things worse, your heart nearly broke when you thought that your father and mother were angry with you, and you could hardly bear it, when all you wanted was to be a good little girl and make everybody happy.

I must have been around fifteen when it was my little sister Gilike's turn to be locked in the bathroom because she'd misbehaved, and Dezső spoke up with his daytime Father face:

"Irmuska," he said to my mother, "poor child's been locked in the bathroom for five minutes already. Go in there, smack her little bottom lightly twice, make her promise she won't do it again, and let her out."

"You always want me to do the dirty work," was my mother's response. "You go and smack her bottom if you have the heart."

The world went blank before my eyes. I thought I wasn't hearing right. Did they also speak like this when I was the prisoner of the bathroom? Do they love me even when I'm bad and being punished?

My father wore his Daddy face only in the evening.

According to the strict house rules, the children had to be in bed by eight in the evening after a bath, with teeth properly brushed. In the first eight years of my life, when I was the only child, usually Daddy gave me my bath. I can still remember the way he stood me up in the tub, wrapped my bathrobe around me, picked me up and out of the tub, set me on the table, and rubbed, rubbed, rubbed, so I shouldn't catch a cold. But the best was yet to come, because next he would pick me up as if I were as light as a feather, fling me over his shoulder, deposit me in my bed, pull over a chair, and tell me stories.

My evening Daddy didn't take his stories from books. There were plenty of people to do that all day long. He told me stories from his head. My evening Daddy was a scholar. Every one of his stories began like this: "Once upon a time, there was a little girl. Her name was Éva," and we all know that if a story begins like this, then everything that happens will happen to Éva, so it must be true. Consequently, it follows that whatever my evening Daddy relates must be a true story, from the first word to the last.

The stories were always spellbinding. Daddy took the subject either from the Bible or from history or some natural phenomenon, the four corners of the earth, the celestial bodies, the Northern Lights, rivers, oceans, the rain, the clouds – in short they had to be (partly) true. I especially remember the story about the eruption of Mount Vesuvius. This story, too, began with: "Once upon a time, there was a little girl. Her name was Éva." "When you're older," Daddy said, "you'll come with us to Italy, to the foot of Mount Vesuvius, where you'll see for yourself what I'm telling you now." Anyway, Mount Vesuvius began to rumble something horrible as a heavy shower of stones erupted from its belly and rolled down to the valley, sweeping everything before it, trees, shrubs, buildings, everything that happened to be in its way. A black cloud of smoke covered the face of the sun, and it got as dark as it must have been in the belly of the earth, where no light ever goes. Then a shower of sparks shot forth, the sparks sizzled and hissed and screeched as they do when there are fireworks, and a mighty fire broke out everywhere the sparks landed. The whole mountain was on fire! Then, without any transition at all, the landscape was illuminated as the fire-red lava burst forth from the mountain peak and, like the ocean at high tide, engulfed the entire mountainside, ruthlessly flooding everything within reach.

I, who was present at the scene, could hear everything and see everything. I smelled the smoke, the birds fleeing towards the clouds, and the animals running and whining, and fear gripped my heart.

"I can show you a picture, if you want," Daddy said, and he brought the Great Révai Encyclopedia for me to read. If only he hadn't! Sitting and turning its pages made me grow this tall! I loved that encyclopedia. It was chock full of novelties and illustrations in colour and black and white. I could lose myself in it for hours on end.

Dear Editorial Board of the Great Révai Encyclopedia! After all these years, I ask you: how could you illustrate such an exciting and colourful subject with such a boring, schematic, unimaginative, and ugly picture? On *your* picture there's a small hill quietly and peacefully smoking, even cheerfully, I might add, whereas in front of my eyes the sky and the earth joined forces, the world began to sway. I am terribly disappointed in you. Where are all the things that my Daddy-faced daddy related to me, the wondrous things that he helped me see and hear? Your picture called for blood! My profound disappointment called for immediate revenge, and I had to say something that would hurt my father to the quick: "I thought you were a scholar, Daddy," I announced. "But now it seems you get your knowledge from books!" I wanted the disappointment to hurt him as much as it had hurt me. He was the only one around. He had to bear the brunt.

If he wanted to attend school past the age of thirteen, my father had to learn to fend for himself just like his brothers. His brains were his only capital. He had to take advantage of that. Luckily, every school has its contingent of poor students, and there are always some poor students with well-to-do fathers. This is how my father paid for his schooling: he tutored other students. He also read everything he could get his hands on. He couldn't get enough of the classical Hungarian and foreign authors. He kept reading them until he developed his own taste in literature. His favourite poet was Dániel Berzsenyi.[1] His hobbyhorse was the accurate, articulate style, a spoken Hungarian that was unsentimental and properly accented. What a long road from the tailor's shop in Fehérgyarmat to get where he got!

He was a self-made man in every respect. He prepared his business ventures with care and circumspection. He was level-headed,

---

1 Dániel Berzsenyi (1776–1836), the only son of a landowning noble family and the outstanding poet of the early nineteenth century, would only be recognized as such after his death.

asked lawyers and professionals for advice, read the pertinent literature, and, just as importantly, provided the material basis for
his ventures. But once he made his decision, he acted promptly
and without hesitation. He made sure that everything was secured
by a contract.

His first business venture was the lumberyard, whose under-
pinnings were provided by my mother's dowry. He was attracted
to the lumber business because of his love of nature. His outings
in the woods were thus a professional duty. He learned everything
about lumber and could tell the species, age, and best use of a tree
from a small sample. He kept the yard in immaculate order. Back
then, lumber was an object of respect. The lumber used for buildings and furniture was carefully dried for years and was kept in
covered, well-aired sheds. It was classified according to size and
quality, and was constantly turned around as it dried.

There were two Sándors at the lumberyard who were employed
full-time; the rest of the employees were hired on a daily basis as
they were needed. One of the Sándors was Sándor Kányádi, the
other Sándor Orbán. Both must have received miserable wages, but
since everything depends on the individual, they managed it in different ways. Mrs Kányádi wore well-starched and ironed dresses
and was always neat. The Orbán family, on the other hand, seemed
to have been put on the face of this earth only so that my mother
could indulge her passion for charity through them. Orbán, poor
man, was shrouded in a cloud of cheap brandy at all hours of the
day. He never missed greeting my father on holidays, name days,
and birthdays. The other Sándor must have done the same, but if
so, this has been lost to memory. Not so the Orbán type of greeting, because he insisted on reciting Marx's *Capital* to us irrespec-
tive of the occasion. The family had to listen to it without twitching
a muscle. When he finished, Sándor always got something for his
diction, while my mother sent Mrs Orbán the flour, lard, sugar,
and other foodstuffs they needed to stave off starvation.

The country was of two minds about preparing for its participation in the war. The governments that came and went in quick
succession were riddled by infighting between the anglophiles

and German sympathizers, but they agreed that the country must stock up on essential supplies. With the war knocking on our borders, bandages became a top priority. Herman Lajos Fahídy, one of my father's brothers who went by the family nickname Louise, was familiar with the business. So Father co-founded the Fahídy Bandage Factory with him in a spacious basement in Csáky Street in Budapest. Since it was a family business with a single accountant and a couple of unskilled workers, the overhead was negligible. Thanks to his good looks and gift for negotiation, my uncle Louise obtained public procurement tenders with ease, though sometimes by a hair's breadth – by a difference of ten or twenty fillérs! Even in those days, public life was no celestial gathering of angels and Grail knights. But no one would dare risk offering a bribe to anyone deciding the fate of government tenders.

When in the 1930s the government came up with the idea that the plains of Hortobágy were just the place to grow rice, my father built the Hajdú Husking and Grinding Mill next door to our lumberyard in Debrecen. (In the late 1940s, for no particular reason, a crusade was launched against the mills, and my father's mill was one of the victims along with the grinding mill a couple of houses down on Szoboszlói Road.)

My personal feelings about the mill were tainted by the fact that, at the age of fifteen or sixteen, I very much wanted to be a big girl, like the rest of my classmates. They, the envied, were already going around in silk stockings, high-heeled shoes, and grown-up fur coats, though not in school, of course, because the strict dress code prescribed uniforms and black ribbed stockings. Though I pleaded with my parents, even my Sunday best had a white sailor collar on it, the only concession being a pair of socks instead of the stockings. And since I was born with flat feet, like it or not, I had to wear high-laced orthopaedic shoes made by Mr Hadnagy. But that fur coat, I could have given half an arm for it!

"I'm building a mill," my father said, "and that costs money. Besides, you're still a little girl." (I was the tallest in my class, with three girls lagging just behind me, and then, after a huge gap, came the others, who were at least two heads shorter than myself.)

Two years later, though, I got the fur coat. It came in very handy, even if not for me. Before we were deported, we gave most of our things into the care of various people. The honour of guarding my coat went to our sincere friend and neighbour, the pharmacist Szabolcs Szoboszlói Szabó. His wife, Aunt Irénke, survived the war in a bomb shelter thanks to my coat. At least it warmed her while I lived through the winter of 1944–5 in a pair of overalls, and to add insult to injury, I had no underwear, or socks, or shoes. There were hundreds of thousands of us in the same situation, so many cogs in the wheels of the German war machinery.

Nagytanya, the great farm, came into my father's possession unexpectedly. My maternal grandfather, Alfréd Weisz, pestered the saints, reminding them that he's no two-penny marlot, until he procured various diseases of the organs: angina pectoris, high blood pressure, vascular stenosis, you name it. When my parents were married, Grandfather, at the height of his powers, was still running the show at Ógyalla. Then, as his illnesses caught up with him, as his former voluminous tenor faded into baritone, he became much like a toothless lion. No one was scared of his fits of temper any more. Even though he continued shouting as before, his shouting became theatrical and ineffective, and those around him exchanged tolerant smiles behind his back. On the other hand, it was very difficult to watch over his health from Debrecen, so the family council convened and decided that he must move from Ógyalla to Hungary. My mother insisted more than the others. She was closest to Alfréd, and she also bore the closest resemblance to him.

Nagytanya became Alfréd's place of residence, where he continued farming with varying results, as it required more and more effort of him. Then another family council was called and it was decided that my father was the financial genius in the family and should put his shoulder to the wheel. That's when literature on farming flooded our home. My father read it with a vengeance. Considering the results, the family council was right – the farm came into its own again under my father's guidance.

One of the reasons for the spectacular improvement had to do with the previously mentioned Wertheim safe in the farm office, because although the income was strictly entered in that certain great ledger, not so the money that was removed from the safe. The minute my father let it be known that it was as important to know what was taken *out* of the safe as what was put *into* it, the accounts were out of the red.

Amusing things happened as well. Our family felt that you had no right to expect anything from others that you couldn't do your-self. Look, this is how to do it! This is why I know how to knead dough for bread, milk a cow, fix a yoke on an ox, hitch and saddle a horse, weave a whip, even snap it, swirl honey, use a spade and a shovel, and many other things that I no longer have any use for, alas, in my apartment on Pest's upscale Váci Street.[2]

Two of my mother's younger brothers, Mr Pali and Mr Sanyi, lived on the farm and were in charge of the alfalfa field planted next to the vegetable garden, which, by the way, made a home for Uncle Sanyi's bees. On the first day of harvest, they had to keep up with the foreman of the reaping brigade. Every phase of har-vesting took everything out of a man. You can't use a scythe if you don't keep up your physical condition, if it's not something you do regularly. It would have been highly humiliating if "Mr" Pali and "Mr" Sanyi were not up to the task and fell behind. And so they mowed that big alfalfa field, just the two of them, every chance they got. This is why they grew alfalfa in the first place!

My father picked up a scythe – for the first and last time in his life – when the day labourers were cutting hay. The countless farm animals needed a great deal of hay, so they cut it down at least twice each spring. They cut down the grass even from the sides of the best-hidden ditches. The day labourers got one out of five stacks. My father made a heroic effort at reaping, but he soon real-ized that reaping was not for him. On the other hand, he learned what a physical effort it was to do the reaping, and since he had his own views on respecting labour, he raised the day labourers' share from one-fifth to one-fourth, this to the dismayed outcry of the neighbouring farmers.

---

2 The famous pedestrian street of upscale shops in Budapest.

He organized the Aryanization of his possessions[3] meticulously, with our so-called friends becoming our fronts. The poet János Arany's lines seemed more relevant than ever: "The midnight predators gather for the kill."[4] He kept the reins in his hand until the moment after the last; he gave the orders even from the ghetto. He trusted his friends. How come he didn't know that a man's real face shows itself when there's trouble? The dirty work was left to me when, having returned from the camp, I put that unwavering, sincere friendship to the test.

I arrived back in Debrecen on November 4, 1945.

The same ragged, grey clouds hung over the sky as in March 19, 1944, when the Wehrmacht occupied Hungary. Nineteen months passed, but I didn't age nineteen months. I aged a lifetime. Without transition, I went from a child to a worn-out adult. I had nothing and no one. I faced the world alone.

Debrecen is a small town, where everyone knows everyone else. The news of my arrival spread like wildfire. I stayed with Dr Barta and his family. He was my father's family physician. I had hardly settled in my chair when two families called us, the Vágós and the Barabáses, saying they'd saved what my mother had left in their care, and when could they bring it over?

During the war, everyone who could fled Debrecen. The Vágós and the Barabáses fled as well. The Vágós had the cutlery that was going to be part of my dowry. I am still using it today. The Barabás family had two large chests that they dragged with them during their flight, and they dragged them back as well. In the Vágó and Barabás families they didn't preach what is commonly known as ethics, honour, and humanity, they practised it.

---

3 The so-called Second Jewish Law (Law no. IV of 1939), enacted by the Hungarian Parliament in May 1939, defined Jews on racial grounds, drastically limited Jewish participation in the professions, and banned Jews from higher education, teaching in state schools, and the civil service. Owners of commercial and businesses enterprises were forced to hand over their business to "Aryans," but in many cases kept managing them through front men.

4 János Arany (1817–1882), leading poet and translator of Shakespeare. Lines of his famous ballads, such as this line from *The Toldy Trilogy*, became part of the vernacular.

On the other hand, the Rácz family never called. They had been our neighbours, and our closest, dearest friends. The single Waldsee postcard I had sent from Auschwitz[5] was addressed to them. Uncle Lajos died before the deportations; Aunt Magda and her son, Csongor, fled to the West, and lived off of what they could sell of our possessions. The Szoboszlais didn't call either. They lived across from us in a house where they also had a pharmacy. I went to see them. Aunt Irénke had kept warm in the bomb shelter thanks to my fur coat. I opened her wardrobe. It was full of my mother's monogrammed bed linen. I pulled it out. I raised the corner of the bed cover. Mother's monogrammed linen graced their bed.

"Pull it off, Aunt Irénke, I'll wash it later."

This is Hungary. During his interrogation, Eichmann said that in no other occupied country did as many people report the Jews as in Hungary – anonymously, I might add. I'm hardly back when I too receive an anonymous phone call that my mother's beautiful Hutschenreuther china set is on a farm near Debrecen. I go there with a police inspector by my side armed with a search warrant. The spout of the teapot sticks out of the large wooden crate. Next, almost the entire set emerges from its depths. I still use it today.

We used to tease Mother by telling her that the parish priest, János Szabó, whom we called Janó between ourselves, was her boyfriend. He used to visit us – probably, in no small measure, because of Mother's irresistible cooking, but especially because of her mushroom, ham, and cheese pockets, his favourite. We gave him the list of the things we had entrusted to the care of others. Altogether, the list weighed about a hundred grams. When I returned, I asked him for the list. He wasn't living in Debrecen by then. He wrote back the following, word for word: "I had better things to do than worry about your list." He certainly wasn't going to get any mushroom, ham, and cheese pockets from me!

---

5 The infamous Waldsee postcards were an invention of the Germans. Some prisoners at Auschwitz were allowed to send these cards with the fictive Waldsee address on them, bearing a set message about how well they were faring.—Trans.

My adamant search for whatever had survived of our things was not only about objects. It was about my father and my mother and what they had taught me, that things must be respected because of the work that had gone into them. The spirit and beauty they embody provided the framework for our middle-class life and that of other families like ours, and defined my childhood, now a dream world lost in the mist of time, the first decades of the twentieth century.

My mother in 1923, at the age of eighteen, when my father fell in love with her. My mother was afraid to show this picture to my grandfather, Alfréd Weisz. Their roles had long since been reversed and my mother was taking care of my grandfather, but this photograph was still too risqué.

My Mother, Irma Weisz

I was seventy-five years old when I made my peace with my mother and hung this photograph on the wall. Earlier, whenever I thought of my mother, I felt like screaming. I was gripped by uncontrollable rage. Why did she bring me into this world? Why did she love me and watch over me and then desert me and leave me alone?

I used to think a lot about who could have been the first on this earth to say "I."

Who did he say it to, where, and when? What did he look like? One thing he didn't say was: "Well, I just said the first person singular of a personal pronoun, which is going to be the most important word in the millennia to come." But if he had the brains to say that most important of all words, which has animated the world ever since, sooner or later he must have also asked himself: "Why am I here?"

In our family, we never had to ask ourselves the question that has inspired philosophers throughout the centuries: *Why are we here?* As sure as day follows night, we knew that we were in this world in order to ensure the widest possible arena for our mother Irma's talent for organization.

Living with Irma made life a joy.

She knew everything as a matter of course, she knew it of its own accord, as it were, and with admirable self-confidence; and she knew it best, too – how to run the household, feed our numerous guests, keep the garden in order, knit, crochet, embroider, drive a horse and carriage, make preserves, turn pork into sausage, and preserve food for the winter. She knew how to dress with simple elegance, how to go to a concert, the theatre, the cinema, how to organize our frequent trips – how to LIVE. And how to exercise, exercise, exercise, even if she was no nymph.

We were always on the go – to my grandfather in Ógyalla, to Aunt Hédi, my mother's sister, in Majcihov, to my father's brothers and his sister Gizi in Budapest. We had a constant run of visitors, too, and not just overnight guests – aunts and uncles, my cousins, and at least once a week my father's friends for dinner, feasts from which we children were excluded. Uncle Matyi Kardos and Uncle Pali Kálmán were regulars, as were our neighbours with their spouses, and of course our uncle Tóni with his family, and also our brother-in-law and Father's physician Gyula Barta and his family. (Mrs Barta's brother Józsi Beck and my mother's younger sister Nuni ended up married. What a coincidence!)

Uncle Pali and Uncle Matyi were responsible for the steady embellishment of Irma's vitrine, the pride of so many households displaying undoubtedly valuable but arguably tasteful objects. (Personally, I can't abide such showcases.) These vitrines, which took pride of place in all self-respecting middle-class homes, remind me of domestic altars where the objects of veneration are not household gods but Alt-Wien, Rosenthal, Capo di Monte and other goblets, vases, pipe-playing shepherds, geese, rococo pairs gracefully leaning towards each other, fawns, and dancing ballerinas frozen into place in porcelain. As they took a light-hearted leave of us, just as if we were off on one of our regular visits to Grandfather instead of heading for the ghetto, Aunt Magda Rácz and Aunt Irénke Szabó, our dear neighbours and true friends, couldn't hide their overwhelming desire for our possessions, and pulled the treasures from our vitrine with hands trembling from excitement. "You won't be needing this anymore, Irmus dear," Aunt Magda Rácz said sweetly, with admirable prescience. She may have known something we didn't.

Irma could always come up with something to make life interesting. Something good happened every day. When I recall the way she was, the following words come to mind: agile, restless, a dynamo always on the move, headstrong, rebellious, colourful, inventive, nimble, loving, soft-hearted, full of mother-warmth – an enduring model.

I do everything I possibly can just as she had done it. She was thirty-nine when I lost her. I'm often shocked when I overhear grown-up women talk to their mothers. I can't believe my ears. They're impatient, ill mannered, even nasty. I can't imagine ever saying: "Now, Mother, come off it. I know better than you!" In my eyes she will remain thirty-nine forever. The dead do not age. I could easily have a thirty-nine-year-old grandchild of my own. For me, my mother is the child I never had.

Those grown-ups whose parents are still alive don't know how kind fate has been to them. The love a child feels for his or her parents can't be measured with the help of quantitative concepts. You can't say if you love your father or mother more. Such love cannot be ranked. You love the one for one reason, the other for another. Regardless of the pains people take, it is virtually impossible to make up for the loss of a mother. The surrogate mother doesn't smell of milk. She doesn't have the body-warmth or the heartbeat we hear for nine months and carry in our subconscious selves forever more.

Regardless of where we were, my mother was always the youngest mother there. She was twenty when I was born. This small difference in our ages came with lots of advantages. I was allowed to romp about. In fact, provided that two grown-ups held my hands, I could even do a quick somersault, even on the street. I had to climb the highest branch of a tree, I had to jump off the top of the rabbit cage, I had to hold in my hands frogs, mice, worms, caterpillars, I had to pat all the horses and dogs. Put another way, I was not allowed to be afraid of anything, because that would bring with it the most offending of all sentences: "If you don't do it, you're no daughter of mine!" Few things could have been more painful, since I desperately wanted to be my mother's daughter. I wanted to please her. I wanted to be a mischievous urchin like her. We shared a venial sin – we were both first-born, but we came into the world as girls. It hurt my father a great deal; he may still resent me for it just a bit. My maternal grandfather was made of different stuff. He was immune to offence and disappointment, and with total disregard for hard fact, looked upon Irma, his first-born, as a boy and brought her up as such. My mother Irma was his favourite, meaning that he noticed when, being first-born, she came into the world, but then he turned his attention elsewhere. But he invested Irma with his chief traits, among them his love of animals.

When we were children, we were allowed to bring home all the discarded and humiliated cats and dogs their owners had got tired of. It never occurred to us that they might harm us. When an animal has been searching for its owner possibly for days, wandering about desperately and not finding him, it will eat out of the hand of anyone willing to give it a sip of water and a bite of food. My mother nursed all the sick animals back to health, then sent them down to the farm, where it didn't matter if there was one more or less of them around. All that has remained of this love of animals in me is that I'm still a dog lover and so will not keep one in a city flat. I'll never know how pet owners can deprive their favourites of the one thing that is most vital to them, their freedom – ample space to move about, their several kilometres' daily run, and so on. The city dog is the embodiment of unrepentant human selfishness. The problem is that by now the dog doesn't seem to mind.

Just like Grandfather, Irma spoke the language of horses. In our house, a whip served only for decoration. I can't imagine how my grandfather would have reacted had any of his coachmen dared to whip his horses. On our farm, people spoke to the horses (and the dogs, too) in clipped, unmistakable, imperative sentences. They understood everything we said. They obeyed and fetched.

As far as my mother was concerned, horses, like all good things in life, were created expressly to make her happy. Irma loved a two-in-hand, especially if she could drive it. I will never forget how she left the farm on the carriage, always observing propriety, with Jani Móré, the coachman, sitting up front, and in the back, Mother, my younger sister, and me. But the propriety lasted only as long as we were within view of Grandfather. (I can still recall the couple of scraggly willows that marked off the boundary of the farm.) As soon as we were out of Grandfather's field of vision, we changed places. Mother sat up front, I sat by her side, and Jani Móré was sent to the back. I bet his stomach must have been in knots, wondering when the axe would fall, in which case he'd bear the brunt of Grandfather's ire. When she was in the driver's seat, my mother threw all restraint to the winds. We flew like birds, leaving a thick cloud of dust behind. Luckily, our horses were well trained, while we children enjoyed knowing what a fantastic mother we had. We were terribly impressed by her daredevilry. It never occurred to us to be afraid. With Mother holding the reins, we felt safe. (In those days, life itself was as safe and secure as the Great Church in the heart of Debrecen. Who would have thought how quickly it would pass?) Then, when we reached the willows on our way back to the farm, we unharnessed the horses, had them walk around a bit until the froth was gone from their backs and they had calmed down, then Jani took his appointed place on the driver's box again and we drove up to the farm at a leisurely trot, our faces as innocent as a little lamb's.

Irma spoke the language of plants as well as animals. Everything thrived under her hands. (We used to say amongst ourselves that we can speak horse-language, cat-language, and plant-language, too, because they obey us – even me.) When I compare today's methods of plant protection with what we practised back then, I see that though they didn't call it organic, that's what it was. We used blue vitriol, Bordeaux solution, and potash-soap, and even then, only when absolutely necessary. The sour cherries, cherries, plums, walnuts, currants, and gooseberries never needed spraying. The tree trunks were whitewashed for winter, and in spring, they were scrubbed clean with a wire brush, and old bags and flytraps were made into rings to protect them. When the trees were in bloom, they were checked almost on a daily basis for any changes, and if we spotted caterpillars' nests or plant lice, we grabbed for scissors fixed to a long pole, and not for the spray can. Anything we cut off we burned without delay. It needed a veritable plague of lice for us to spray the plants with nicotine.

Regardless of how many apple or pear trees we had, we left only two or three fruits on each branch, and when the trees were still very young, we covered every piece of fruit with a paper bag that had to be replaced only after a major storm. This way the fruit matured without toxins. When autumn came we picked the fruit and took it down to the apple cellar amidst great rejoicing. We placed the apples on stands made of wooden boards with empty rows between them so we could walk around. We stored the pears while still green in the shed where we kept the grain for the pigs, and didn't touch them till February. By then they were yellow, juicy, and sweet as honey.

Irma kept her orchard in tip-top shape and was proud that, thanks to the deluge of fruit that the garden produced, she was able to supply her friends in Debrecen who did not have gardens with preserves, jam, compote, and dried fruit with which she filled her larder, cellar, and attic, and if something remained on the trees after that, we'd call in a couple of Gypsy children, who finished the devastation.

Every year she put aside a jar or two of compote for my engagement and wedding. When my little sister Gilike was born, Mother did the same for her. These jars were stored separately in the larder, and I was uneasy to observe that with the passing of time, they had a tendency to dry out. We didn't take these jars to the ghetto with us. They remained in the larder on the separate shelf we held in such esteem. Every jar had the year and the name of the owner on it: Éva's for her engagement, Gili's for her wedding, and the other way around. I wonder who ate the compote instead of us?

Irma had a high regard for talent and was fond of saying that we all bring a talent for something with us, it just needs to be discovered. In the vicinity of Nyitra, Pozsony, and Érsekújvár,[1] where she grew up, there were a lot of Gypsies. Back then the name Gypsy was not considered pejorative; there were no Romas and Sintis. My mother taught Gypsy children to read scores, because she valued their music. Following her example, in the early 1950s, when I was sub-department head of adult education – and not realizing that you can't make people happy against their will – I also wanted to do something for the Gypsies.

In the early 1950s, the majority of the Gypsies of Baranya County had not yet settled down, and they lived as freely as the birds of the air. They went about in wagons, stopping in one place, then another, at temporary lodgings, on the edge of the woods, by

---

1 Érsekújvár: Nové Zámky in southwestern Slovakia.—Trans.

the banks of a stream. They practised their traditional trades well: tub-making, nail-making, basket-weaving. But first and foremost, they played music.

The cultural policy of socialism made no room for Magyar-style mock folk songs, of which Kodály had once spoken approvingly, and which were so much a part of life in pre-war Hungary – they were part of everyday life, of elegant evenings and nightly revels, and Gypsy band leaders and generations of Gypsy musicians made a living from them. Every place of entertainment worth its salt had a Gypsy band, whose members were better informed about the world than most citizens who never crossed the outskirts of their town or village in their lives.

Wanting to follow in my mother's footsteps, as an enthusiastic educator of the people I went from village to village, telling the local teachers that the Gypsies should come to the schoolhouse at a certain date, when they could participate in a course for illiterates. But I wasn't thinking like those I meant to help, who must have regarded my efforts as part of the same Communist shenanigans that made them settle down and have a permanent work place. The town crier appeared, advertised the course, and quick as a wink they were in their wagons, and in two days' time there wasn't a single Gypsy left in the place. There was only one exception, the village of Erdősmecske, where the town crier did not publicize anything, and where the old schoolteacher was an experienced and wise man. If I could remember his name, I would put it down here in capital letters. He picked up his blackboard, put it on his back, and went to the Gypsies in the woods. He hung the board on a tree, and it was up to the individual to decide if he wanted to learn how to read and write or not. Thanks to his efforts, a couple of Gypsies learned to write after all.

How one moves does not depend on one's physique. I've seen very thin Barbie-like bodies move awkwardly and heavy bodies move with grace. Irma belonged to the latter group. She started using the wall bars out of necessity, because she had inherited "the family spine" from my grandmother.

Grandmother passed down her bad spine to each of her three daughters. The family used to say that they spent half their lives at Pöstyén[2] sitting up to the chin in a mud bath, and the other half torturing themselves with gymnastics. As far as the mud bath is concerned, there was a grain of truth in what they said, but the torture was not true, because all three loved to exercise.

Irma enjoyed thinking like a heretic and talking like a priest. By way of excusing herself, she used to say that only an ox never changes its mind. What person will not change his opinion from time to time? As long as you truly believe what you say and stand by your convictions, you're okay. Even Anatole France wrote somewhere in *The Gods Are Athirst* that a man who was not a revolutionary in his youth will never grow into a proper petit-bourgeois.

I paid a high price for my own revolutionary leanings, whereas I thought that it was the only path to salvation, along with the Lord, of course. I was born a simple soul, and a simple soul I have remained, because I continue to believe in things that will lead to my salvation – sometimes a certain diet, sometimes its opposite, but always in all sincerity while it lasts. One thing, though, that I have never changed my mind about is exercise.

Irma was wonderful at bolstering my self-confidence. When she was young, she may have been embarrassed by her height. But she taught us that it's okay to stick out of a crowd. Just make sure you're humble about it. "Don't gild the lily, they'll notice you anyway," she advised, and wouldn't let me wear more than one piece of jewellery at a time. "You're no Christmas tree!" She knew that I was born with a flat chest, a curveless spine, knock-knees, and flat feet, but she inspired me to do things that would guarantee that I wouldn't feel bad about my infirmities. "If you're elegant, you're elegant naked, too," she used to say, "because elegance comes from within." How did she know that she must prepare me to survive the humiliation of the naked Appels with inner elegance and a head held high?

Still, like the other grown-ups, Irma would occasionally say things that made no sense. I was taught that if you don't know something, you should ask, just don't pretend you know what you don't, because you'll be found out and be an object of ridicule, and

---

2 Pöstyén, today Piešťany in Slovakia, was a spa famous for its hot springs.

that's such a contemptible, uncultured thing. However, Irma had a sentence I didn't understand, but never asked about. Sometimes she'd say, "Even the spade handle will fire away, if I want it to." This intrigued me, but I could never recall the context in which it was said. But right away I imagined the spade handle as it straightened up and started firing a round of sparks in all directions and then, having spent all its sparks, sank into a corner. Except whenever Mother said this, an unfamiliar, I might say impish smile appeared on her lips. For lack of background knowledge, I couldn't make heads or tails of it. Luckily, if we apply ourselves, such lack of knowledge can be remedied; and I was always the studious type.

The central axis of our lives was food. Everything revolved around it. Mother, my governess Ruth, and the cook of the moment put together the week's menu with the greatest of care and circumspection, and only after several consultations. Once a week we even had a meatless day. I like to amuse myself by thinking back on the baked and cooked foods of those meatless days – the leavened and kneaded doughs, the puff pastries, puddings, custards, pies, pancakes, and white wine sauces. I don't think we had two identical meatless days in a year. But they were very careful to make sure that the day the laundry-woman, Auntie Lazányi, was due, the day should not be meatless.

Most of the ingredients, the vegetables and fruit, grew in our own garden. Flour, sugar, and game were brought up from the farm. But we had a chicken coop and at least two pigs in our own sty. My mother was firmly convinced that only what came from our own hands was healthy and hygienic; everything else was a poor imitation of the real thing. Accordingly, we even made our own ice cream and never went to a confectioner's in Debrecen. Even we children learned to look at the cakes and sweets available in cafés and tea rooms with suspicion. The one exception was Pest. By some miracle, everything in Pest was considered authentic, so we could eat at Gerbaud's [3] and dine at Gundel's. [4] Little wonder, considering that the former was celebrated for its cakes and the

---

3 An elegant old patisserie in Budapest, founded in 1858.
4 Opened in 1894, the Gundel was considered the top restaurant in the pre-war era.

latter for its cuisine; and we drank water from the tap, because back then it didn't taste of chlorine.

I don't know how we managed, but we ate as much in one day as we do now in a week – all of us, that is, except for me, because I nearly starved to death, mainly because they kept urging me to eat, chocolate if nothing else, but I couldn't swallow it. It had a repulsive colour. I couldn't understand how anyone could allow something down one's oesophagus that bore such close resemblance to human excrement. I transferred its colour to its smell as well, and it even *smelled* like that, I swear.

We had to eat at least five times a day – a light breakfast with a couple of soft-boiled eggs, or an omelette, or ham and eggs that we called "hemenegs," brioche with two or three kinds of jam, rolls or buns. The noonday meal consisted of at least three courses – soup, meat, vegetables, salad, cakes, and fruit at the very least, and for the grown-ups, coffee. A good thing that we had plenty of cooked vegetables and fruit, because I liked to eat them in great quantities and continue to do so even today. The dinners were "light," too – a bit of cold meat or fish, ham, sausage (home-made, of course), and luckily, salad and fruit, and some cake as a matter of course. The grown-ups drank spritzer with their meal, and the children drank water or raspberry juice that Mother made from the raspberries she grew in the garden.

Irma drank her coffee or tea without sugar, and I drank my cocoa without sugar. Never in my life did I drink either tea or coffee with sugar, because I wanted to be like my mother. When towards the end of 1944 in the camp at Allendorf I lost nearly a third of my original weight, all the food I wouldn't eat when I was a child and all the sugar I didn't put in my coffee smarted like an open wound.

The twice-yearly marathon washing and ironing was a spectacular ceremony that lasted several days. Aunt Lazányi was in charge. She always came in the same black coat and kerchief, she always carried the same big bag in her hand, and everything proceeded in exactly the same manner every time. She had hardly crossed the threshold, she hadn't divested herself of her coat yet, but she would already gulp down a shot of pálinka. She wouldn't even talk to us till then. But with the pálinka down her gullet, she turned sweet and talkative. Aunt Lazányi didn't just wash and iron, her primary occupation was to attend religious processions. She carried the banner with the Virgin Mary personally, and sang religious songs. She sang beautifully, with good timing and piety, so it was easy to imagine her going up front, climbing up the side of the hill with the coveted banner in her hand. She basically lived from one procession to the next, and in between, she told us about her experiences.

Her arrival was preceded by excited preparations. The large laundry chest, which was as tall as a man and had a door at the top and at the bottom, was relieved of its contents. The dirty laundry was dropped in at the top and pulled out at the bottom. Bed linen, table linen, and kitchen towels were washed twice a year; underwear was washed during the frequent so-called "small wash days." But the "big wash days" were the real thing. The laundry was carefully separated according to colour, quality, and material. Then, with Aunt Lazányi at the helm, the dirty linen was washed for days, boiled in a copper cauldron, rinsed over and over again, starched and whitened, then taken up to the attic to dry. In winter, the wash that had been hung in the attic was so hard, it crackled. Then two women would roll up their sleeves and pull at the pillow cases, duvet and eiderdown covers, sheets, tablecloths, and kitchen towels in a diagonal as well as a parallel direction, then in the days to follow, they put everything through the two rolls of the mangle worked with a crank. This was the pre-ironing. Next they sprayed as many pieces with water as they could iron the following day.

Once washed, everything had a predetermined, non-negotiable size. The small and large pillowcases, the sheets, the covers, and so on were always folded into the same size, and pink tissue paper was placed under the embroidered surfaces. Everything had its appointed place in the commode, measured out to the last inch. The freshly ironed things were placed at the bottom of the neatly arranged column. This way, every piece was used equally. As Irma said, order is the soul of things, and I quite agree with her.

The grown-ups' underwear, my father's shirts, the nightgowns, pyjamas, and socks were stored on the shelves of the wardrobe in the bedroom. The shelves were also lined with pink tissue paper, and the edges were decorated with crocheted ribbons my mother made, pinned to the sides with thumbtacks covered in enamel.

Every kind of clothing came in summer and winter varieties, as well as varieties for school, and so on. Also, since in those days we still had spring and fall in Hungary, there were also so-called transitional coats and suits. On March 15[5] we went to the ceremony in socks and a sailor's dress and didn't have to wear a coat, because spring had arrived. On November 1[6] we put on our galoshes and placed a wreath on the tomb of the Unknown Soldier in the cemetery, because winter had come.

Along with our book, school, and toy shelves, we children were also put in charge of our own wardrobe. If we didn't keep our things neat, Mother never reprimanded us. She just took everything off the offending shelf and placed it on the floor.

Making dried pasta in the summer was always great fun and took several days. We made vermicelli noodles, thin noodles and wide noodles, square noodles of various sizes, shell-shaped pasta, pasta for stew, and also egg barley in a variety of sizes that were put through sieves brought from the mill, then sorted according to size. They were dried in the sun, placed in plain net sacks, then hung up in the pantry to dry. I've forgotten the secret of making dried fruit, but the taste of the dried plums pitted and stuffed with walnut still lingers in my mouth.

We also put an incredible amount of compote away for the winter. When we suffered from a cold, we ate cherry compote, otherwise compote made from peaches and apricots, pears, and so forth. The latter three were inedible because they were processed while still green, then cut into shape with the help of special knives. The cooks added sulphur to preserve the colour. They placed the fruit on huge sieves, then placed a small stick of sulphur under the sieves, lit it, and covered the sieves. Then they soaked the fruit seventy times to get rid of the smell of the sulphur. Since that made the fruit hard and sour, they proceeded to cook it in heavy syrup.

---

5 The anniversary of the 1848 Revolution, March 15 is a school holiday.
6 November 1, All Saints Day, is followed by the Day of the Dead, commemorated to this day by a visit to the cemetery.

We children were expected to cut the stone-hard compote with a teaspoon without it leaping off our dessert plate.

We loved the process of preparing jam. There were two kinds. One was made in the kitchen in a pot, and when it was ready, it was placed in jars and kept warm to prevent it cooling down too fast. Mother wrote the name of the jam and the year on small labels. We also made jam from all kinds of uncooked fruit made with 50 per cent sugar and stirred for one hour.

But the fun came when we made plum jam. They brought the large copper cauldron used for boiling the dirty linen out of the laundry room. They built a makeshift brick fireplace under it. The cauldron was sterilized under my mother's watchful gaze. When it was as bright as the sun at high noon, it was deemed ready for use. Several women sat in the garden pitting the plums. Then when there were loads of plums made ready, they lit a fire under the cauldron and stirred the plums, taking turns, because it was hard work. The handle of the wooden spoon was bent at a ninety-degree angle with a large ladle at the end for stirring. The trick was to make a fire that wouldn't burn the plums. The women continued the cooking even at night. This jam and the mixed jam made out of the leftover apples, pears, and plums, prepared in the same way, were placed in wooden boxes. They were pretty little wooden boxes of the same size, lined with grease-paper. The hot jam was poured into these. More grease-paper was placed on top, and the lid was nailed down. No sugar or preservatives were added. When we tipped the jam out of these boxes in winter, we could cut them with a knife. The last boxes that held the yield from 1943 my father gave away in the ghetto before we were taken to the brick yard prior to our deportation.

The pig slaughtering was not an entirely positive event, because by the time the two piglets grew old enough to be slaughtered, they had names like Grunty and Fatty, or Pinky and Nosy, whatever suited them best. I'm not exaggerating when I say that they grew up to be our personal friends, and you don't go around eating your friends without giving it a second thought!

Pig slaughter was also preceded by feverish preparations. People spent days scrubbing the wooden tubs and vats for the ham, bacon, and so on that would be set aside for curing. They cleaned out and filled the smoke hut with fresh straw to receive the bacon, flank, ham, pork cheese, and liver sausage to be cured. Rolls soaked in milk were added to the blood sausage, buckwheat mush was added to the tripe sausage, and we bought a couple of pork livers to add to the liver sausage, because you can never have too much liver sausage around.

Irma conducted the proceedings like a true professional. She wore a kerchief on her head and covered almost her entire body with a big white apron. All she was missing was a baton. For two days and two nights she orchestrated the butcher and the women who busied themselves in the summer kitchen making soup, stuffed cabbage, roast meat, sausage and hard sausage, some with lemon, some with garlic, and some plain. After curing, the dry sausage was removed to the attic. When the smoking was finished, they removed the ashes from the fireplace that reached to the ceiling – a mere bucketful for an entire year! We used sawdust wrapped in paper bags, and it doesn't produce much ash. They brought the dried sausage down from the attic and wrapped each stick in grease paper. They put the ashes through a sieve, placed them back in the fireplace, and placed the sausage on top. Throughout the summer, we took what we needed from there.

Needless to say, we made our own pickled preserves as well from the cucumbers, peppers, and green tomatoes grown in our garden, and from the baby corn and baby melons brought up from the farm. We also made pickled plums, cauliflower, beets, and so on, all prepared with vinegar.

The most fun, though, was making sour cabbage. Going against ancient custom, we didn't grow our own cabbage, though. Irma bought it at the market. I might add that I'd have hated to be a cabbage vendor where my mother was the customer. Still, year after year, she managed to find mounds and mounds of cabbage that was just right and that was delivered on the grower's cart through the side gate.

Like any culinary activity, making sour cabbage also began with an eye to hygiene. They brought out the cabbage barrel that had been meticulously scrubbed months before, right after we'd

scraped the last bits of cabbage out of it at Easter, when the last of
the ham was brought down from the attic and the last stuffed cabbage of the season was cooked, because it was winter food. Once
we ate the last bit, it was time for spring and summer to arrive, and
these seasons of the year called for different kinds of food.

When the cart packed half full with cabbage arrived, Irma acted
as if the barrel had never been scrubbed, ever. They launched the
attack on the barrel, the lid, the press, with lye ashes. Then they
spent at least two days chopping and grating the cabbage. I don't
know how their arms held out.

Filling the barrel was also great fun. They added all sorts of
things to the grated cabbage, ingredients that they scrimp on today.
Here's the list: coriander, mustard seed, juniper berries, allspice,
bay leaves, marjoram, savoury, quince, apples, red hot peppers.
Even so, I'm bound to have left something out. And of course there
were many heads of cabbage for next winter's stuffed cabbage.
Then they started turning the press, which had heavy wooden
boards under it. Once the sour cabbage was ready for consump-
tion, we children couldn't wait for the quinces and apples at the
bottom, because they tasted so deliciously sour.

The sour cabbage barrel was kept in the apple cellar, a circumstance of which one thing has remained, namely that to this day
I can feel the mixed scent of sour cabbage and apples, and that the
smell of one will invariably bring to mind the smell of the other.

A thorough house cleaning before Christmas and Easter formed
an essential part of our household rituals. There was also a major
restorative cleaning in August, while we were away on the farm.
All sorts of workmen would show up and repair the falling plas-
ter, the blemishes on the walls, the cracks on the painted doors
and windows. Generally, as soon as anything needed repair, it
was repaired. As a consequence, everything always seemed new.
During the eighteen years I spent at home, I can recall only two
instances when the house needed painting.

We hated these major house cleanings because they interfered
with our daily routines. But there was no way around them. Irma
acted as if house cleaning were the preeminent reason for living,
and as if every object were created only so it could be washed,

scrubbed, dusted, or shaken out. When this didn't happen to them, they could consider themselves to be in a state of grace. I never understood the need for these marathon cleaning bouts, considering that everything was being cleaned all over the house all the time. The clean smell that characterized our home is still in my nostrils.

Irma organized Santa Claus Day, Christmas, Easter, name days, and birthdays with the greatest of care and with an eye to their special character. Presents made by hand were valued the most highly. For Christmas, we gave each other presents we made ourselves. Irma set the example. I remember one Christmas when all my dolls – I must have had more than ten – received new clothes. Irma sewed and crocheted the little dresses herself, and she even made shoes, bags, and hats to go with them, enjoying every minute, I'm sure. We children also did our share, making drawings and paintings with great care or else collages from shiny paper. We made boxes from coloured raffia, and when we were older, we embroidered handkerchiefs and knitted or crocheted shawls and gloves to give as presents. We began making these objects in October so they'd be ready by Christmas. The first Christmas I can remember, a real angel stood under the tree.

The bunny always came to our garden to hide its presents among the shrubs and bushes and we went looking for them with great excitement. Santa Claus put what he'd brought in the window – books, nice notebooks, and pretty Faber pencils – not your usual Christmas stuff. But no chocolates. I wouldn't eat them anyway.

From what I have said above, one would think that Irma got up at five in the morning, rolled up her sleeves, and blew her bugle. But no such thing. Despite her seventy-five kilos, she was a sleepy little kitten. She liked to say that she was like a pumpkin flower, she bloomed in the evening. She hated going to bed early, and the only thing she hated even more was getting up early, just like me. Nor did she. But she organized everything perfectly, my father's breakfast, our getting to school, and setting the housekeeping chores in motion. Cleaning, the ritual of rituals, was begun at the spot farthest from the bedroom. By the time the cleaners reached the bedroom around ten a.m., Irma was out of bed and in the bathroom, from where she emerged bright as a button and smelling like heaven. One would have been hard put to decide what was more important to her: food or her vanity. She loved to eat well, but she also wanted to look good. Luckily for her, in those days the ideal female figure bore no resemblance to a broom handle. A bit of plumpness here or there didn't damage one's femininity. Irma had plenty of plumpness of her own, and she compensated for it by wearing a girdle. She had an evening girdle with a low décolletage and she had a special one to wear under her swimsuit. She had girdles of various colours, especially salmon pink, of which there was the most in her girdle for day. (But no black ones, because they were too risqué and not proper in the least.)

The lady who made Mother's girdles and other undergarments was called Lujza, just like that, Lujza. Her salon was located in a side street between St Anna and Kossuth streets. She was a true artist and called my mother "esteemed." There were mountains and mountains of silk in her salon, brilliant pink, salmon pink, azure blue, apple green, sun yellow, and lilac, and flower prints, large and small. There were also show pieces with embroidery, openwork, Richelieu work, and tulle inserts. You had to choose a colour and the handwork from among the samples. Then you bided your time, and the masterpiece was ready. Until I was fifteen, my undergarments were made out of fine cotton by our domestic seamstress, Honorea Berkovics. From the age of fifteen I was considered a big girl and old enough for silken underwear. Lujza even had my name embroidered on my slip, and not just my monogram, but my name in full, like this: Éva.

I never saw my mother without a girdle. She even wore one of her everyday girdles on her way to the gas chamber at Birkenau.

There were things in our family that are not easy to understand in retrospect. For example, our entire family, and that includes all our relatives, near and far, felt it incumbent upon themselves to be frugal. Luckily, they were not frugal with everything. They were not frugal when it came to food, for instance, which meant not only the food we ate ourselves, but also the food that the live-in servants ate. In our home, the food for the maids, washing women, and so on was not rationed, the pantry was not locked, not even the wardrobes and commodes. I was firmly convinced that a bunch of keys hanging from a ring around the belt of the housekeeper was the invention of English novelists.

On the other hand, they saved for the sake of saving, the way there's art for the sake of art. "L'art pour l'art," which we twisted into "pourlapour." Luckily, I was the first grandchild, and that status came with advantages. I had no one whose clothes I'd inherit, while, on the other hand, everything I had worn made the rounds of the family. Some of it even came back round to my little sister.

In short, I always had new clothes. But don't think I was taken to a shop and picked out what I liked, then we paid for it, and I wore it. No such thing. Gizi, my paternal aunt, had a children's clothing salon in Fehérhajó Street in Budapest. In her heyday, she had a dozen girl apprentices. Anyone else making my clothes except Gizi was out of the question. For one thing, she was a member of the family and therefore could be depended upon, and for another, since she was a member of the family, we felt it our duty to take our business to her. The loyalty was mutual – we had her make our clothes, while she charged us at cost.

When my mother decided that I had nothing to wear, meaning that I'd outgrown my clothes yet again, we had to brave the distance between Debrecen and Budapest. Because of our "pourlapour" frugality, the obvious solution of taking me up to Gizike, who'd take my measurements, and staying in Pest until the masterpiece had materialized was out of the question. No way. My mother went through the contents of the discard wardrobe, a white three-door affair standing in the hall that held only stuff we did not use but would never think of discarding. Having found the most ragged piece of threadbare bed sheet, Mother rolled it around me very tight and sewed it up. Then very carefully, she cut the sheet in half up front, and mailed it to Gizi in Pest. Then, based on the sheet pattern, Gizi would make me several sailor outfits.

Gizi had an invention that was not popular with us children. We called it "growing clothes," meaning clothing that grew along with us. Wherever possible – up, down, on the side, inside every blouse and skirt – she would leave an extra ten centimetres. These ten centimetres were cleverly tucked in, and as we grew, the hidden dimensions of our "growing" clothes came into play, which meant that our clothes would simply not go out of use. On the contrary. When the next child in line inherited a garment, it could be reduced or enlarged at will. Still, it is impressive that those materials would serve several children, and, in their final metamorphosis, the garments made from them would be turned inside out and worn that way.

Aunt Gizi's trademark was the fine white cotton apron. I had countless white aprons with lace, open-work, embroidery, pleats, Seumchen basting, ruffles, and various combinations of all of the above, and I paraded in these aprons from morning to night. I certainly learned to take care of my clothes! I even wore white cotton aprons to elementary school, which was no small feat, considering that we wrote with pens dipped in ink, and the ink would easily drip on its way from inkpot to paper. I learned that saliva is one of the most effective spot cleaners. Just try it. The taste of the ink we used back then is still in my mouth.

I will pine after my mother's empire as long as I live, its rigorous rules, the motherly omnipotence tempered by gentleness, care, and love. Irma organized our lives, but the way she went about it, we never even noticed. The fact that there is no bringing her back is painful beyond words, the fact that nothing whatever has remained of her – my mother as a grown-up – when she was the same age as I, her child, would become, not even a simple photograph. The way I lost her, which was a far cry from family custom whereby the loving family nurses the old at home until they give their soul back to their Maker – in short, the way I lost my mother, my father, and my younger sister, the cold-blooded, cruel, premeditated murder that I didn't even recognize for what it was when it happened, will remain an open wound through a lifetime, be it ever so long. We couldn't even take our leave of each other. To this day, I try to avoid farewells, if I have the chance.

My mother made me feel that I was the most important person in her eyes, and so was my sister, and that the most important person in all our eyes was my father. How did my mother manage it?

The cliché that time heals all wounds is a lie. It depends on the wound. There are wounds that never heal. They remain open. Some wounds hurt and burn and smart and bleed without letting up.

All we can do is learn to bear it.

Me at the age of three.

The True Story of My Birth, or, My Birth As It Really Happened

We were never short on imagination. This had its good side and it had its bad side. The good side was that I was never bored, I always had something to preoccupy me, I just had to imagine something. The bad side was that I could never be quite sure if something had really happened, or if I just thought that it had. In short, these two things got all mixed up inside. One thing, though: I never told a lie. I was taught that we Fahídies never lie, because it is below our dignity.

I loved fairies, the reason for which will become evident to the reader when he reaches the end of this chapter. My daddy told me true stories every night, and sometimes they involved fairies, which is probably one reason. So it was no surprise when I met one on the front stairs of our home.

We had a beautiful covered set of stairs leading up to the main entrance. It had thirteen steps. (We were not a family riddled by superstition.) The steps were dark red. I can still smell the odour of the wax, diluted with methyl alcohol, that was used for polishing them. The stairs were covered with red coconut matting. The white runner going up the middle had a red stripe going up either side. The matting was held in place on each step by a brass rod fixed to rings, while on the right and left of each step stood a green plant. It was all very impressive.

I was just hastening out to the garden when I saw a fairy one step below me. This fairy looked just like me. She wore a fine white cotton apron, her hair was arranged in two braids tied with white ribbons, she was holding a doll under her arm that looked just like mine, and she was holding it in the same manner that I used to hold mine. I wasted no time in calling to her:

"Dear little fairy, wait for me, please!"

The fairy was not friendly in the least, though, and ran away as if she were fleeing, as if she didn't want me to catch up with her. I was terribly excited, but no matter how I hurried down the thirteen steps, I couldn't catch up with her, and by the time I reached the bottom of the stairs, the fairy had disappeared without a trace. I could hardly wait for evening to tell Daddy about my fabulous adventure.

Grown-ups are difficult for me to understand, often even today. If someone tells me a true story – but what am I saying, not one but many true stories – involving fairies doing all sorts of things, why can't it be true that I had also seen a fairy? And then my daddy, the same daddy who taught me in the first place that fairies exist, tells me that I am lying. So let me solemnly repeat: a Fahídi does not tell lies, and neither do I. And I stand by what I said, that I saw a fairy on the stairs. If you don't believe me, prove me wrong. That's what I was told, too, at the end of every story.

My special relationship to fairies is connected to a true story, the most exciting of all true stories, the one I heard most often, even if with slight variations. My daddy could never tire of telling me the story, because when he asked what story I wanted to hear, I always chose this one. This true story was special because, for one thing, it didn't begin like the rest: "Once upon a time, beyond the Seven Seas, there lived a little girl and her name was Éva." This true story began in a much more intriguing way. Here it is:

Once upon a time, beyond the Seven Seas, there lived a girl and a boy. The girl had black hair and dark eyes, and she had a way of looking with these eyes, sometimes full of mischief, at other times full of gentleness, a way, I say, so that once the boy looked deep into these eyes, he could never think of anything else. The boy had blond hair and deep-set grey eyes, and he had a way of looking with these eyes so that even stones began to tremble when he looked at them.

The boy and the girl loved each other very much.

The boy loved to go into the forest. The trees were his friends. He hardly glanced at them and he knew what kind they were and even how old, and if he happened to glance at a tree that had been sawn in two, he could even tell when there was drought in the tree's life, and when an abundance of rain. He knew which tree would serve for what.

Though the boy loved the trees, he also loved the plants and the flowers of the forest, and every evening would bring large bouquets home to the girl. During his forest strolls, he was also amused by the animals. He loved to listen to the pecking of the woodpecker and the distant cooing of the cuckoo bird, because the cuckoo bird will not sing in the presence of humans, that's why its song is always distant. The boy was also familiar with the goldfinch and the thrush, the jay, the rabbit, the little fox – always the little fox, as if there were no big foxes – the weasel, the squirrel, and when he ventured into the distant forests of Transylvania, he even met some bears.

For her part, the girl was diligent. She tended her garden, and she cooked and baked for the boy, and always waited for him with a beautifully laid table. She also knew the art of sewing and darning, she could sing and play the piano, she played tennis and loved to dance, but she loved gymnastics best of all. The girl grew up on a big farm and could talk to the animals. The dogs and the cats and even the horses did her bidding, even though she spoke to them in a whisper.

The boy and the girl lived together in harmony.

They lived together in harmony, but after a while, something was missing from their lives. They didn't understand at first what that something might be. After all, they had everything they could wish for. The boy had a lumberyard where he worked diligently, and the girl had a house and a garden to tend and to keep her busy, and they loved each other very much.

Then one morning upon awakening, the girl laughed and said to the boy:

"I know what's missing from our lives. Our child."

"Now why didn't I think of that?" the boy said. "You are quite right."

And they set about diligently looking for their child. They started with the house first. They climbed up to the attic, climbed down to the cellar, they pulled out every drawer and opened every door of every wardrobe. They looked behind every piece of furniture and under it, too.

They went to the mountains and they went to the sea, they visited strange cities, including Budapest, where their parents and brothers and sisters lived, and they visited all their relatives, near and far. They searched for their child everywhere they could think of, but could not find her.

There was a lovely, long autumn that year. It was October already, but the sun was still warm in the afternoon, even if the days were growing shorter. Pleased with the lovely weather, the boy and the girl drove out to the forest. When they got there, they got out of the cart and walked deeper into the forest on foot. They were both enchanted by the familiar magic of the forest – the way the birds, the trees, the plants, and the flowers communicated with each other.

The girl and the boy walked silently side-by-side, holding hands. They liked walking along like this, in silence. To them the silence meant that they didn't need words to tell each other of their love. This is how they chanced upon a small clearing when they heard the sounds of beautiful music, so they stopped, hoping they could discover its source. The music was coming from the clearing! There were fairies all around, dancing and singing!

The girl and the boy stopped lest they disturb the fairies, then retreated on tiptoes, sat down under a bush, and listened to the music. They didn't even notice that the air had cooled down, the sun was about to set, and the music had long since stopped. It was time to go home, and so the girl and the boy set off towards the edge of the woods.

But suddenly they stopped, because they heard a plaintive cry from inside the forest. It was the crying of a child. They ran in the direction of the sound, because it was getting cooler and darker by the minute. Meanwhile, the sound of crying came closer and closer to them. Panting, they stopped in front of a bush. They bent the boughs to the side, and lo and behold, they saw a little fairy with real wings on its back lying on the ground and crying for all it was worth because it was shivering from the cold.

"What are you doing here in the middle of the forest in the dark of night shivering from the cold?" the boy asked.

"We were playing hide and seek, and the Fairy Queen said she would blow her fairy pipe when it was time to go home, but I hid inside this bush so well I didn't hear anything, not even the sound of the pipe. And now here I am, shivering with cold and not knowing what is to become of me. Boohoo!"

The girl and the boy looked at each other and had the same thought. The girl spoke first:

"We were just looking for our little girl. You look just like her. Would you like to be our little girl?"

That's all the little fairy needed to hear. She stopped crying and amid her trickling tears she answered with a smile:

"Yes."

The boy removed the little wet wings from the back of the fairy girl and left them behind under the bush, wrapped the trembling fairy in the girl's kerchief, then said:

"If you want to be our child, you must never forget that you were born a fairy. It's not something you can cast off like your wings. If you should ever forget, just reach back and touch your shoulder blades, and you will feel the memory of your wings. If you are born a fairy, you must act like one all your life. Don't be conceited because of your talent. We all bring something into the world with us, some this, some that. Never ever look down on anyone because they're different, or poorer, or not as smart, or not as good-looking as you. You are here to help those who are not as smart as you, to provide for those who have less than you, and to protect those who are smaller or weaker than you. Learn as much as you can. Sooner or later, all that you have learned will come in handy. Listen to everyone who turns to you in good faith, and if you can't give them anything, don't give them advice, but words of kindness. Don't tolerate injustice. If you feel you are right, stand by your convictions. Learn what should be taken seriously, and what should not. It is often better to laugh than to cry. If you work, do what you need to do with all your heart and to the best of your ability. Your name will be Éva Fahídi. You may not lie, you may not cheat anyone, you may not cause pain to any man or animal on purpose. Even your monogram will be FÉ,[1] which in German pronunciation means fairy.

According to contemporary views on the education of children, it was not of the essence to enlighten a toddler about the biological facts of life. But since I spent a lot of time on the farm, I knew quite

---

1 FÉ: The initials of Fahidi Éva, the author's name in reverse, in the Hungarian order.

a lot about life and its origin. So needless to say, I knew how *other* children came into the world.

For instance, I knew that a lot of children were born on the Nile, where there were lots of little babies on the beautiful lotus leaves floating among the even more beautiful water lilies. They love it there and play the whole day long, but if Daddy and Mommy decide that they want a baby, the stork appears over the Nile, chooses the prettiest one, picks it up in its beak, and drops it where it is wanted the most, at which there is much rejoicing, because Daddy, Mommy, Granddaddy and Grandmother, aunts and uncles – in short, everyone – is happy that the new baby has arrived.

I also knew that French babies don't have it so good because they're born inside a cabbage. Personally, I love cabbage, including sour cabbage and stuffed cabbage, but each has its own function and, most especially, its own characteristic smell. Cabbage doesn't smell anything like a newborn baby should, so I would certainly not like to wait in that cabbage smell until Mom and Dad find me, take me out of the cabbage, and cry with joy, "Mon petit choux!" – pretty little cabbage. I'd hate to be anybody's petit choux, unless a goat's. I felt sorry for French babies and was glad I wasn't one myself.

I also heard that some babies grow inside their mother's belly, and, once they have grown nice and big, they come out. But this was just another one of those silly grown-up tales, because it made no sense how a baby could get in in the first place, and once it was in, how it could get out. I much preferred the version of my own birth.

The tale Daddy told me is exemplary even by today's standards. It imparted a strong sense of self and taught me what I should be doing in life. It taught me to stand on my own two feet, and it taught me that I shouldn't be the one asking for help but that I should give it. I was also taught that I should be guided by the basic human values of honour, empathy, tolerance, and compassion, and that I should remain honourable even in the most absurd situations. The rules in that story were always my guides. I'm so glad Daddy told me the story so many times! Where would I be without it? Life has been hard on me, but whenever something pains me, even to this day, I recall that I am a fairy child.

Luckily, life is full of humour; you just have to tune in your antennae to receive it.

In September, 2004, Berlin was preparing for two unusual exhibitions.

Though Germany lost the Second World War, not so German big capital. The prominent Nazis were sentenced at Nuremberg, but their fortunes remained intact. Long live the inviolability of private property! And so the condemned spent two or three years in jail while their money quietly continued to multiply, and once they were out of jail, these Nazis went about increasing their fortune in the booming postwar economy without impediment.

The Flick family is the prototype of this scheme, most especially the grandfather Friedrich Flick and the grandson Friedrich Christian Flick. (According to family chronicles, the generation in between had no talent for finance.) By the 1940s, Friedrich Flick, the founder of the dynasty, had already amassed a substantial fortune. He came by it through the Aryanization of the Jewish factories,[2] and multiplied it manifold in the munitions industry. During the Second World War, he had fifty thousand forced labourers work for his various ventures. I was one of the thousand women labouring at the munitions factory at Allendorf, where Friedrich Flick was on the board of directors, and which he would buy after the war. None of his descendants inherited their grandfather's genius for finance, and in the end his fortune went the way of so many others. It was dispersed.

Exceptions prove the rule, and the grandfather, Friedrich Flick, did not abide by one of our favourite family sayings, whereby only an ox never changes its mind. Well, he proved to be very much like an ox, because the moment the thought of compensating forced labourers came up, he announced that he would never lay out a penny. No way. Not one. Nor did he, then or ever. For a long time, his favourite grandson, Friedrich Christian Flick, followed his example, though it is only fair to say that when Flick left this vale of tears and the Deutsche Bank took over his fortune, thanks to pressure from the German people, we, who were in forced labour

---

2 See note 3 on page 69, above.

in Flick's empire, were promised four thousand Deutsche Marks compensation. We received half. If anyone should decide to ask what happened to the other half, that will make two of us.

I tried, as usual, to slip inside the skin of the Flick heirs, poor things. It can't be easy living with an ill-reputed name like theirs. Two of the Flick grandchildren, a lady and a gentleman, paid their share of the compensation into the German till, and have been trying ever since to distance themselves from Friedrich Christian. For his part, F.C. Flick set up a foundation against racial discrimination, etc. But being his grandfather's best pupil, he did not pay compensation for years. After all, it's none of his business. He wasn't even born yet when his grandfather made his fortune, he merely inherited some of it (and oh, yes, how it must hurt him). But once again public pressure won out, and in late April of 2005, Friedrich Christian Flick dished out one hundred Euros per head as compensation to his grandfather's fifty thousand forced labourers. That's five million Euros. A good thing that few of the fifty thousand are still alive. What would they do with the one hundred Euros?

Once he'd had enough of the life of the smart set that was his birthright, F.C. Flick decided to wash the family name clean of odium. Through the years he amassed an impressive collection of contemporary art and decided to put it on public display free of charge. Since he lived in Switzerland, he decided to offer the honour to the city of Zurich. Though money has no smell there either, as the saying goes, those decent Swiss decided, with the hypocrisy of the outsider, that because of the ill-gotten gains that made the collection possible, it had no place in their clean and honest Zurich. Their moral title to this claim could hardly be supported by their actions during the Second World War, when they turned away the Jews at their borders begging for asylum. They knew as well as anyone else that this was tantamount to signing their death warrant. However, since then a third generation has grown up there, as elsewhere, and they were not asked by their grandfathers what they should or should not do in those shameful years.

The city of Berlin had no such qualms. They were more than happy to put on the exhibition. In response, the heads of the Fritz Bauer Institute of Frankfurt, who are in charge of the Frankfurt documentation centre that serves to educate people everywhere about the history and effects of the Holocaust, felt that it would be advisable to show Germany the other side of the coin as well – and in fact, its third side, too, and so extended an invitation to me and asked me to bring along some of my former camp mates so we could talk about our lives in the factory belonging to the Flick empire under the Third Reich. They also organized an excellent exhibition from the material at their disposal. In short, interested Berliners could see two exhibitions simultaneously, both related to the Flick dynasty. One was down to earth and had hard facts to illustrate how the other exhibition, devoted to art, could come about in the first place.

The F.C. Flick Collection on public display is enormous. It is so rich that there is no exhibition hall large enough to display it in its entirety.

In short, the F.C. Flick Collection was put on permanent display at the huge exhibition complex of the Hamburger Bahnhof in September 2004. The opening address was delivered by Chancellor Schröder. In Germany, those critical of the event pointed out that both Schröder and F.C. Flick belong to the generation that is both personally and politically heir to the generation that not only lived in Nazi Germany but helped make it work.

The day before the exhibition, the Fritz Bauer Institute held a press conference with our participation and with the participation, I might add, of all the major German newspapers, journals, and television channels. Every miracle lasts three days, as they say, but for those three days the media was all abuzz with what we said.

Personally, I was worried about the upcoming press conference because I didn't know if our host, the Fritz Bauer Institute, would agree with what I was planning to say. The way I saw it at the time, no one is responsible for the place of his birth, and no one is responsible for anything, except his own actions. I do not live in Germany. I am an old woman. I have come to terms with hatred and contempt. I no longer have hatred in my heart. I want to die in peace. I am not interested in daily politics.

The press conference had a vibrant atmosphere. My fellow former inmates described our slave labour at the DAG (Dynamite Nobel Joint Stock Co.) German munitions plant with the conviction and authenticity that comes from personal experience – the starvation, the cold, the work that defied human strength, the humiliation, and so on.

Since I like to voice unorthodox views as much as I like to play, I didn't wait to be asked the most exciting question of the evening regarding my views on the F.C. Flick collection. Instead, I asked those present if they would play along with me. Once they agreed, I asked those in the audience who had been asked whether they wanted to be born to put up their hands. There was a moment of puzzled silence. They didn't understand what I was getting at. Then I asked those who had been asked before their birth where they would like to be born to put up their hands. By then there was sporadic laughter in the room. They suddenly understood that F.C. Flick had not been asked these questions either. When next they asked me what I thought about the Chancellor taking sides by opening the exhibition, all I could say was that he must know what he is doing. After all, he's the Chancellor. By now there was laughter all around.

The next person asked me why I don't have hatred in me, why I don't lash out at F.C. Flick, and which philosopher's views I agree with. At that point I took out my book in German and opened to my father's story about how they found me as a little fairy girl under a bush, and read it to them. It was my father's legacy, what he gave me to start my life. Some people inherit one thing, some another, I said. Some inherit money that has blood on it, others inherit a moral conscience. It went off very well. Daddy had to tell me the true story of my birth many times so that, nearly eighty years later, it could make Germany think.

And now comes the true story of the true story, because it was as difficult for my mother to tie the knot as for my father. It's simply a matter of how you look at it. If we look at it from the point of view of the young man – in this particular instance my father Dezső – finding a suitable spouse involves the following considerations: where is the girl who is pretty as well as intelligent, but won't want to wear the pants in the family? If we look at it from the point of view of the marriageable young lady – in this particular case my mother Irma – the following considerations must be taken into account: where can she find a clever young man who won't waste his inheritance, who can be depended on, doesn't drink and will make a good father, and, though no Adonis, still looks somewhat better than the devil, and is nearly a hundred and eighty centimetres tall? He'll let his wife try her wings, won't lord it over her, is relatively well educated so that he'll be able to engage in conversation on a number of important topics, will have a reasonably lively imagination and won't be deadly dull, and will be a good companion wherever he goes with his wife. From which it will become immediately clear how much more difficult it must have been for the girl – in this particular instance, my mother Irma.

Desirable young men were not to be found on every corner of Ógyalla even back then. As for poor grandfather Alfréd Weisz, he never noticed that he suddenly had three daughters of marriageable age, which called for three wedding feasts, three dowries, and, last but not least, the need to conjure up three suitable matches for them. Clearly, he couldn't be expected to work his magic without leaving the vicinity of his Lipizzaner horses, and so the situation called for a helping hand. In a typical Kaiserliche und Königliche[3] family like ours, untold numbers of uncles and aunts, as well as all their relatives, friends, and acquaintances, close ranks, waiting for the signal to charge, like so many battle horses waiting for the sound of the bugle, so that by activating all available manpower they can help a member of the family reach safe harbour. So it was with Irma. They took her up to Budapest from Ógyalla for the "season," meaning the winter season, putting her into the care of Uncle Árpád and Aunt Sári, my grandfather's sister and her husband, with the unannounced but quite obvious intention that they should find Irma a proper bridegroom and prospective husband. In short, Irma bided her time in Budapest hoping for the best on what is today Béla Bartók Road, which at the time was still decidedly quiet and tranquil, just across from the Hotel Gellért, and while she waited she attended concerts, went to the theatre, and visited the museums – in short, she lived the big-city life of a small-town girl.

---

3 Imperial and Royal; see note 5 on page 62. Here, the label refers to the fact that the author's family lived all over the former territory of the Monarchy.

I have far less information on how Dezső came on the scene. In any case, when Irma was seventeen years old, he was already twenty-seven, the embodiment of a serious, dependable, marriageable young man. The fact that he was not wealthy did not count in Irma's family, where Alfréd – meaning my grandfather Alfréd – could remember quite clearly how he started his own career and how it was boosted by my grandmother Ernesztína's appreciable dowry. But by the time he was twenty-seven, Dezső had become an expert on timber, and had a steady job and an air of respectability. He had read an impressive number of books, and, last but not least, was a sight for sore eyes. Anyway, once Irma was in Budapest, the "family marriage broker service" sprang into action, and after some feverish searching, Dezső ended up on the hook.

This is how it went. As is the custom in these cases, an accommodating friend of the family told Dezső that he would soon be introduced to a young lady who had come up to Pest from Ógyalla in far-off Czechoslovakia, and that the young lady had a lot going for her, not least of all her expectation of a handsome dowry. His plebeian pride got the better of Dezső, and in full cognizance of his moral superiority, he announced, "I have no need of some village goose from the back of beyond, not even if she's stuffed full of banknotes from top to toe, so don't mention it again."

Irma was also prepared for her meeting with the serious, reliable young man, but without waiting for her informant to end her say, she gave full vent to her indignation thus: "He can be as reliable as a tax inspector, for all I care. I won't have anyone who is after my money. I'd rather be an old maid!"

A stalemate. Except Dezső and Irma underestimated the determination of friends and family who had conspired to unite them in holy matrimony and so arranged a meeting between the two that for all intents and purposes looked as if it was due entirely to chance.

It was love at first sight.

True love is born in an instant and matures in heaven. With his blond hair and grey eyes and with her dark hair and dark eyes, Dezső and Irma made an ideal couple. Both of them had grown very tall, but luckily, Dezső had grown just a bit taller than Irma.

The winter season had come to an end in Pest, and Irma had to go back to Ógyalla. Except, there was a hitch, because the shameful border created by Trianon now stood between them.

Dezső began to experience strange things. In his industrious working life, this was the first time that during the day a pair of black eyes, shapely ankles, and a huge crown of black hair should dance before his eyes – not to mention the night. He had to admit to himself that, be it day or be it night, he couldn't help thinking of Irma, and he followed up the realization by paying her frequent visits. Dezső was living in Debrecen by then, but an inner necessity forced him into the two- to three-day trips to Ógyalla in Czechoslovakia where time flew by so fast, he had to return to Hungary almost as soon as he got there.

He was constantly at odds with the customs officers, because have you ever seen a man in love who didn't take flowers to the lady of his heart? Well, he did, too, whereupon they made him pay customs duty, and the sum was so unreasonable that he flung the flowers to the ground. What a scene! At Komárom the Czechoslovak customs agents had him leave the train and made him pay a colossal sum for the bouquet, and even so, he could count himself lucky that the train didn't leave without him.

I mention only in passing that this was the start of our family's loose morals vis-à-vis Czechoslovak customs, because from then on we took pride in getting the better of them every chance we got. Some years later we went to Czechoslovakia to attend Hédi's wedding. She was Mother's younger sister. We took her a silver tea set as a wedding present. The cups were lined with crystal goblets, and the set had every piece one could wish for: a small pitcher for lemon juice, a small bottle for rum, sugar bowl, teapot, and milk pitcher, everything placed on a silver tray of considerable size. I have no idea why we lugged it from Debrecen instead of buying it in Bratislava, but lug it we did. According to regulations, anything in use was exempt from customs duty. By the time we reached the border and were waiting for the customs agents, the convertible table under the window was laid, the freshly brewed tea was steaming in the cups, and every jar, bottle, and sugar bowl was filled to the brim with whatever it was supposed to be filled with, and there we sat with serious faces, trying very hard not to giggle as we sipped our tea and felt as heroic as St George when he slew the dragon.

Our other favourite story of how we got the better of the customs agents, which centres on Irma's own dowry, owes its existence to the fact that in those days a dowry without Brussels lace was no dowry. There were lace catalogues, and you could order the item you wanted on the basis of the number in the catalogue. One of the family uncles was charged with going to Brussels to bring back fifty metres of Brussels lace, which cost a pretty penny even back then, and was subject to a hefty customs duty. Poor uncle bought the lace, put it in his travelling bag, and headed back to Czechoslovakia with his booty. There's no border without a customs agent, and so he too was asked if he had anything to declare.

"Fifty metres of Brussels lace," he said in all seriousness. The customs agent saluted and left the compartment. He thought uncle was in a joking mood; if it were true, he'd never declare it, because the customs duty would be prohibitive.

Meanwhile, Dezső kept commuting between Debrecen and Ógyalla, the number of his sleepless nights being directly proportionate to the realization that the proposal of marriage could no longer brook delay and would have to be made.

The world inhabited by Irma was altogether strange and unfamiliar to Dezső. Dezső spent his childhood under strained circumstances. Furthermore, his parents were very religious Jews. He worked his fingers to the bone for everything he achieved. To him, money was there to be saved, always in the interest of some specific aim.

To Irma and her family, life was there to be enjoyed. They were also Jewish, but not observant. They never talked of money because it was as natural that they should have it as it had been in Dezső's childhood to be without. A natural good cheer was also part of life, the coming and going, the extensive housekeeping, the flood of guests. During his first visit to Ógyalla, Dezső nearly fainted when a two-horse carriage with a liveried driver came to the station to pick him up. He'd never been on such a thing before. Irma did not go to greet him personally in case he got ideas into his head.

On the particular visit to Ógyalla that Dezső had been preparing for, it was already in the air that he must propose, or else they'd send him on his way. Alfréd Weisz was perhaps a jot more reserved when he greeted him, but possibly Dezső thought so only because of the promptings of his conscience. So there they sat in the salon when at last Dezső pulled himself together, took a deep breath, and said, "Alfréd, sir, I'd like to ask for your daughter Irma's hand in marriage."

Alfréd acted as if this sentence had been thoroughly unexpected and had caught him off guard, and so he called his faithful helpmate Ernesztína to his side and, last but not least, his daughter Irma, the object of the proposal.

Ernesztína was there in an instant, wiping a tear from her eye in keeping with the occasion, while Irma barely had time to peel her ear away from the keyhole of the salon and run back to her room, only to emerge with a face as innocent as a newborn babe's. And while Irma's slightly envious younger sister Hédi, who was closest to her in age, now took her turn at the keyhole, Irma stood by her teary-eyed mother gravely and demurely, listening to what her equally moved father had to say, at some length, I might add, about what he and Dezső had agreed on some time ago.

When both Dezső and Irma were gone and I got married myself and had to learn to accommodate myself, I thought of them with the highest respect and admiration. I am quite sure that there must have been a lot of tension between them because they hailed from two such different worlds and must have had very different values. For instance, I can't imagine Irma not getting what she wanted when she wanted it, just as I can't imagine Dezső not buying something that Irma felt was important but that he didn't.

I am shocked again and again when I look around me. With few exceptions, married couples can be very hard on each other. They slight and abuse each other, at home and in company. But that's the lesser evil. The catastrophe is that they act the same way in front of their children, regardless of their age, thus depriving them of their sense of security. I look at photos of children today. They look pretty and sweet. But I've seen ten-year-old children with eyes that have more knowledge of life in them than I had in mine at the age of eighteen. How come their loving parents don't die of shame?

If I had nothing else for which I could be grateful to Irma and Dezső, I'd still have plenty to be grateful for, because they spared us, their children, from feeling the tension between them. We did not have to judge them and decide who was right. In our eyes they were equally important, and they were inseparable. We were naïve and happy children. How did they do it?

The Ballad of Alfréd Weisz

When the unparalleled and shameful privatization law came into effect in Hungary after 1989, I needed to acquire documents in lieu of evidence once again. Granted that since 1939 my family had had lots of practice in this, now, having no family left, all the work fell to me.

Though I loathed it with all my heart, I had to prove once again what was the most natural thing in the world – that I had forebears on this earth, that they lived somewhere and owned things, that every regime stripped me of all I had, what luck that there was something to strip me of! The plunder, by the way, did not end then. Anyway, in the Hungarian National Library I found the *Financial Compass* for the year 1924 that contained the records for the foundation of the Fahídi Brothers Lumberyard and Lumber Processing Company, and to my surprise, I found Alfréd Weisz, my maternal grandfather, on the board of directors. That's when I realized that this was Alfréd's way of staying "online" with respect to the fate of his daughter Irma's dowry. Now I had one more piece of paper to acquire, because I also had to have him declared dead. I wrote to the Gelej Township Council, who sent me the letter and protocol on the left. It warms my heart to know that sympathy and good will have not disappeared from the face of the earth. Since my grandparents died in Auschwitz and not in the township of Gelej, which prevented him from issuing a death certificate, the town clerk Pusztai, who is not my relative, just my namesake (by my married name), decided to find the person who took them to the ghetto in Mezőkeresztes and was the last to see them.

Gelej Községi Polgármesteri Hivatal
Telefon:Gelej 52-717
439/1992. szám.-

        Pusztai Béláné asszony
        BUDAPEST Váci-utca 11/B. 1052

            Tisztelt Asszonyom !

        Sajnos kérésnek nem tudok eleget
tenni. Ennek oka benti jegyzőkönyvből
kitünik. Halotti anyakönyvi kivonat
csak akkor állitható ki, ha az elhalt
halálesete az anyakönyvbe is bejegyzésre került. Ahoz, hogy nagyapja halálesete anyakönyvezésre kerüljön most már
csak holttá- eltüntté nyilvánitás lehető-
sége kinálkozik. Ehez polgári biróság
rendelkezik hatáskörrel.
        Amennyiben a kárpótlás iránti
igénybejelentés elbirálását az segit-
hetné jegyzőkönyvileg meghallgattam
KÉKEDI BERTALAN geleji lakost, aki
tanusitja, hogy nagyapját és nagyanyját
lovasfogattal ő szállitotta a mezőcsáti
GETTOBA.
        A geleji polgármesteri hivatal
részéről bizonyitjuk, hogy WEISZ ALFRÉD
és felesége Gelej községből történő
elszállitásuk óta Gelej községbe nem
tértek vissza. A MEZŐCSÁTI GETTO-ba
összegyüjtötteket az akkori hatalom
Nyugatra tovább szállitotta.
        G e l e j , 1992 évi november 6.

                        Tisztelettel:

                        Dr. Pusztay Béla
                           jegyző

(Above and opposite) Letter and records of the Gelej Township Council. The
letter and the protocol are the stuff of ballads.

439/1992. szám.-

JEGYZŐKÖNYV

Készült Gelejen a Polgármesteri Hivatalban 1992 évi november hó
6.-án KÉKEDI BERTALAN /an. Virágh Zsuzsanna, Szig. szám: AC-II. 658154/
Gelej Deák Ferencz u. 5. szám alatti lakos meghallgatásáról.

Jelen vannak alulirottak:

Felkérésre megjelent a polgármesteri hivatalban Kékedi Bertalan
geleji lakos. Előtte ismertetésre került PUSZTAI BÉLANÉ Budapest
Váci-utca 11/B. szám alatti lakos 1992. 11. 02.-én kelt megkeresésé-
ben foglaltak. Jegyző előadja azt is, hogy a HALOTTI BIZONYITVANY-t
kiállitani nem tud, mert a GELEJI ANYAKÖNYVBE csak azon halálesetek kerül-
tek bejegyzésre akik Gelejen haltak meg, vagy birósági itélet geleji
anyakönyvezésről rendelkezik. Mivel egyik eset sem forog fenn, lehetőség-
ként csak az marad, hogy WEISZ ALFRED Gelej községből történő deportálásár
nak körülményeiről meghallgassunk olyan személyt/eket/ aki, illetve akik
WEISZ ALFRED volt geleji lakos GETTOBA hurcolásáról tájékoztatást tudnak
nyujtani. Kéri Kékedi Bertalant az előzőekkel kapcsolatban adja elő
milyen ismeretekkel rendelkezik. Ezt követően Kékedi Bertalan a követ-
kezőket adja elő:

" Én 1923-as évfolyambeli vagyok, igy 1944-ben még nem voltam
katona. Személyesen ismertem WEISZ ALFREDOT és feleségét. Gelejen földbér-
lők voltak. Mivel nevezettek gazdasági alkalmazottjait a háborus helyzet-
re tekintettel katonai szolgálatra behivták, igy alkalmilag én segitkeztem
a gazdálkodás vitelében. Ilyen minőségemben került sor arra, hogy 1944-ben
WEISZ ALFREDOT /1876, Réce/ és feleségét az ő tulajdonukat képező lovasfogattal én szállitottam be a MEZŐCSATON volt GETTOBA. Mezőcsátra érve
a GETTÓ előtt álltunk meg, WEISZ ALFRED és felesége bement a GETTÓBA.
Onnan én Gelejre visszahajtottam a lovakat. Azóta NEVEZETTEK hollétéről
nincs tudomásom. Ide Gelejre nem tértek vissza. Sajnos nem tudok olyan
személyt sem megjelölni aki az általam előadottakat tanusitaná. Illetve
tudnék, mert háztartási alkalmazottjuk is volt, de az Igrici községből
származott, de hogy ő is hova lett azt nem tudom."

Jegyzőkönyv felolvasás után hh. aláiratott.

Kmft.

Dr. Demeter József
polgármester

Dr. Pusztay Béla
jegyző

Kékedi Bertalan
Szig. szám.: AC-II. 658154

My namesake was right. You could enter the ghetto of
Mezőkeresztes, but no one could ever come out of it alive. Not
even Alfréd Weisz and Ernesztína Gross.

Having acquired all the necessary documents, I was now ready
to be privatized the Hungarian way. Both in its capacity as official thief and receiver of stolen goods, the government declared
that whatever socialism had nationalized was now the property of

democratic Hungary. (Democratic? What a joke.) And it rid itself of part of the stolen goods, mostly by selling them below their price and value. Only one thing mattered – that none of it should go back to the rightful owner.

When we judge someone for his sins, I often think: If the circumstances are not known, how can anyone be judged? I'm thinking of that certain "I did it under duress," because I, too, bought the apartment I had been living in as a tenant, but which had never been mine. Who is crying over it now, I wonder? It was possible to demoralize me to such an extent that the state was able to turn me into a receiver of stolen goods myself. The sin is no less deplorable if many people share it. And one's hands are forced into doing worse things than this. Someone who has never been in a similar situation can't be sure how he or she would react under the circumstances.

Before I saw the application of Marxism in practice and wanted to believe in something very much, something that – naïve dreamer that I was – would give substance to our lives, and felt, too, that we must do something for the community, I thought of the Communist heroes with awe. I have no doubt that they underwent horrible torture. I know that some refused to talk. I have always been grateful that I never had to face such a trial, because I would not have been a hero. I am sure that I would have talked. If you haven't experienced it, you don't know what physical pain can be like and the psychological terror that is no less painful, what it is like when you are between the devil and the deep blue sea. I can only laugh at the braggers who condemn those who have acted under duress when life hasn't even put them to a test by depriving them of matches when they're on the verge of a nicotine fit. They should try it once, and then judge their fellows.

Roasting bacon in Debrecen, 1943. I'm the second person on the left leaning forward. My father and my mother are sitting in the corner on the upper right, with Gilike standing next to them. My cousin Boci is sitting up front on the right. Lajos, her husband, is the third in the row.

Asteria

"You study for the sake of life, not for the sake of your teachers," our teachers told us as they filled our heads with knowledge. But I don't think anyone in the convent school taught us about life. Or maybe just what life, with a capital L, could be like.

The times when I attended school had many advantages over the times when those attended who are now fifty-five or sixty years of age. For one thing, there was no contradiction between home and school in what we learned about basic things, so our parents didn't have to warn us, "Don't say that in school, it could get us all in trouble." We didn't have one set of principles for home and another for public display. Our guiding principle was always to tell the truth. What a horrible way for parents to send a child into the world, having to caution him not to say what he thinks!

In Debrecen, I attended the Svetits Young Ladies' Boarding School run by an order of teaching nuns and named after Our Lady of Hungary. We followed each other in eight-year intervals: my older cousin Boci was eight grades above me, while my younger sister Gilike was eight grades below me. Boci and I were still tried and true Fahídies and therefore eager beavers, while Gilike, in keeping with the new times, was a hedonist. As far as she was concerned, life was one big game.

Back then, little girls wore teeny-weeny little skirts, and their panties sometimes showed from under them. This was the fashion. The fashion in the convent, regardless of age, called for skirts that covered the knees as well as uniforms, and we had to dress accordingly. Gilike didn't like her skirt to reach her knees and refused to wear it, and we didn't force her, unlike one of the Reverend Sisters who disapproved of the length of Gilike's skirt and said to her, "Tell your father, dear, he's not a poor man. He can afford to buy you a longer skirt!" Gilike excused her father without delay. She looked into the eyes of the Reverend Sister and said, "I don't want to wear long skirts. I have no intention of becoming a nun!"

Teachers had only one job, to teach the children. This, too, was one of the advantages of a convent education. The Order made sure that the nuns who taught us, provided they made suitable teachers, should have the highest possible qualifications.

Even from sixty years' distance, some of my teachers seem to smile at me with kindness. I loved Sister Albertína very much. She was our homeroom teacher in the first four years of gymnasium.[1] She was like a mother hen. Her wings always offered a safe, warm haven. As much as I loved Sister Albertína, that's how much I hated Dr Mária Kornélia Hoszták, our homeroom teacher in the upper four grades. I can still hear the cracking of her jaws when she forced herself to smile. She certainly never did it of her own accord. She was a good teacher, but to call her a good person would have been an offence. Still, I owe her a debt of gratitude because she made me learn Latin and Hungarian grammar, which I am making good use of to this day. I needed many languages during the course of my life, and I was glad to see that not only the grammar of the Latin languages but even Russian grammar is based on Latin. Kornélia fanned the flames of the fire that my father first lit at home – the embers of my love of reading. The only difference was in the books they selected for us to read.

I still think of my teacher Asteria, who taught us German and French, with love and affection. I took private French lessons as well and was reading German literature when my classmates were still struggling with the rudiments of grammar.

Asteria was a star in more than her name. She had stars in her eyes, the bluest of blue forget-me-not eyes, with the iris bounded

---

1 Gymnasium or high school started at age ten and had eight grades.

Gilike with Lackó, her playmate, and Pajkos, the dog, Nagytanya, 1938.

by an even more intense blue to make her eyes seem bluer still. She could look at someone with so much warmth and she could say with so much love, "It's not enough to speak a language, you must know the grammar inside and out," that I learned everything there was to learn just to please her. I have been grateful to her for this for the rest of my life.

I experienced everything and its opposite, too. This also was part of my contract with fate. So I was not surprised when, on the morning of April 5, 1952, I found myself out on the street with my furniture because, from one day to the next, the City Council of Pécs deprived me of my job and my home. Like so many descendants of families like mine, I became déclassé and was turned into an unskilled construction labourer.[2] That winter I had the privilege of pouring the cement for the floor of the pressroom of *Szabad Nép*[3] headquarters in Budapest. My wardrobe consisted of two overalls; one was on me, the other was hanging, freshly washed, on the clothesline. But every morning I left for work in clean overalls. I need hardly say that, since I hated the cold, I was made to work all winter out in the open. My hands and feet were freezing; I couldn't find ankle boots big enough to fit me, and for years afterwards I was treated with X-rays because the frozen spots on my hands and feet would hurt when the temperature dropped. But then, that's the nature of frozen hands and feet, I guess! After work I warmed up at the Alliance Française, where, strange as it may sound today, no one was the least bit surprised when an unskilled labourer was able to converse in French.

I thought of Asteria with a grateful heart, because the itemized knowledge of German and French grammar rendered me a great service back then. I figured that since there was no hope of the

2 During the Stalinist dictatorship, between 1949 and 1953, members of the former aristocracy and bourgeoisie lost their property, were expelled from university, banned from living in Budapest, and interned to the countryside, and they could not find employment in their field.

3 *Szabad Nép* [Free people] was the Communist Party daily.

I exercised my whole life – even today!

government allowing me to engage in any intellectual endeavour, I might as well have written proof that I spoke foreign languages. From the 1950s through the 1990s, any Hungarian who wished to have his knowledge of a foreign language recognized officially had to appear at the fearsome Rigó Street Language Accreditation Centre. The Academy for Foreign Languages, of which it formed a part, was the only official forum for taking a language exam to prove your proficiency. The teachers at the academy were kind to me, because, despite the fact that I walked in from the street without having studied with them, they immediately granted me a certificate of the highest level in both German and French, all thanks to Asteria.

I loved her very much. She was almost as thin and transparent as my older cousin Boci, whom I held in awe. She also had something else going for her that I envied and admired – she spoke Slovak. Like my mother, she hailed from Upper Hungary or some other

Slovak-inhabited area. When they discovered this, they embraced each other eagerly, and from then on they spoke Slovak to each other with joyful abandon.

We did not talk about politics openly in the convent, but I may have had a better ear for such things than most people. For all I know, no one else noticed when, in the years following the Anschluss,[4] Asteria said, "Henceforth, the name of that man [Hitler] will never pass my lips again." At a time when the Viennese branch of my family had already been eliminated, this was a weighty message.

When the religious orders were disbanded under socialism, Asteria went back to her village. She couldn't have been young any more, and it couldn't have been easy for her to get used to civilian life, which must have been very unpleasant for a nun back then. I heard that she died when she climbed up a tree to pick plums and fell to her death. It's not the kind of end one would wish for a nun. Elderly Jews say that if God loves you, he grants you a quick death. Asteria deserved to die suddenly, without the fear of death, so she could go knocking on the pearly gates in heaven. If anyone, then she most certainly is trailing her forget-me-not blue eyes at the celestial urchins, telling them that it's not enough to speak a language, you must learn the grammar backwards and forwards, Amen. May her memory be blessed!

In the convent, making anti-Semitic remarks was as much frowned upon as any talk of politics. Since the leadership of the school did not resort to discrimination, the children made no hurtful comments either. On the other hand, I didn't feel very close to them. I was too busy with my own world, chock-full of so many wonderful things: gymnastics, sports, the piano, books, music, and art. I was also wrapped up in the friendship with my classmate Éva Kende, who remained my best friend for the next forty years, that my schoolmates never had a chance to get close to me. Not that they made much of an effort. Of course, neither

---

4 Anschluss: on March 12, 1938, Austria was annexed to Nazi Germany.

did I. Now that we are past our sixtieth graduation anniversary, I find that they're on my mind a lot more. Now that every year one or two out of the twenty-eight of us pass on to the celestial school up above, our ties are becoming tighter, and it has become important for us to be able to say to each other, "Do you remember when ... ?" And so we gather together from South America, the US, Debrecen, and Budapest, and joyfully, we remember, and remember some more.

Road to the crematorium. Source: *Das Auschwitz Album. Die Geschichte eines Transports*. Yad Vashem/Wallstein Verlag, 2005.

Unwarranted Optimism

A couple of decades ago, when some medieval Jewish houses were excavated in the Castle District of Buda, they found cellar doors connecting three small houses. Being no strangers to pogroms, our ancestors were prepared to flee. While they were breaking down the door upstairs, the inhabitants could flee to their neighbours, and from their neighbours, somewhere, anywhere. Were they optimists?

History first came into my life in 1938 with the Anschluss. The many *tantes* and *onkles* living in Vienna suddenly had to get away. But before that – the first loss in my life – I had to part with my governess Ruth, because her mother became incurably ill and she had to go back to Vienna.

Our family was the sort of typical Kaiserliche und Königliche family of which there were many in those days. We were dispersed throughout the territory of the former Monarchy. We had relatives everywhere.

The Treaty of Trianon was a tragedy for us. It brought to a sudden end the situation that had been taken for granted by the generation before me, when you could travel from Ógyalla to Vienna, Abbazia, Budapest, or Prague as easily as from one Hungarian town to another.

I never could get my maternal relatives straight – my grandparents' brothers and sisters, their cousins and their families living in Vienna. Regarding the end result, it doesn't make a difference, though. Not one of them survived. Their age, if nothing else, destined them for the gas chambers of Auschwitz.

Of the *tantes* living in Vienna in 1938, whoever could do so fled to the protective wings of their relatives in Czechoslovakia. They were not blessed with the gift of foresight. They lived there only for a short time before the Germans marched in.

Our family chronicles preserved the story of two Viennese relatives, Riki and Regina. Both ladies were famous for showing off. Once when Riki was strolling down Vienna's elegant Graben,[1] the ribbon that held up her underpants came untied. Bowing to the law of gravity, the panties began to slip, slip, slip, unencumbered. Riki could already feel her undergarment around her knees, then her ankles, and next thing, there it lay in the middle of the Graben, in full view, the be-all and end-all of the art of underwear manufacture, my aunt Riki's underpants decorated with ruffles and lace and embroidery.

When first I heard this story, I immediately saw my aunt Riki turn from deadly pale to crimson red, and I imagined what I would have done in her place – a natural, down-to-earth reflex. Certainly not what Riki did, because Riki did not turn deadly pale and then crimson. Instead, she turned up her cute little nose as high as she could and stepped over the frothy pile as if it weren't even there, because a gentleman remains a gentleman even in hell, and a lady remains a lady.

Being engaged in noble competition with Riki, Tante Regina didn't want to fall behind in showing off. The family used to whisper behind her back that she was always so decked out that there was no telling her from a Christmas tree.

My aunt Regina's story would not be complete without Bernard – just like that, the French way, because it was the only way he responded – Bernard, the Bernardiener of the moment, one of my grandfather's many favourite dogs. Bernard deserved all the praise that was heaped upon him. He was a perfect gentleman, and as such could make delicate distinctions, as one would expect of a St Bernard. We children pummelled him, used him as a pony, sat on his back, put our fists in his mouth, pulled his ears, and wrestled with him, but he didn't mind, he knew he had the advantage over us. He put up with anything from us and laughed

---

1 Graben is the elegant shopping street in the old centre of Vienna.

superciliously at us. If worst came to worst and he tired of us, he gently flung us off his back.

My grandfather trained Bernard not to bark – he had his other dogs for that. Bernard had to flash his friendly smile at everyone whom he did not regard a close member of the family. This was no ordinary smile. For best effect, Bernard sneaked behind the person in question, and raising himself on his hind legs and placing his front paws on the shoulders of the incriminated individual, with a friendly flashing of teeth, he would look the visitor in the eye.

Regina came to visit my grandfather after sunset. She was impeccably dressed, as always, wearing her best grey flannel suit, an eggshell-white lace blouse, a pair of white and yellow shoes, with hat, handbag, and gloves to match, and with at least three more pieces of jewellery than she should have. Except, she forgot about Bernard. Actually, everything went as it should. Everyone acted as they should, Bernard, and my aunt Regina's bowels, too.

Being one step ahead of the Germans, the two ladies relocated to Bratislava with their families. Their flight turned out to be short lived, though, because in the cautionary tale, Death catches up with his man in Ephesos, while the Germans caught up with Aunt Riki's and Aunt Regina's families in Bratislava. From there the road to the gas chambers was straight as an arrow.

The other event that touched me personally was the fact that Ruth, my beloved governess, had to go back home to Vienna. They say that you can't remember what happened when you were three. This is not true. I can safely say that my very first snippets of memory are from the age of three, and they have to do with Ruth. They must have left a deep impression on me, that's why they survived. For instance, I remember perfectly well the time she first came to us from Vienna.

The prehistory is to be found in the thrilling Viennese magazine *Blatt der Hausfrau*, or Journal for Housewives, that the postman brought to us at regular weekly intervals. It contained important information: recipes, advertisements describing the secrets of the lotions and potions to maintain a white complexion and luxuriant long hair, an ad for the same vacuum cleaner every time, and advice on removing wine, beet, grease, candle, and ink stains from tablecloths and garments, as well as the latest society gossip from the Austrian capital. There were also lists of the latest books, and lots of other advertisements as well, because even back then, that's how newspapers made their money.

It was in the *Blatt der Hausfrau* that my mother first read about Rudolf Steiner, who was well known by then, it being the mid-1920s, and who wrote about a lot of things that made a great deal of sense, especially on bringing up children. My mother liked every one of his views on the subject. He even ran a school where they taught the Waldorf method to kindergarten and primary school teachers.

A Viennese au pair office was among the advertisers in the *Blatt der Hausfrau*. They recommended governesses trained in the Waldorf method, and after an exchange of letters, Ruth Stein appeared in our lives. A couple of years later, Erna Riess came to care for my younger sister through the same channels.

I was three years old when, after being carefully prepared, I was told that my mother wished to share the heavy burden of looking after me with a hag I didn't know and who, adding insult to injury, was coming from Vienna, and we had to go meet her at the station. They kept showing me Ruth's photograph – her dark hair with a large wave on one side of her coiffure, her warm brown eyes, her slightly disappointed smile, and her all-dominant forehead. Ruth's IQ veritably radiated from the picture. Like water off a duck's back. I decided then and there that I would hate her and make her life a living hell. Let her go back where she came from, the sooner the better, I won't have her share me with my mother!

So off we went to the central station in Debrecen and waited for the Budapest express to arrive, which it did. A Breitschwanz, a beautiful black Persian lamb coat just like my mother's, got off of first class, and above it a very discreet but all the more elegant brimless hat, a so-called box, a pigskin travelling case, and no luggage. She looked just like the picture they'd shown me of Ruth. It wasn't quite what I had expected.

Even back then, I knew how to ingratiate myself. If a fur worthy of its name came towards me on the street, I tore myself away from the hand holding mine, brushed my face against the fur, and said, "Kitty." This way I made everyone adore me and, as an extra added plus, I gained familiarity with many kinds of fur, how they smell and what they're worth, which is why I would never have a real fur coat as a grown-up. By then I kept seeing those wide-tailed little black Persian lambkins as they come out of their mother's belly, and before they have a good look around, they're slaughtered to make fur coats. I would feel the same way about the beautiful little minks and cute little moles bred only to be turned into elegant coats.

Anyway, there was the Breitschwanz coming towards me at the Debrecen railroad station, whereupon I tore myself away from my mother, ran over to it, buried my face in it, and said, "Kitty," which effectively sealed our common fate with Ruth. From that moment on, I simply adored her.

The cabin trunk with Ruth's clothing arrived the following day. She had silken underwear! I had never seen anything like it. What a surprise! But Ruth herself was even more of a surprise to me.

Originally, Ruth had planned to get married and become the mother of five children. I must say, I started out with the same plan, except it wasn't to be for either of us. After being disappointed in love, Ruth decided to take the Waldorf course and get as far away from the scene of her pain as possible. This is why her choice fell on us in far-off Debrecen, and on the foreign-sounding name Fahídi – the distant unknown. Add to this her mother's divorce and the fact that she couldn't see eye-to-eye with her new stepfather.

Through the years, my mother and Ruth developed a deep friendship. They made my life miraculous. Ruth was a partner in all things. Like Mother, she let me jump and leap about to my liking, she taught me to knit, crochet, cross-stitch, embroider, make boxes out of coloured raffia, sew a tablecloth from large size beads, make dresses for my dolls, paint, draw, sing, and use my imagination to make something, anything, out of paper, wood, feathers, roots, chestnuts, pebbles, susla (random bits and pieces) – in short, anything we could get our hands on. We even built a puppet theatre with sets for our own stories. Whatever props were missing we ordered from Vienna.

This is how I got a child's sewing machine that was like the sewing machine used on the farm for making sacs. It made chain stitches. I also got a child's gramophone with records to match that played the "Radetzky March," "The Turkish March" from Mozart's "Sonata in A Major," and parts from "A Little Night Music."

Ruth told me lots of stories. I enjoyed my children's books except for one, the *Struwwelpeter*,[2] which was very popular back then. As far as I'm concerned, this book contains everything that should not be taught to a child. Every one of its illustrations and every line is enough to make your hair stand on end. Luckily, it is not given to children today to read. But the rest of my books were wonderful – the illustrated poems of the Busch brothers, including Max and Moritz, the richly illustrated Grimm and Andersen tales, Livingstone's journey, *Nelli und ehr Puppen*, and so on.

Ruth and I had our own secret language. Ruth had a gesture for everything, and gesticulating like that, we understood each other perfectly. A shame that I've forgotten it just as I've forgotten the Morse code from my cub scout days. But the essence has remained. I can make all my troubles go away by moving, just like Zorba the Greek. I feel sorry for today's generation hooked on their TV sets and PCs. I'm not surprised that there are so many psychologists. Under the circumstances, they're sorely needed. Most of the people around would rather die first or swallow a hoard of painkillers; they will start moving only as a last resort. In my house you won't find tranquillizers, sleeping pills, or painkillers, but you will find wall bars, a big ball, and a stationary bicycle. It's all a matter of preference.

Before I got to see the ocean, I was fascinated by it. I had an illustrated children's book with Gothic German lettering that recounted the legend of the Flying Dutchman. I loved that book. In the first illustration, a wild north wind puffed up the sails of the Dutchman out of all proportions, and I could even hear the muted, regular snap, like the beating of drums, as the sails strained to hold out against the ravaging storm. A gigantic mast stretched towards the sky, and though it was as thick as one's waist, I could hear it creaking and moaning as it fought the tempest. The waves

---

2 *Struwwelpeter*: Heinrich Hoffmann's classic children's book first published in 1845 that used rhymed stories and graphic illustrations to show the horrible things that happen to children when they misbehave.—Trans.

reached the sky and crashed against the ship, threatening to engulf it. I could even hear the rumbling thud of the drops of water as they assaulted the deck. And in this infernal noise there stood the Dutchman, his head nailed to the mast, and the nail sticking out of his forehead at least an inch. His eyes were so sad, defeated, and lonely! I don't mean to demystify him, but they were those of an ox.

Has anyone looked an ox in the eye? I have. The eyes of an ox are always teary, even when it is eating and is as contented as can be. It is always looking into the distance, into some far-off place, at the essence behind appearances, perhaps at Africa, its original home before it got hitched to a wagon. It is so lonely and there is such cosmic sadness in its eyes that they are just like the Dutchman's, who was under a curse to wander the restless seas and never find a home or another human being to talk to. I might add, though, that while the Dutchman can find redemption, the domesticated ox cannot. Civilization has pulled its home ground from under it, and at this point all it can do is stay right where it is.

I'm sorry I'm not romantic, because from what I've said about the Flying Dutchman it would follow that I would want to be Senta, the girl who flings herself into the waves in order to save the Dutchman. But I don't. For one thing, being pragmatic in nature, I have no talent for dramatic heroism, and for another, after several marriages and wonderful love affairs, I have not yet met the man for whose sake I'd throw myself into the freezing ocean in a north wind. I simply have not found him yet. But I haven't given up trying.

After Hitler's rise to power in 1933, the Anschluss of 1938 did not come as a surprise. But, as the French saying goes, no one is as deaf as a man who will not hear. We in Hungary were highly optimistic. I wish I could remember what on earth we were hoping for. Anyway, Ruth returned to Vienna, where the Anschluss caught up with her. She married the manager of the Viennese Carlton Hotel, and, what we considered great good luck at the time, they fled to Shanghai. She couldn't take her mother with her, who was very sick and lay in a water-bed and could not be moved. Ruth died of a guilty conscience. She was sitting in front of a typewriter in Shanghai, wanting to write a letter to someone, put her hand to her heart, and died. My mother continued to correspond with her husband.

At the time I didn't know that Ruth was just the first of the many people who would leave a gaping void in my life.

The world around us had turned topsy-turvy, and we'd have met Germans on all our frontiers, had we crossed them, so we stayed put, constantly worried about those who had remained in Slovakia and who made up an appreciable part of our family.

We children were treated as if Hungary had a certificate of guarantee that it would stay clear of the war and as if we were not under any threat. I went to school and learned German literature from Aunt Mici, French from Aunt Éva Leitner, the piano from Mrs Füredi née Margit F. Halácsi, and musical harmony from Emil Szabó. I studied artistic gymnastics with Aunt Karola, and I had youth season's tickets to the theatre and concerts. In the summer, until it was time to go to Grandfather on the farm, I played tennis every morning, then went to the Great Forest[3] to swim, with a servant bringing our lunch after us. As I said, we no longer went abroad, but by great good luck, we had relocated Grandfather from Ógyalla to Debrecen years before. In short, we were very optimistic. Why?

"Oh, the Russians are already under the Carpathians and within the week they'll be in Debrecen," my mother chirped dreamily in early March, 1944. (That's when the troops of the Red Army reached the Northeastern Carpathians at Czernowitz.)[4]

"I still remember that during the First World War when I was a little girl, we had Russian prisoners of war on the farm in Ógyalla to replace the servants who'd been requisitioned into the army. They kept stroking my hair and some said, 'I have five of my own at home, this size,' and they indicated the height with their hands. Besides, they sang so beautifully," my mother continued, warming to the memory, "and they even took our horses and gave us dirty little Russian horses instead, who didn't understand gidde'up, which was fun, actually, because we had to say to them, *prrrr*. And when the Russian POWs went home, they even cried."

---

3 The "Great Forest" is a large natural resort, with swimming pools, in the suburbs of Debrecen.
4 Today Chernivtsi in Ukraine.

Group picture of my high-school graduation.

Well, we got back the Russians my mother was so keen on. But first, we got the Germans.

As a result of our self-imposed deafness, not only did we not hear, we did not even see what was happening around us. Put another way, we refused to take notice. Anything might happen in Germany, Austria, Slovakia, Romania, Yugoslavia, Poland – anywhere in the world – we said, but one thing is certain, it is not about to happen in Hungary. Miklós Horthy[5] will protect us.

---

5 Admiral Miklós Horthy (1868–1957) was regent and head of state of Hungary between March 1920 and October 1944. His role in the post-1919 counter-revolutionary
paramilitary violence and at times reluctant collaboration with Nazi Germany in
the Second World War and the Holocaust make him a controversial figure. He was
allowed to live out his life in exile in Portugal.

Besides, he has Jewish friends. He even has Jewish relatives. Also, our family is full of heroes who received high military awards for their participation in the Great War. We were always faithful Hungarians and gave our blood, if that's what was needed, and our money, too, not like the Hungarian gentlemen of old who'd give their blood to Empress Maria Theresa, but not their oats.[6]

My father did not take seriously the fact that one anti-Jewish law followed hard upon the next (1938, 1939, 1941), that they pulled the rug from under our feet and took our factories, companies, and shops away, because he found and continued to direct those Aryans who bought our enterprises on paper. He thought he could trust them. Anyone with brains left everything behind and fled the country. Material goods can be lost, but they are replaceable. Not so lost lives. How come my father didn't think about this?

It took many years for me to understand my father.

He was born into nothing, his father was a tailor who had a small workshop in Fehérgyarmat and ten children, and yet he made something of himself. He learned everything on his own, how to eat with a knife and fork, how to behave in polite society, how to conduct a business transaction, how to develop a reliable taste in literature, how to play tennis, how to start not one but several businesses, how to establish plants and manage them. This was too much compared to the nothing from which he had started out. He could not leave his life's work behind.

After graduation from high school, I wanted to attend the Academy of Music in Budapest. Playing the piano was part of family tradition. Everyone in my mother's family played the piano, some better, some worse, while Boci, my older cousin from Father's branch of the family who was eight years my senior, and whom I loved and admired, had already graduated. Everything could be had for money, even back then, and though both sets of

---

6 Empress Maria Theresa (1717–1780) ruled the Habsburg Empire between 1740 and 1780. Popular myth holds that on her coronation as King of Hungary (ancient laws did not have a stipulation for a female ruler), the gallant Hungarian nobles offered "Vitam et Sanguinam," their lives and blood, but later refused to support her wars and reforms.

my grandparents were Jewish, I was admitted to the Academy as a private student.[7] Corruption is not a modern invention.

As if I were living on the last island of happiness instead of Eastern Europe, which would soon turn into the inferno that was raging around us, I played the piano day and night and read books and more books – and, of course, engaged in sports and gymnastics. I, too, wore the family blinders.

On March 19, 1944, dirt-grey tattered clouds hung in the sky. It didn't rain, but the sun didn't show itself either. That afternoon we were invited to Uncle Anti Barabás, who also had two children, though they were closer in age to my younger sister than myself. The Barabás family were wonderful. They could tell the good from the bad, just like us, and they were profound humanists. The two families became acquainted through the children, then it was discovered that Uncle Anti was also a lumber merchant and that he had partners in Transylvania who also had business dealings with my father. A deep and sincere friendship developed between them. My mother and Ica, Mrs Barabás, also got on like a house on fire. I always thought of the Barabás family as if they were my own. After the war when, for all intents and purposes, I lived in Érsekújvár in Czechoslovakia but would go to Debrecen now and then, I stayed with them several times.

Early that morning, we heard strange sounds, the intermittent roar of airplanes above our heads. A continuous line of traffic was not typical of the local airport, where no more than one or two planes would take off or land every day. At first we didn't think anything of it, and in the afternoon went to visit the Barabás family, who lived close by. Meanwhile, the planes continued to roar overhead. That's when we learned that "in town," meaning the central area of Debrecen, because we lived further off, "on the outside," German vehicles had been parading down the streets nonstop. (We learned only later that some sharp-witted locals had made a note of their licence plate numbers and realized that the German

7 The 1920 so-called numerus clausus law limited the enrolment of Jewish students at universities to 6 per cent, and enrolment was further restricted by the Second Jewish Law of 1939.

vehicles came in at one end of town and went out at the other, and then made their way back again.) It was time to acknowledge that the Wehrmacht had invaded us.

When we got home from the Barabáses, with a ceremoniousness that was highly unusual for him, my father herded us into his room. His countenance had a mixture of suffering and nervousness spread over it, and something I had never seen before: fear. At last he understood what was happening. There was an awkward silence as we sat down, awed by the strange expression on his face.

"We were always a close and loving family," he began, his voice full of fear, "and now that bad times are upon us, we must stick together more than ever. Don't worry, it won't last long. We'll just have to hold out till then."

I found Father's new face very, very strange. But I knew right away that if my father speaks this way, he must have a pressing reason for doing so: we're in very big trouble.

What happened to my father happened to me as well. In an instant the feeling that would soon be my frequent companion swept over me – the feeling of uncertainty, of contingency, the fear of the unknown that grips you by the throat and unsettles your stomach, the premonition that what was about to happen would be inevitable, fated, and fatal.

The phones were still working on March 20, so we received news of various atrocities. We hastily removed some of our valued possessions into the care of neighbours, and my mother lined Father's short fur overcoat with a great deal of money. We also called Grandfather on the farm and all our available relatives, and waited, paralysed, for the axe to fall.

We didn't have to wait long. On the morning of March 21, an ear-splitting ringing of the bell shattered the peace of our home. We could see the gate from the window with German soldiers standing there. There was no time to lose. Father put on the fur coat lined with money and ran down the back steps to the garden, which had a gate so small that it wasn't visible from the outside. Ever since, when I've looked for an apartment, the most important criterion was two entranceways located on two different corridors. I live in a place like that now, too, in case they should come and

Hungarian Jews in the ghetto. Source: *Das Auschwitz Album. Die Geschichte eines Transports*. Yad Vashem/Wallstein Verlag, 2005.

want to take me away – a persistent, centuries-long fear embedded in the genes, a reminder of the cellar doors of the medieval Jews of Buda, the claustrophobia. Even though I was brought up to be so brave!

The soldiers asked after my father. Sweet as pie, in her best Viennese dialect, my mother told them that he'd just left, a wonder they didn't bump into him. It turned out that their interest in Father was only in his capacity as the head of the household, because they just wanted to inform him that on the following day, March 22, the commander-in-chief of the local German military police, a certain Captain Kaiser who we later learned hailed from Dresden, would be moving into our house along with his orderly. I don't believe in miracles, but I can't understand to this day why they allowed us to stay in our own house, even if it meant being crowded into one room. Maybe it was the Viennese dialect.

True to his word, Captain Kaiser moved in with his orderly Fritz in tow. Which meant that we could keep our radio and telephone (not that we had anyone to call, since everyone else's phone had been removed), and we could keep our gardener, who also acted as our janitor, plus our maid. For some unfathomable reason, the captain decided to show us that a commander-in-chief of the Nazi military police of the Third Reich could be a noble and high-minded man of culture and good breeding. He was a charmer. He would come sit with us in our one room almost every night; he ate at our table and engaged in conversation with us about literature, music, and art. We mutually avoided unpleasant subjects, so there was no mention of Heine, Schubert, and Lessing, as if they'd never existed, as if their works had not been publicly burned in Germany. I knew a bit more about classical German literature than he; I'd read Klopstock,[8] he hadn't. He knew only *Die Meistersinger von Nurnberg* by Wagner, and only because Hitler liked it. Honestly, we didn't try to show off our cultural superiority!

During happy peace times, his orderly Fritz – what else could he have been called? – had been a baker, and from the outbreak of

---

8 Friedrich Gottlieb Klopstock (1724–1803), German poet, best known for his epic poem "The Messiah."

the war, an officer's orderly. Could he have been the only German who didn't fight and didn't kill anyone, just polished his superior's boots? In any event, he was a caring father, because every week he sent his wife a kilo of potatoes and a kilo of onions in Berlin. They came out of our stock. After all, we had plenty. Wasn't that great news? What sort of empire is it that has no potatoes and onions in its capital? Is there anything that could give more cause for optimism? Here's proof positive! Let's be optimistic!

In the discussions with the captain there was no mention of the future. So it happened that on April 29, the last day the Jews were forced to move to the ghetto, we had to make do without his congenial company, and left our entire house to him without a word of farewell – all the furniture, the carpets, the paintings, all the accoutrements of a proper bourgeois household. It was only on my return from the camp that I learned that Mr Kaiser took the turning over of our house literally. When he left, German trucks came and packed up everything that was moveable in the house. They pulled the last nail out of the wall.

In the ghetto we stayed in the house at no. 30 Hatvan Street. Before moving there, we spent days transporting flour, sugar, several containers with baked meat and lard inside, and countless bottles of compote to serve us there. We spent days baking all sorts of pastry that keeps, and also conveyed a large container with grain, and poultry in large cages. We had food enough to last us several years; we wouldn't have had to go hungry, if it came to that. In the end, just before we were taken to the brick yard, my father gave everything away. The ghetto was full of poor Jews who had nothing to eat.

In the ghetto the two Fahidi families, those of Dezső and Antal, were assigned a single room of about forty square metres – the four of us, and the three in Antal's family, because Antal's sister-in-law, who was a physician, came with them. Also with us were my cousin Boci and her husband, Lajos Fuchs – he was lame on account of his childhood polio so he was not taken for labour service – and their six-month-old little boy, Ferike. We didn't know yet what a luxury it was to have four square metres of living space per person.

In the ghetto, we all invented some feverish activity to keep us from losing our sanity. My father took on the yard: he swept and kept it clean all day and, with the help of bribes, he kept in touch with his front men.[9] Still, he resembled nothing as much as a caged lion. My mother and her sister-in-law, Aunt Margit, cooked, did the dishes, washed the clothes, cleaned, did all sorts of household chores with a passion. Auntie, on account of being a physician, made herself useful in the so-called hospital and I helped her, even if I was never interested in medicine. Uncle Tóni suffered greatly from the lack of freedom. He was the one who used to stand at the gate of the lumberyard and banter with anyone passing by. Boci and Lajos were preoccupied with their baby Ferike and with each other. It was a luxury for Boci to have her husband around when all men of his age were taken for labour service. At least they were given this gift, to stay together and love each other until the last moment.

We all shared a feeling, deep in our hearts: the unbearable anxiety over an uncertain future.

We didn't stay long in the ghetto. On June 20 they began to transfer its inhabitants to the Scherli Brick Factory, where we could enjoy nature's blessings to the full – with no roof over our heads, the less than gentle rays of the sun during the day, and at night, the starry firmament. What great good luck that it didn't rain.

Fate always meted out a bitter irony to me; as far as I'm concerned, fate has nothing but bitter irony. One of the gendarmes guarding us was from Szentistván, a small village where, just as in any other village, everyone is related to everyone else. He was related to Pista Hegyi, our estate manager. "Give me the young misses," he said to our parents, "I will hide them so nobody will be able to find them." I disagreed. After all, even the dogs knew us in that village. There are no secrets in a village or on a farm. If a young mother appears with a new shawl around her shoulders after she gives birth, people are bound to know who gave it to her. (For instance, my grandfather, Alfréd Weiss, especially if the newborn was the spitting image of him.) On the other hand, my mother

9 The commonly used expression was "stroman" or front men and referred to the Aryan business partners who took over Jewish businesses, while the former Jewish owners maintained management.

gave her wedding ring to the gendarme, asking him to deliver it to Pista Hegyi. I never had the chance to ask if he'd ever received it.

Between June 25 and 27, three transports took off from the Scherli Brick Factory of Debrecen. Boci had a classmate from the Scherli family. There was also a boy. He had the time of his life over the whole thing, and for days wouldn't stop snapping pictures of us.

When on June 25 they started herding the Jews into the cattle cars, my mother and I took two big cans of water and two mugs and stood by the roadside as the columns passed. When the water ran out, I hurried back to refill the cans. This continued for two whole days. Then on June 27, the third day, they put us in a cattle car along with the ghetto's store of medical supplies that were in Tanti's care. Except, by then, there was no one left to give us water.

The translation of the above letter:

Addressee: Géza Weil MD

Hermann Paper Works, Slovakia

Sender: Irma Fahidi

Hatvan u. 30, Debrecen, Hajdú County, Hungary

My Dears, I haven't heard from you in a long time, I hope you are enjoying good health. We are relatively well, we are all healthy. Our parents have gone away, and at the moment I don't know their address, but as soon as I find out, I will immediately pass it on to you. Nuni and family are going to Kaposvár on May 25th. I would like to hear from you, too, as soon as possible, so write! We all send our love, Irma.

PS Nuni has received your wire, it made all of us very happy.

A Coded Cry of Despair

Anyone who reads this postcard from Irma to her sister and brother-in-law will find nothing unusual in it, whereas every word is a cry of despair and every sentence signals a mortal tragedy for our family. I will now write this postcard as my mother could have done, exposing the meaning between the lines:

> My Dears, I haven't heard from you in an alarmingly long time, what is happening with you? For the love of God write, I'm so worried lest something terrible has also happened to you. We're getting on best we can; at any rate, we are all still healthy. Our parents have been deported, there is no news of them. Do you think we shall ever learn their whereabouts or what has become of them? Nuni and family must go into the ghetto in Kaposvár no later than May 25th. What will become of them? Nuni is alone with the three children! Write without delay!
>
> PS Nuni received your telegram. What a relief! At least we don't have to worry about you.

And now I will write down how Géza and Hédi understood the letter:

> It is clear from the address that our aunt and uncle are no longer living in Majcihov, where my uncle Géza was district physician, but in Hermanec, where his friends got him out of danger's way for the time being by employing him as a physician at the Paper Factory. It is also clear from the addressee that my mother and family are not living in our own home on Szoboszlói Road any more, but at a strange address,

from which the addressee can figure out that our family are locked inside a ghetto.

Since Géza and Hédi had first-hand experience with the German occupation, they must have also known – since they were familiar with our house in Debrecen – that it was now the residence of some German of importance, as indeed was the case, namely, the commander-in-chief of the German military police. Being more experienced as well as wiser than us, they also knew that Grandfather and Grandmother were deported permanently, and Mother was waiting in vain for them to send news from some normal address. There was no post office in the gas chambers of Auschwitz.

Nuni's situation was by far the most tragic. She was the youngest of my grandfather's three daughters, an eternally happy little puffball. Nuni had three children, two boys, an eleven- and a nine-year-old, little devils both, and a two-year-old little angel of a daughter with black hair. Her husband had been called up for forced labour some time ago. Nuni had to bear the burden of managing the thousand-hold estate at Jánoshalma, but she was one of Alfréd Weisz's daughters, and there was no reason for concern. On the other hand, her having to go to the ghetto in Kaposvár where she'd have to fend for herself without anyone there from the family to help her was very much a matter of concern. With three small children there was only one place she could wind up: the gas chambers of Auschwitz.

And another interesting thing: the wire from Hédi and Géza.

While packing her things for her move to the Kaposvár ghetto, Nuni received a telegram from Slovakia from her older sister Hédi, of whom we'd hear nothing for a long time. All we could do was hope that they were still alive. Nuni had enough presence of mind that, before moving to the ghetto herself, she made sure that Hédi's telegram would reach my mother. This is how close we were as a family.

Hédi and Geza thus had confirmation that we knew that for the time being they were out of danger, that they were able to make themselves invisible, and that they were still in Hermanec, at the paper factory. But not for long. In those days, fate marched through Europe in German military boots.

Soon after the arrival of my mother's card from the ghetto, my uncle Géza was warned that he should get away before he was dragged away. They packed what they needed into three knapsacks and went to Besztercebánya,[1] joined the resistance, and took their daughter Gerti, who was nearly the same age as me, along with them. Géza put his knowledge of medicine to good use, because before long he bandaged and kept a Russian paratrooper alive, who also joined the resistance. The partisans didn't have a moment of peace. The Germans discovered and smoked them out, and Géza's life was hanging in the balance. Even two of the knapsacks were lost. They watched them roll down the hillside, but had to continue their flight and could not retrieve them. It was the condition for their survival.

The one surviving knapsack that now represented their entire fortune contained the postcard, the last my mother ever wrote. Hédi kept the postcard, though she didn't know at the time for whom. It was for me. She gave it to me when Uncle Géza tried to find what remained of the ruins of our family and took us to Érsekújvár,[2] where after 1945 he became a district physician once again.

---

1 Today Banská Bystrica in Slovakia, where the Slovak National Uprising was launched in August 1944.
2 Today Nové Zámky in Slovakia.

Women and children on the ramp waiting for the selection process upon arrival. Source: *Das Auschwitz Album. Die Geschichte eines Transports*. Yad Vashem/Wallstein Verlag, 2005.

1 Cattle Car = 100 Bullocks

If I meet a complete stranger I've never seen before, have never heard of, and I know nothing about his ancestors or progeny or any of his relatives – I have no idea whose son or calf he is, as we used to say back home; in short, I know nothing about him, but if he's been to Auschwitz, the information surfaces during the first five minutes. From the way we immediately recognize each other, one would think that those who'd been to Auschwitz were under a pheromone cloud all their own. We communicate without having to elaborate. We speak the language of accomplices.

"From where did they ... ?"

"How many days did it take to ... ?"

"Oh. The ramp? When?"

"Anyone else from the family?"

"They gave your little sister to your grandmother?"

"To Brežinka?"

"Which camp?"

"Your Blockälteste?"

"And how long were you ... ?"

And what everyone relates during the first five minutes: The trip in the cattle car. The first selection.

The words "cattle car" had pleasant associations for me from my pre-Auschwitz life.

There were extensive fields on my maternal grandfather's estate, where I became familiar with some wonderful examples of the flora growing in Hungary that are now either on the list of extinct plants or on the list of protected plants. One of these fields was fallow and couldn't be used for anything but grazing. However, since this lovely field had saline soil, wild chamomile grew on it in abundance, and come spring, its flowers were gathered with the help of big wooden combs, dried, stuffed in sacks, and taken to the railroad station of Mezőkövesd-Mezőnyárád, where the sacks were loaded onto wagons and dispatched to one of the pharmaceutical plants in Pest.

I didn't see the spring chamomile because I was at school then. But once in a while, when I had a tummy ache, I drank chamomile tea, because Grandmother sent us chamomile by the bagful. We even had our hair washed in it. But in late July I watched the sea lavender or *Limonium (Statice) gmelini* blossom with its branching lilac arms stretching in all directions, and towards the sky, too. The whole field looked as if it had been covered by a big, soft, lilac eiderdown. Under it was a chorus of millions upon millions singing a soft pianissimo, because all the bugs, bees, and wasps that existed in this big wide world seemed to be there, busy with the sea lavender, dancing around it, sucking its honey, using it as a swing. Yet it has a strange smell, unpleasant to the human olfactory organ. Bugs, of course, have a right to their own opinion, and so do I. Today, the *Limonium gmelini* is a protected plant. But every August I hastily pick a lapful from the vicinity of one or another underpass and head home with my booty as happy as a lark. Just like the bugs, I love its tart smell. No wonder. One whiff and I'm back home on the farm.

Everything has its use, even a field of saline soil, because apart from the chamomile and the sea lavender, this meadow also produced a good grade of grass. Every April, on the day of St George, meaning the 24th of the month, we bought a hundred bullocks. Our only overhead was the single young herdsman who watched them. In September they were sold and put in cattle cars in Mezőkeresztes-Mezőnyárád, just like the chamomile. The clear profit was what they ate on the saline meadow and for which they showed their appreciation by gaining weight. It made perfect sense.

I like to ask the provocative question: Who knows what a bullock is? We all know the umbrella term "cattle." The male of the species is the bull, the female is the cow. But what about the heifer? And the bullock, which still has a lot to learn before it can become an ox? Well, for your information, it's like this. The calf, when it is born and we think it is as cute as can be, is a calfkin, but nevertheless, it still has a gender. If it's a girl, then it's a heifer, if it's a boy, then it's a bull. And once the *joi de vivre* is excised from it, it's called a bullock, and after it studies diligently and grows nice and big and is hitched to the yoke, it's an ox.

All I meant to say with respect to the above is that for us there was something joyful about being able to put something in a wagon, at times chamomile, at times bullocks, sugar beet for the sugar processing plant, rapeseed for pressing oil, and wheat, corn, oats, barley, reed, and who knows what else. Logs also came by wagons to the Fahídi Lumberyard to be turned into boards, laths, and firewood. Everything related to train wagons had good associations for us. The one thing we never dreamed of was that one day they might also herd us into a wagon, and that it would be unbearable. How unbearable? No need to exaggerate: a person can bear *anything*.

By June 27, 1944, only one trainload of people were left at the Scherli Brickyard in Debrecen, but even then, the Scherli boy was busy taking pictures of us. He had no time to lose. They were removing his favourite subject. We must've made an uplifting spectacle as we gathered our belongings, deciding what to leave in the dust of the brickyard and what to take with us, after which the Hungarian gendarmes began herding us into the wagons with their fists, if necessary.

It would make a separate book to answer the question: What does a person need to survive?

You take for granted that you are living in a yard that has a pig sty, a chicken coop, rabbit cages, a barn, granary, and tool shed, countless fruit trees, a sand box, sports equipment, and who knows what else there is. You take it for granted that you are living in a house with rooms for various functions, a kitchen and several bathrooms and what have you, each equipped in accordance with its function, a lot of furniture, paintings, chandeliers, carpets, a piano, books, music scores, etc. You take it for granted that you have closets full of summer and winter clothes, shoes, coats, hats, toiletries – you have *everything*. And then suddenly you have to decide what to take of all these things, what little bit you can carry, what you think you cannot do without. This is the last phase. It doesn't happen overnight.

The Hungarian authorities made sure not to startle us but to deprive us of everything we had, including our favourite objects, gradually. First they deprived us of our opportunities, our shops and factories that guaranteed our income, then our houses and gardens, then whatever we were able to take with us into the ghetto, and then, when we went to the brickyard, we could take only what we thought was absolutely necessary. But we were wrong. Even many of those things remained behind in the brick-yard, my father's warm navy blue house coat, for instance, which he used to bundle me up in at night because there too I was cold, of course. And the Bunsen burner Mother used to cook our meals.

Everyone in the family had a knapsack, a haversack, and a small carrying case in one hand so the other could be free. The knap-sacks, haversacks, and carrying cases were chosen to suit our size and strength.

Still, there were exceptions. Gilike carried my small wooden stool because she loved it, and she carried her teddy bear and her favourite Kruse doll.[1] Boci and my mother carried a big clothes hamper between them in their free hands with heaps of diapers, baby toiletries, bibs, and baby clothes, with Ferike, Boci and Lajos's six-month-old baby boy, on top.

It is wonderful when you have a cousin eight years older than you. She has a beautiful long blond braid, attends the same school, and when she graduates, you take her place in gymnasium. Boci – Anna Borbála was her real name – studied at the Academy of Music in Budapest, and by the time she graduated I was admitted. She was a real grown-up. She was very slim, not our thick-set kind at all. The circumference of her waist was the same as the circum-ference of her head, incredible as it may sound. Her wasp waist would have put any real wasp to shame.

---

1 Kruse dolls: German-made dolls known for their high quality and lifelike appear-ance, much in vogue in the interwar period.

Boci had many suitors, but her choice fell on Lajos, even though Lajos walked with a limp, the remnant of the polio he had as a child, before the Sabin vaccine was invented. This is why Lajos was not taken for forced labour. There was no other young woman near or far whose husband was at home. They were all in Ukraine or at the front, though a couple of lucky ones were serving at home in Hungary.

Boci was happy. For the first time in her life she weighed more than fifty kilos. She was nursing Ferike, and she was a very beautiful mother. She was radiant, full of the joy that cannot be put into words, the feeling that connected her to her little son, the meaning of her life, her happiness. We walked around them on tiptoes. Having this tiny island of normalcy in the horrendous upheaval, the uncertainty, the fear of the future, and the filth was like a gift of providence – the charmed lives of Boci-Lajos-Ferike hovering above our own existence, something that all of us would have liked to safeguard as long as it was humanly possible.

All my life I loved to travel. In those days we travelled to faraway places by train. We did a lot of travelling because we had relatives at great distances, a lot of relatives, and so we were always on the go. After the Anschluss of 1938, there was no one we could visit in Vienna, because the *tantes* had fled to Bratislava. Then, when Slovakia also came under German occupation and we still had most of the Fahidi branch of the family there – from the Weisz branch my aunt Hédi, my mother's younger sister, and her family, as well as Mother's various uncles, aunts, cousins – we couldn't visit each other because by 1942 they had started deporting the Jews. We were happy to just receive news that they were still alive.

Human adaptability is nothing short of miraculous, the way we steadily slipped into our own annihilation. When a shipwrecked person finds himself on the open seas holding on to a board split off from the side of the boat, he is hoping that another boat will pass by and he will be saved. Then a piece of the board splits off, but there is still something to hold on to, there's still hope. And when the board gets even smaller and he can hardly hold on in the rough seas any more, he is hoping more than ever, because a miracle *must* materialize! But no miracle materialized. What materialized were the cattle cars that took us away on June 27, 1944.

I had pleasant memories of getting on a train in groups, such as school outings and cub scout camping trips, the innocent little pushing and shoving as we boarded, the cries of the children calling to each other, because it was very, very important to sit next to your friends, the pleasant chirping, like that of a flight of starlings alighting on a branch, that you hear when many people get on the same train.

Our train of June 27 had nothing in common with these memories. The train pulled into the Scherli Brickyard along the rails with loud screeching and jolting. It wasn't a passenger train but a cattle train whose steps couldn't be reached from the ground. They laid planks against the sides so we could climb up.

The ghetto's medical supplies had been put in charge of Tanti, officially known as Dr Lenke Szerényi, the sister-in-law of my uncle Antal Fahidi, and who, being part of the family, lived with us in the ghetto in forty square metres divided up to house ten people, which counted as a veritable luxury. We took good care of the medicine, thinking that it would be of great service for all the people from the ghetto once we caught up with them.

Thanks to these small crates of medical supplies, when the cars were backed up and everyone ran amok without regard for the others, dragging their bags behind them, trampling their neighbours underfoot, elbowing them out of the way as they shouted the names of family members, the gendarme on duty held back the crowd in front of our wagon. We dragged in the crates of medical supplies and, since all saints point their fingers at themselves, may God forgive us, we dragged in our own possessions as well. In fact, the whole lot of us were the first in the wagon. Tanti went up front with outstretched wings as the royal guard of the medical supplies, my uncle Antal, kicked and beaten beyond recognition, his wife, my aunt Margit, my mother with Boci, and between them Ferike in the laundry basket, Gilike, me, and my father and Lajos, Boci's husband, pushing some important package before them that they felt could not be left behind for all the world.

We ended up in the most distinguished place, under the palm-sized opening of the cattle car that they called a window and that was covered in barbed wire, lest someone should attempt to escape through that hole of about fifty centimetres. We even had time to arrange our bags to serve us as seating and place Gilike's small stool so she could look out the tiny window if she stood on top.

Once we were in the wagon, all hell broke loose. The gendarmes let go and the whole group charged like a herd of cattle, wanting to get on the wagons first. The mêlée was indescribable. Those who were stuck at the back pushed those in front of them with superhuman strength. Those in the front rows lost their balance and, tripping and stumbling, cursing, jerking at the handles of their bags and sacks, were still calling the rest of their family, while, once inside the wagon, they tried to find a secure place for themselves from which the flood of people would not be able to dislodge them. As the wagon filled up, with the decrease in the available space the possibility of movement decreased, too, yet many were still shouting and pushing their way in. At that point the gendarmes came to the rescue; they beat the breathless crowds until they were all crowded inside the cattle cars to the last man, along with his last bundle.

Since you can't change your ways in the blink of an eye, once we were settled in our miserable nest, we first of all accommodated ourselves to the hell around us and tried to keep to ourselves as much as possible so that the outer world should filter in to us in a manner we could deal with. Then, since only a saint can step over his own shadow, we began to hope. For what?

The mythical Eldorado.

"For one thing, we don't know where they're taking us."

"For another, we're completely uprooted. We're in a vacuum."

But we're together, we're strong, we're healthy, we are very close and love each other very much. So many things working to our advantage must surely guarantee a bright future.

We'll be there soon ...

We'll be somewhere ...

Somewhere where they are expecting us, where they need us.

We will work.

We will be together.

And together, we can survive anything.

Even the little time that's left before the war ends.

Then we will go home ...

To Debrecen ...
To our garden, our house, the farm.
They pulled the door of the cattle car shut, then locked it. We waited for the train to start. And then they opened the door of the wagon again, and shoved Uncle Laci Falk inside, then they braced the door again.

Uncle Laci Falk's brush factory was to the east of the fence of the Fahídi Brothers Joint Stock Company. We loved Uncle Laci. He had a great sense of humour; he was kind, very cultured, and extremely musical. It was said of him that he wanted to be a concert pianist, but his father wouldn't hear of it. He sent him to Germany to learn trade and finance at one of the best colleges. In Germany, Uncle Laci wasted no time in falling in love with the first woman within arm's reach, married her, bought a Bösendorfer,[2] and, to the consternation of his family, showed up on their doorstep with the love of his life.

Women as such – how we see them, how we rank them, saying what makes one woman the way she is and the other the way *she* is – held pride of place in our family storehouse of prejudices and preconceptions. For instance, there was the Viennese woman; she was *nonpareil*, the be-all and end-all. She was elegant, tasteful, charming, cultured – nothing but superlatives. (Not so the Parisian woman, who you could be sure would be wearing makeup, but you couldn't be sure that she'd bathed first.) At the opposite end of the spectrum was the German woman. She bathed, all right, but she was as hefty as a barmaid, had no taste, and didn't know how to dress or cook. It was a mystery what made her a woman at all. Luckily, the exception proves the rule, because going against all family prejudice, Uncle Laci's wife, the German Friedl, was the embodiment of the ideal woman. She was all smiles, sweet, elegant, charming, the way a woman should be, and to top it off, she even had a heart and brains to go with all her other good qualities. Still, although Friedl was one hundred per cent Aryan, Uncle Laci was, by all criteria, a Jew, and though he stayed behind, his hiding place was discovered, and in the last moment, they shoved him in the cattle car with us.

---

2 Bösendorfer: A concert piano considered the best in Central Europe at that time and a status symbol for well-off families.

June, as we know, is a summer month, and the cattle car was ruthlessly assaulted by the sun, and the technical minimum of people who were stuffed into a car headed for Auschwitz was eighty souls plus their belongings.

The sun is beating down on us, the temperature inside the wagon is rising.

There is no water. There is no water for anything!

There is no drinking water, there is no water for you to wash your hands or place a wet cloth on your throbbing forehead, no water to clean a baby's bottom, or for a sick man to take his medicine. There is no water!

The sun continues to beat down on us, the temperature inside the wagon continues to rise. How many degrees could it be? Thirty Celsius? Or thirty-five? There is no water!

Your throat is dried out, there is no saliva in your mouth, your tongue sticks to the roof of your mouth, and you are sweating as the temperature keeps rising. It must be as hot as hell, because it couldn't be any hotter there either. Ferike, long since divested of his clothes, is suffering naked, save for a diaper, atop the hamper. We take turns fanning him.

Gilike doesn't say a word. She does not weep, she does not cry. She's a big girl, she's eleven years old. I'd like her to cry or scream, shake her fist, curse. Anything! But Gilike just looks. I shall see her eyes as long as I live. Gilike just looks, taking us in, mute and soundless. But her eyes speak for her. They are accusing us, questioning us. Why? What have I done? I'm such a good little girl, I've never done harm to anyone in my long eleven years of life. So why? Why? Why?

Uncle Tóni is quietly moaning and dying, his huge body one gaping wound. Having been kicked and beaten, he is covered everywhere in black and blue spots, open wounds and bruises. Tanti is applying creams, giving him injections, trying to alleviate his pain as best she can. His wife, my aunt Margit, is fanning him to alleviate his suffering.

Boci and Lajos, the always cheerful, jocular Lajos, are sitting dejectedly side by side. Pimi and Pami. That's the pet names they gave each other. They don't say it out loud, but the question hovers above their heads: What will become of us? And what of Ferike, the apple of their eyes, given to them to bring them joy and happiness? What will happen to them? What? What? What?

My father and mother still feel that they must serve as a good example to the others and must keep everyone's spirits up. They say they know that we'll arrive at a place soon where we can all live normal, proper lives, and where we will be given work worth doing. We will all work. The work may be more strenuous than what we're used to, but we're strong and healthy, and what is most important of all, we're together and will stay together. We're inseparable. Besides, the Germans have as good as lost the war, we just have to hold out for the short time till their ultimate defeat. We just have to survive this short trip.

Meanwhile, besides the lack of water in the wagon, now there is also a lack of air.

At the far end of the wagon someone goes insane and starts screaming incoherently. There is no stopping him. We're all sweating and we smell. The air grows heavier. We're suffocating in the heat. Our lips stick together. Our legs are heavy and swollen.

We are human beings. We are biological beings. We are subservient to the laws of nature. We have human needs that must be met. There is no toilet in the cattle car. In the cattle car there is only a pot – one pot for eighty people. Who is the unfortunate human being standing next to the pot and why is he being punished by fate this way? The pot fills up in a minute, and its smell lingers and lingers. And what happens once the pot is full? You can't order the laws of nature to suspend themselves.

Gilike is standing at the "window," looking out the hole. At least, I don't see her accusing glance. She smiles and waves.

"Who are you waving to, Gilike?" I ask.

"Uncle Laci Falk is so funny! He's rolling down the embankment. I'm waving to him." Thus Gilike.

Lo and behold, when I came back home I learned that, before we reached Kassa, Laci Falk asked the gendarmes to throw him out of the wagon upon his own request and responsibility, and probably not a little of his money. He told me that he indeed waved back to Gilike. But this time he managed to hide so well that they didn't find him.

To complete Laci Falk's story, it should be recalled that after the war he and Friedl reopened their brush factory and revived their pre-war business connections. Brushes made by the Falk Brush Factory were exported to several countries, including Sweden. Laci had a good nose for business. Before they could nationalize his factory, he packed some of his machines among his brushes, and got out of the country with his wife. Later, they helped a lot of people from their new home in Sweden.

Meanwhile, our train reached Kassa. It is evening, the sun is not shining. The temperature in the wagon is a bit more bearable. They push the wagon door open. We're given water and an empty pot. The orders are issued in German. Along with the pot, a gun barrel also appears in the wagon door, and we hear the order: Hand over any gold you still have because if you don't we're going to start shooting! And there was some gold we could hand over to them. In fact, whenever there was a change of guard and the same orders were given, we still had some gold left to give them.

After the relatively bearable night, the daytime heat continues, the horrible stink, the lack of water. Those who have lost their minds continue to scream, those who have died continue to lie among us, a bunch of inanimate corpses. Those who are ill continue their death agony. But the train is patient, it continues on its way for two whole days, three altogether, until we arrive at our destination where we can disembark.

It was dawn. It was just getting light. There was no station sign. We had no idea where we were.

They pushed the wagon door open and amid ear-splitting yelling and cursing we were dragged out of the wagon. Whoever couldn't get out was thrown out. But we were standing on the ground at last, on something solid. We could stretch out. The fresh early-morning air felt invigorating.

There were a lot of strange characters around. I didn't know what to make of them. They were wearing ugly grey and black striped pyjamas. They had funny-looking sailor's hats on their head made out of the same striped material. They were shouting in a strange language that bore some resemblance to German, but wasn't. I didn't even see any Germans around. These striped figures must have been the bosses around here, or so it seemed. They certainly acted like people in charge.

The striped characters told us not to mind our belongings, they would be brought to us. The babies were taken away from their mothers and given to the grandmothers. They told us we would be marching on foot. Those that couldn't come with us would be taken by bus. We were even happy for the chance to put our numbed bodies in motion. Those who looked young were asked their age. If anyone said they're less than sixteen, the striped characters screamed at them: you're sixteen, and don't you forget it! If anybody asks, say sixteen, understand? Don't forget. Sixteen. You're sixteen!

We didn't even notice that we'd been separated into two groups, men and women. Tóni must have stayed behind in the wagon. He was alive, but he couldn't get off. My father and Lajos got off, but the next second disappeared from sight. I concentrated on staying by Mother's and Gilike's side, so I didn't see how or why the men had disappeared. We were busy with Ferike. Mother and Boci had placed him on top of the hamper again, just as when we'd got on the cattle car. One of the striped characters told them to hand Ferike over to my aunt Margit, but they said he's not heavy, they don't mind carrying him. – And so they did.

The first order was given:

"All doctors step out of line!"

Past fifty and in full knowledge of her responsibility, Tanti came forward.

We had formed nice, regular rows by then. I was walking on the outer side of our row, next to Boci, who was still holding one handle of the hamper with Ferike on top. Mother was holding the other handle in one hand and Gilike by the other. My aunt Margit stood at the other end of our row. It felt good to be able to walk and move at last. Day was breaking, the sun was coming up, and along with the new day the hope inside us was renewed; see, we've made it, we're going to get decent work and we will do justice to it, we'll get by, we'll stick together, the family is together. Besides, the war is almost over.

That's when we spotted the Germans, just a few of them, a mixed group of men and women. They were standing where the column was heading, so we had to pass by them. When the lines reached them, they spoke to us in a quiet, almost friendly way. Upon hearing them, some of us went in one direction, some in another. And if anybody wanted to remain with the person who was told to go to the left, the Germans told them not to worry, it's just that the strong would continue on foot, while the weak and tired would be taken after them by bus. They would soon be together again. Which, needless to say, put everyone's mind at rest. What else.

Our row reached the group of Germans. Since she was nursing a child, Boci was slightly more corpulent than usual. The eight years of difference between us didn't show on her. Also, we resembled each other. When we reached him, a friendly German gentleman asked us, "Are you twins?"

"No," we said, and following the gesture of his arm, I ...

... *went to one side,*

Boci, the hamper, and in the hamper Ferike, and on the other side of the hamper my mother, Gilike, and Aunt Margit ...

... *went to the other.*

The next row was already standing in front of the Germans, who continued to motion with a friendly wave of the arm: this way and that.

The greatest tragedy of my life had just happened to me and I didn't even notice.

In a second I was all alone. I lost my father, my mother, my little sister – all of my closest relatives, except for Tanti. My childhood was over. I turned into an adult. From then on I had no one to rely on except myself. Of course, I didn't know this at the time, I didn't understand it at all.

The temporary show of kindness ceased the minute we were at some distance from the selection committee and, as I later learned, from Mengele, who was in charge of the selection for most of the Hungarian groups.

We were put in charge of the SS Aufseherin,[3] the whips were cracking and so were the curses and orders, slaps were flying, and so were hits in the back and kicks. We were formed into rows of

3 Aufseherin: Female SS guards.

five and driven on the run to the bath at Brežinka, whether we wanted it or not.

Anyone who would like to know what the multi-chamber entrance area was like that ended in the shower room at Brežinka should go to Buchenwald, which was built on the same model. There they can also see the furnace in its original condition. In Auschwitz, the Germans blew up the crematoria and the rooms that led there before the Russians reached the camp. In 2003, they pieced together a furnace so that President Bush could have himself photographed in front of it, but the entrance area did not resemble the original. To see the original you must go to Buchenwald. On my first visit to Buchenwald, I felt at home right away and walked through all the rooms familiar to me from Brežinka, the rooms where our heads were shaved and our body hair removed, where we were sprayed with animal disinfectant, and where we entered as human beings and emerged as Häftlings.

Anyone who has been a Häftling once will never be the same person again. Something inside you snaps and can never be soldered into one again.

Gypsy with baskets, Dicsőszentmárton, 1911. Source: Ethnographical Museum, Budapest. Photo: Artúr Adler.

Where Am I?

When the men in striped pyjamas dragged us out of the wagon, when we'd stretched our arms and legs and breathed in the cool early-morning air, what did we see? Something we'd never seen before – the Gypsy camp of Auschwitz, the family Gypsy camp of Auschwitz. The Germans knew that family ties were so strong among the Gypsies that even they couldn't sever them, so they had to keep the Gypsy families together, even at the camp.

There was always something attractive about the romantic view of Gypsy life, even if it was not strictly true. That attraction involved freedom, beggarly as it might have been. What a wonderful feeling to fly free as a bird, not to have a permanent place to live, to sit atop rambling wagons, to set up camp along the banks of a stream, to sing, dance, and make merry. The beautiful Gypsy girls wear rose-patterned skirts, and the young men wear vests with metal buttons. And when they feel like it, they break camp and move on to new paths and new destinations. Do the horses need fodder and the children food? Who cares! That would mean a paying job.

When I was a child, life had already advanced beyond that. The Gypsy king still owned a palace in Pozsony (Bratislava) and the buttons of his vest were set with real diamonds. But of the former freedom only the nostalgia remained. Some of the Gypsies made a living from the traditional handicrafts, but most lived in need, and the Gypsy way of life was but a dream. There were no horses, no wagons, only the hovels, ignorance, superstition, illiteracy, and penury.

We the non-Gypsies have always ostracized the Gypsies, meaning that we did not accept them. But we asked them why they wouldn't assimilate.

Our family belonged to the better type, because we generally considered any being on two legs as a human being (even anything walking on all fours). We knew the Gypsies in and around the farm and even in Debrecen by name, and helped them. But regardless of age or gender, we used the familiar form of address with them. So much for human dignity and equality.

On the farm, my grandmother had two favourite targets on whom to vent her generosity, and she had plenty of opportunities to do so. One was the shakter, the kosher butcher from Mezőkeresztes, and the other was our Gazsi, a Gypsy who had no official place of residence. These two men had one thing in common: no year passed by without them remembering their duties and presenting their family with yet another offspring. The shakter was truly dutiful in this regard, though Gazsi had nothing to be ashamed of either. Their families were later prevented from being overpopulated by the crematoria of Auschwitz, where their wives and countless children were sent upon arrival.

Once the shakter had panhandled his way through the village with no more hope of finding another morsel for the many mouths he had to feed, he would walk out to the farm, and as luck would have it, he always happened to have an empty sack or two with him. We didn't keep a kosher kitchen, so we didn't need the shakter to kill the chicken for frying or the hen for soup. But that's not why he came. The small bags were filled up, the children now had something to eat, and he was also given a goose or two to carry under his arm.

For his part, Gazsi needed no excuse. He showed up without any. But that's not so. He had a very good excuse. His family was starving, and the latest addition was on its way. Gazsi would bring this to our attention with admirable eloquence and expression. He didn't need to nudge my grandmother long. He also got his goose and his bags of food, and off he went, just like the shakter. Except the gendarmes would usually bring Gazsi back.

"This infamous good-for-nothing rascal says he was actually given the goose!" fumed the indignant gendarme, Ferenc, because as far as he was concerned, Gazsi must have stolen it. If he's a Gypsy, he's a thief. That's just how it is, right?

At such times, Grandmother saw the situation at once and, turning to Gazsi, reprimanded him: "Gazsi, didn't I tell you to take two geese? What did you do with the other?" "Jean Valjean," we older grandchildren whispered behind Grandmother's back, citing Victor Hugo. But Grandmother didn't learn mercy from *Les Misérables*, she had plenty of her own.

The gendarmes were not over-scrupulous when they had to keep order in the village or on the farms. They were put in charge of a specific district and usually went around in a pair. One of the regulars of the pair was Feri. The gendarmes enjoyed a privileged protocol. They could go into the summer kitchen, where they were offered a spritzer. A large pack of virgin tobacco was also made ready for them. Tobacco was subject to state tax, and we grew lots of first-class tobacco leaves. It was the gendarmes' duty to discover and report anyone owning virgin tobacco without having paid tax on it. They nevertheless didn't mind getting theirs for free. There's nothing new under the sun.

If they chanced to meet any member of the family, they always offered a polite greeting. They even chatted about horses with my grandfather, because they had very good horses themselves. I wonder what Feri said to my grandfather when he met him in the ghetto of Mezőkövesd, because they must have met. Mezőkövesd was Feri's official terrain. Did he feel a sense of shame, I wonder?

Historians still owe us an explanation for the reserves of brutality evidenced by the Hungarian gendarmes during the deportations. Where had it been till then? Or where did it come from all of a sudden? Not that it made a difference. The Jews of rural Hungary would have been deported in any case.

The gendarmes hit and beat and kicked and slapped and cursed. This was not part of their orders but a voluntary contribution that they prided themselves in. Whatever was of value they plundered. This, at least, was something human and understandable in their actions! It is the simplest way of acquiring possessions, and the opportunity presents itself only in rare situations. No wonder they took advantage of it, now that they had a chance. But there was no need for the cruelty. Why did they resort to it?

It would be wonderful if I could be writing instead that the Hungarian gendarmerie acted heroically, that they sheltered and saved the Jews of Hungary wherever and whenever they could, that they tried to minimize their victims' pain, and that through their actions and attitude they unequivocally expressed their disapproval of the deportations. I wish I could say that the deportations were forced on the Hungarians by the Germans.

But the truth is that Eichmann came to Hungary with sixty or at the most eighty men. In *The Last Chapter* by Christian Gerlach and Götz Aly, published in 2002,[1] and whose first Hungarian reader I most probably was, the authors examined the interrelationships and contingencies that made the genocide and the confiscation of Jewish property desirable for every segment of Hungarian economic life and, vulgarly speaking, even for the last dog in Hungary. (I'd have much preferred to read this from the pen of a Hungarian historian, though.) The book has just appeared in Hungarian. It is a real eye opener.

Let us assume that every one of Eichmann's attendants was a very important person. Each had his own driver, secretary, and orderly, which still makes just barely over one hundred people. They were very clever and experienced. But it was not those hundred, but hundreds and thousands of Hungarians and, with few exceptions, the entire Hungarian state apparatus that, in a matter of fifty days, deported four hundred and thirty thousand Jewish Hungarians to Auschwitz.

---

1 Christian Gerlach and Götz Aly, *Das letzte Kapitel: Der Mord an den ungarischen Juden* [The Last Chapter: The Murder of Hungarian Jews] (Stuttgart: Deutsche Verlags-Anstalt, 2002).

I have the greatest of respect for János Arany. He is one of my favourite poets. I read his "Gypsies of Nagyida" again the other day. I always read János Arany with great pleasure and am much taken by his inimitable command of language, his lightness of touch, his factual knowledge. There's not a morsel of hate, contempt, or prejudice in that poem, only understanding and forgiveness. If a Gypsy cheats a bit and steals, well, that's part of the package, it's only natural. After all, he's a Gypsy. And all this is written with such humour, so ingeniously and convincingly! And with something my ears are especially sensitive to: condescension. Since I've become familiar with humiliation, my senses are especially sharp. János Arany hails from among the better of his kind. Those who are not as good do not condescend, they hate. What a difference! And despite all this, he is still János Arany.

On the early morning of July 1, 1944, the romanticized Gypsies of Nagyida were furthest from my mind. The scene shocked me to my core. Women, all skin and bones, in filthy, ragged rose-print skirts with the ubiquitous baby lying on their empty chests, men, also of skin and bones, in vests with metal buttons, and skin-and-bones children with black eyes grown wide with accusation.

I couldn't pay much attention to them, because I had plenty of trouble of my own. But on August 2, 1944, you could not avoid paying attention.

When the deportation of the Jews in the countryside was begun in May 1944, Auschwitz was soon filled to capacity. The Hungarian authorities wasted no time. The transports followed each other in such rapid succession that the crematoria couldn't handle all the bodies, so they had to dig ditches in which to burn the dead on open fires.

Those who were sentenced to life also had to be put somewhere – until they served their purpose, at any rate, and didn't become corpses themselves. There weren't enough camps equipped to handle the influx of Hungarian Jews, so there was great need for a smoothly working camp with all the amenities of Auschwitz – guard towers, electrified barbed wire fences, and searchlights, just like the Gypsy camp. I'll never know what weighed more in the balance, the lack of space or the Muselmann[2] state of the Gypsies. Probably both. So on the night of August 2, 1944, the Gypsy camp was freed of its inmates. Nobody sounded the bell for them. The Germans annihilated them without further ado.

I always knew the reason that the SS couldn't talk, just shout: because they were afraid. When a person is afraid, he lets out a loud sound. Under normal conditions, he sings. In the SS scale of values, singing was replaced by shouting. The louder the sound, the less you hear the stirrings of your conscience as it peters out, so you shout until it's gone – meaning the bad conscience. What remains is the shouting as a way of life.

On the night of August 2, 1944, the SS were howling. They surely must have known that the innocent inmates of the Gypsy camp had never done anything in their lives for which they should be annihilated to the last man, woman, and child. Their only sin was having been born a Gypsy. The SS had to do something so that they could convince themselves that there was a reason behind their actions. As they drove the Gypsy camp to the gas chamber, they had to let out blood-curdling shouts, curses, and invectives. The Gypsies knew what was awaiting them.

When I reach this point in my recollections, I begin to doubt that maybe what I see in the mind's eye is a concoction of a too lively imagination, because I remember an explosive brightness caused by fire and I can smell the smoke seeping in through the closed window of the barrack.

Erzsi Brodt – today Mrs György Szemes – was lying by the window that night and looked out. She saw an SS soldier standing with legs spread apart as he trailed his flame thrower on the barrack crowded with people and set it on fire. The cruelty of the SS outstripped the wildest leaps of the imagination.

Those who heard the wailing, the prayers, the swearing, the crying, the sobbing, the cursing, the desperate screams and howls, will never forget it. There are no adjectives to describe

---

2 Muselmann: From the German word for Muslim; in the lingo of the concentration camps, inmates who were sick or starved beyond help and condemned to selection and the crematoria.

it, there are no words to tell it. Piercing, unearthly, agonizing, ear-splitting, spine-chilling, raving mad – so many empty words. You had to hear it.

I know that there is no justice on this earth. It would be comforting to know that those who brought about this horror will hear it for all eternity in Dante's hell, where they will suffer till the end of time.

Éva

Anikó

August 13, 1944. The picture above is from the Auschwitz Album found
in Dora-Mittelbau by Lili Jákob. It was taken in Auschwitz on August 13,
1944, when they herded one thousand women sentenced to slave labour into
wagons. I ended up in the group headed for the DAG (Dynamite Nobel Joint
Stock Co. AG) munitions factory in Allendorf. It offered the only chance for
survival. Of the two women marked on the photograph, the first is Anikó,
my "other half." The second is me.

Who Is Who?

When I think back on the methods of child-rearing they pestered us with, I am moved to tears. "Show me your table manners, and I'll tell you who you are," we were told amidst smiles, while, with a book slipped under each arm, we had to learn to eat with easy elegance and without moving our head, the spoon just touching our lips without spilling a drop of the soup.

If there's trouble, you don't have to ask who is who. It takes less than a minute to find out.

The foundation stone of life in Auschwitz, as in all the German camps, was the row of five, because they counted us at least twice each day. They also counted those who dragged themselves to the Revier but could not drag themselves back, as well as those who stayed behind in the bunks as corpses (only in the better camps, of course, where there were bunks; and they stayed *in* them because the bunks were just like open coffins) and who were taken to the Revier wrapped in a blanket, their arms and legs dangling. The truck that had brought our so-called food then removed the bodies on its return trip. After all, one had to be economical. The remainder of the mass of humanity stood on the Appelplatz waiting to be counted by fives. One would think that adding by fives is no big deal, which is true, but it got the better of the Aufseherins, which meant that we had to stand on the Appelplatz for what seemed like eternity.

Who you stand in line with in a row of five makes a great deal of difference, because you form a community. You eat out of the same bowl, you sit together under the scorching sun because no one is allowed to go inside the block. You depend on each other at all times. You never know what atrocities are in store for you; everyone around you is shouting, the Aufseherins are cracking their whips, the Blockältestes can slap or kick you or beat you over the back at any time, God only knows why. You can't live in constant fear. After a while you must grow a hard shell around your heart, otherwise you can't bear it.

When I think of the time I spent in Auschwitz and in deportation, the first person singular loses its significance. It's not me, but "us." We were so close to each other and supported each other so closely, we were really one person. Our particular row of five took shape almost immediately, as soon as it was forced on us in Auschwitz. It was modified only at the labour camp in Allendorf, where Anikó Weisz and I always stood in the same row of five.

We arrived in Birkenau on July 1, 1944. At Brežinka near Birkenau, where the bath was, we didn't know yet that there were showers that let out gas instead of water. We were turned into Häftlings in accordance with the regulations of the Third Reich: bald head, body deprived of all body hair and sprayed with disinfectant that burned the skin, and instead of clothes, torn, smelly, and filthy rags taken from other women. We looked at each other and laughed. We laughed fit to burst! It was absurdly implausible and comic that we could be the spoiled children from Debrecen whose parents placed such emphasis on their education, their books and music scores, on their learning languages, engaging in sports and being cultured and properly dressed. When we saw ourselves in the window of the barrack, we didn't recognize ourselves.

The feeling of belonging together developed in us without any effort. It was a feeling without which, and I say this with certainty, we wouldn't have made it back home. There was always one out of the five who would keep up the spirits of the rest; there was always one who made the others eat the inedible food or found words of comfort. In my own group, three were as close to me as if we'd been sisters: Anikó Weisz from Debrecen, and the two sisters, Lili and Klári Glück from Miskolc.

I have never set foot in the home of any of them, but can tell you all the same how they lived.

Lili and Klári's father was a fancy leather goods maker and had a thriving business on Miskolc's main street. The workshop was in the basement, under the shop. Papa Glück was a master of his trade. He cut the patterns himself and knew all about leather. After he'd cut the pattern, his assistants and workers assembled it flawlessly under his direction. He was proud of his reputation and had only irreproachable items on his shelves. The better part of his time was thus taken up with acquiring the raw materials and preparing them for his staff to work on.

Lili and Klári's mother was in charge of sales upstairs. The customers liked her. She knew how to talk to them, not that this was a prerequisite, since the many beautiful handbags, wallets, eyeglass cases, and the rest spoke for themselves. Their mother also ran the household, which was in the same building as the boutique and the workshop.

There was also a grandmother in the family, a true original who kept up with the others. She supported herself from a space no bigger than a gateway. She sold pants made of rough linen. The ironworks in nearby Diósgyőr employed a lot of men, and they needed the rough linen pants. The grandmother sold pants on credit, so customers kept coming back to her.

Lili was a pretty young girl, the proverbial Brünhilde – natural, lovely blond hair, light eyes, a strong, well-proportioned figure. She wanted to continue her education. She had brains and she wanted to make use of them. But she was not admitted to the local High School, where they didn't want any dirty Jews, so she spent her mornings in her father's workshop and became a certified fancy leather goods maker. Her afternoons were taken up with her studies: she studied languages, mathematics, and art history. Her father paid for her tutoring.

Klári, on the other hand, was like a dark-feathered little bird fallen out of its nest. When they arrived in Auschwitz, the inmates from Kanada[1] screamed in her ear: If they ask, say you're

---

1 Kanada: The inmates who were assigned to collect and sort the belongings left in the cattle cars and on the ramps worked in the warehouse called Kanada (the German spelling of Canada) in the Auschwitz lingo.

Papa Glück with Lili and Klári.

sixteen. Lili and Klári were about four years apart. Klári was only fourteen. She was a thin little thing, almost transparent, who had grown tall too quickly, a child who, being an adolescent, should have been living in the bosom of a loving family with lots of pretty clothes, shoes, a joyful life, school, good books, and nourishing food. Instead, the sun was now beating down on her on the plains of Auschwitz, where she went without food or water, because nobody could make her swallow the inedible food. Lili watched with concern as Klári's physical condition rapidly deteriorated. They'd already been through several selections, and while Lili was deemed capable of work, Klári was always selected out. And every time this happened, Klári would run to the same side as Lili. Of course, this resulted in a lot of yelling and cursing and the Aufseherin running after them to take Klári away. But Lili and Klári planned ahead: as soon as Klári reached the side of the ones not selected, she would hide among the naked women. So the Aufseherin could not find her. Another young girl was separated from her mother, who had been "selected," but she voluntarily rejoined her – and thus signed her own death warrant. But Klári stayed with Lili, and Lili always knew what to do with Klári to keep her alive. Sometimes with strict orders, sometimes with kind words, she always got her little sister to do whatever was needed for her to survive. If it were not for Lili, Klári would have never made it home.

Anikó attended the same convent school in Debrecen as I, but she was one year my junior. In the cloistered world of a girls' school, we look up with awe at the older girls in the upper grades, while we take no notice of those below us, since they're just little brats. Still, we knew that the dark-haired pretty girl Anikó had a great talent for drawing and reciting poetry. She and her family lived in the Golden Bull apartment house. Everyone in Debrecen knew her mother, who was a great beauty. Anikó's father was also very good looking. He was an engineer and the local representative of the Fiat Company. They made a handsome couple. When I wanted to comfort Anikó I said to her, "You know, I was just thinking how beautiful your mother is," whereas she was at best beautiful ashes by then.

That is because Anikó had a younger brother, the child of sinful optimism. Every normal woman wants little children around her, and the later they come, and especially if they come unexpectedly, the more they are treasured. Anikó's mother, who was no exception to the rule, gave birth to a baby boy just sixteen months before the deportations. The little boy took her along with him to the gas chamber.

On August 12, 1944, they held a naked selection at Camp BIIc in Auschwitz to pick out one thousand women for work. The main gate of BIIc was flung open, and we were herded to a nearby empty camp. There were no provisions, but we didn't notice. We were too nervous and anxious about our future. Since we were all healthy and able-bodied, we were hoping that, once we got away from our old camp, things would get better. The following day they took us to the bath, where we were given grey linen clothes and kerchiefs for our shaved heads. Then they put us in wagons. This is the moment that was captured by the photographer of the Auschwitz Album, who was either Bernhard Walter, the head of the SS Identification Service, or his assistant, Ernst Hoffman. They both had special permission, because photography was strictly forbidden in Auschwitz. When I first saw the photograph, still in the late 1940s, I couldn't believe my eyes. I spotted Anikó in her striped socks and, a little behind her, myself in my cork platform sandals made by Uncle Hadnagy in Debrecen, now tied to my feet with a rag because the sharp, pointed stones of the Auschwitz Lagerstrasse had ruined them. There's no knowing why, but in Auschwitz they let us keep our shoes. They took them away only in Allendorf to replace them with wooden clogs.

And so, six weeks after my arrival in Auschwitz, I found myself in a cattle car once again, and once again with eighty others, except this time we had no belongings, just one package of cheese and a quarter loaf (250 grams) of bread. The day before had passed without food or drink, so the food they gave us when we left for the work camp we ate right away. Nobody told us that our portions were to last for three days! But at least I learned what it is like to eat ripe cheese and then, to add insult to injury, to go without water for two days.

In short, the wagon jolted under us, and off we went into the wild blue yonder – and, just as in a folk tale, on the third day we caught sight of the king's castle revolving on a duck's leg, this time in the shape of a station with the sign:

Weimar-Buchenwald.

I had no idea what Buchenwald was. On the other hand, I knew all about Weimar.

May God bless Aunt Mici as long as a single grain remains of her ashes, and even beyond, because it was Aunt Mici, our tutor in Debrecen, who taught us German literature so well that we didn't forget it even after a passage of seventy years. She spoke even about Klopstock with such enthusiasm and insight, her words were so engaging and her stories about writers so interesting, that she made even a young adolescent like me listen with riveted attention, which is no mean accomplishment. I began studying with her at the age of ten and took lessons with her as long as it was possible. It is because of her that I acquired a thorough knowledge of classical German literature. I read everything she gave me to read, and she helped me develop a literary taste of my own. She also encouraged me to have an opinion about what I'd read, and to go on reading as much as possible.

Her lessons and my father's preferences coincided beautifully, because he also loved books, as did my mother, who read mostly in German, and when I turned fifteen I was given free access to their books and could read to my heart's delight.

I was sixteen when my father told me to read Zola so I could learn about life, as he put it. He didn't realize that there are other kinds of misery than in *Nana* and *Germinal*. I would have learned about life even without reading Zola. But at the time, we didn't know that.

So then, there stood our train at the freight station of Weimar, and I was reminded not only of Aunt Mici, but of my mother as well. "Don't be impatient. These bad times will pass quickly and we shall take you to Weimar, where you can look at everything and read all about your Goethe and Lotte and Schiller."

It was there, under the station sign of Weimar, that it dawned on me that life snubs us at every turn. There were few things I had wanted as desperately as to see Weimar, and now my wish had come true. I sometimes think that you're better off not wanting things lest your wishes are granted.

After a while, the train started moving again, but before long, we caught a glimpse of the station at Allendorf, where the train stopped, and we got off. We had reached our destination.

We dragged ourselves off the wagons exhausted, broken in mind and body, and, as usual, hungry and thirsty. The chief engineer of the factory where they were going to take us flew into a rage. He was expecting strong men in good physical condition who would help resuscitate the German war industry. Well, he was out of luck, because he got us instead! Adolf Wutke SS Hauptscharführer,[2] the commander-in-chief of our new camp, surrounded by a wreath of women, a group of SS Aufseherin, was in attendance.

From the station we didn't need trucks or trains. We reached the singular (!) little camp with the usual cement columns and barbed wire on foot. There it was, in its glory, and not surrounded by countless other camps, like in Auschwitz. We dared hardly hope that this luxurious single camp would be ours. But it was. There were very few barracks, just enough to accommodate a thousand women. There was a Revier as well, and, luxury of luxuries, a washroom of sorts with unlimited supplies of water available at all hours of the day, water you could wash yourself in as often as you liked and drink as often as you liked!

The interiors of the barracks at Allendorf were also luxurious. After Auschwitz, we couldn't get our fill of them. That is because, thanks to the overzealousness of the Hungarian authorities, transports to Auschwitz arrived in such quick succession that there was no time to finish the barracks, let alone furnish them with bunk beds or any other furnishings. At night, order was guaranteed in the simplest possible manner. We had to sleep on the floor. Moreover, since there was very little space, we had to lean our heads on each other's laps or lie on our sides pressed close

---

2 Hauptscharführer (German): SS major.—Trans.

together, like canned sardines. If anyone needed to turn around because her side hurt, since she was lying on the bare ground without a blanket on top of her or a sheet under her and was being pressed from both sides by the others – in short, if someone was adamant about turning to her other side, the entire row had to turn around with her. Not so in Allendorf.

In our very own sweet little camp in Allendorf, we even had bunk beds in the barracks! They were double-deckers with straw mats, a separate mat for each inmate. That was the extent of our bedding, plus an incredibly threadbare, stinking, prickly, ugly brown blanket. I couldn't help thinking of my grandfather Alfréd Weisz's horse blankets. Those were made of camel hair, were rounded off at the four corners, and edged in copper. They were supplied with the AW monogram, and let off one of the most pleasant smells in the world, the smell of horses. I'd have much preferred being a horse on my grandfather's farm.

After the managers of our future factory spent their rage over the inferior quality of their new work force, meaning us, they decided to improve our stamina for the time being, but only for the time being, so we would not get used to it.

Our new life promised to be like something out of a children's tale. I learned that I was in Kur-Hessen, where the Grimm brothers collected so many beautiful German folk tales. What luck that I knew them all by heart. It took no special effort to imagine myself in the situation of Hansel and Gretel. The wicked old witch locks Hansel in a cage and fattens him up so she can eat him. Why she checked his little finger to see how fat he was getting is her problem, that's the place it shows the least. But she kept checking.

We, too, were fed by the "Dinamit AG witch," and we also stretched our little pinkies out through our cages, day after day, so it could see how nice and fat we were getting. And it didn't take long before we were declared fit for work, even though we had certain reservations, especially after we came face to face with what we were required to do – work for strong, healthy men. After our all too brief fattening cure, when we were given potatoes and a third of a loaf of bread, they gave us cattle-turnip and a quarter of a loaf, and towards the end, only a fifth. Then came the day when we began our working lives in the interest of bolstering the munitions industry of the Third Reich. We worked in two or three shifts depending on the availability of raw materials, which meant spending either twelve or eight hours in the factory. At first the trip there and back took an hour each way, but as we grew weaker, this time grew longer. We stood in line for Appel twice a day, which took another hour to an hour and a half.

We made shells for cannons, grenades of various sizes, as well as bombs weighing between five and one hundred kilos. The raw material was trinitrotoluene, trinitrobenzoene, and potassium nitrate. When they built the munitions plant in the late 1930s and early 1940s and put it into operation, it was staffed by German workers. There are pictures of them working in safety boots, safety gloves, safety helmets, safety masks, and huge leather safety aprons, doing the same work we had to do. And they were duly photographed, while nobody bothered taking pictures of us. We didn't look half as good. We wore no protective clothing at all. We worked with highly toxic materials. We handled everything cavalierly, without gloves, masks, or protective aprons. We inhaled all the toxins and walked knee deep in potassium nitrate. The locals called us lemons, because we'd turned yellow. The few scraggly strands of hair that began to grow back took on a violet hue. Inside and outside the factory, we felt the bitter taste of the toxins on our skin and lips. There was no way to get rid of it, since the whole area was contaminated.

There was no distinction between easy and hard work at the munitions plant, where everything was organized with an eye to expediency and economy, meaning, with the help of slave labour. There is nothing new under the sun. They had plenty of examples to draw on from thousands of years ago. Furthermore, I cannot stress enough that the work required able-bodied men, but by default, it fell to us, and this surpassed our capabilities from the word go. And because of our steadily deteriorating physical condition, it became more and more of a struggle.

Since at this stage of my life my contract with fate included a clause that it would keep snubbing me, and since in my previous life my weakest point was my spine, my so carefully tended, so meticulously nursed and exercised spine, it came as no surprise that the work they put me to was guaranteed to wreak havoc with it. This was due partly to my height and strong physique, though neither proved strong enough for the purpose. I worked in a pair with Lili, who was also tall and strong.

The technique of making shells is very simple. The materials, which are in the form of powder, must be taken to the upper level, meaning that a group of my fellow Häftlings were carrying fifty-kilo sacks to the upper floor. These contained the tri and saltpetre, meaning the trinitrotoluene and the potassium nitrate. The two components must be poured into a cauldron in a certain proportion, then heated to eighty degrees Celsius. By then it is a liquid mass. This concoction is let down into a smaller container located on the floor below that has a tap at the bottom for opening and closing it. A tray made especially for this purpose is rolled under the tap. It has neat rows of empty shells open at the top, waiting to be filled. Only a funnel is needed, and the first phase is done.

Anyone carrying a bag to the top floor that is too heavy for her constantly comes in contact with the trinitrate and saltpetre, because there is no paper bag, regardless of its strength, that won't be damaged while it is being moved about. Besides, anyone who is charged with opening and closing the tap, letting the liquid explosive flow from the container to the grenade shell, swallows a portion of the toxic steam with every breath.

The next phase is the so-called sticking. As the liquid explosive solidifies in the shell, there must be no air bubbles left in it, because apparently it may not explode. It also may not explode if any foreign liquid gets into it. Accordingly, as it cools, the contents of the shell must be repeatedly stuck with a stick longer than the shell itself. Those who worked this phase peed into the shells every chance they got. Perhaps they really won't explode! But they breathed in an appreciable portion of the poisonous gases while sticking the shells.

The half-finished, cooled-down grenade then begins its journey. It is transferred to the part of the factory where a hole is cut in the neck. The neck had a beautiful name, "Mundlochbüchse," mouth-cavity purse; this is where the wick and the paper were placed which start burning when the grenade is expelled, thereby detonating the explosive inside. Whoever cut the hole worked in a cloud of toxic powder. After this operation, the top of the grenade was sealed with a cap, and it was ready. All that was needed now to get it to the front were the two of us – Lili and I – plus the Russians who loaded the explosive devices onto the wagons.

Lili and I and Anikó plus another young girl did the unloading. We worked in pairs. The unloading meant that, like so many athletes, we had to stand at the end of the conveyor belt on opposite sides, with me facing Lili. The grenades came rolling down the conveyor belt in neat rows, one behind the other, and the two of us would pick up the first, Lili one end, me the other, then we ran with it either to a wheelbarrow, into which we could fling the grenade at the height of our waist, or a crate that was on the ground, and the two grenades for which it was designed had to be placed neatly inside. Then we had to hurry to be back by the time the next grenade reached the end of the conveyor belt to prevent it from falling.

We have all gone through the experience of remembering something from childhood that seemed so big, and then, ten years later, when we saw it again, we noted with astonishment how small it was. I have horribly oppressive memories of the work I did in a pair with Lili and which became more and more difficult as our physical condition deteriorated. I've tried to recall how heavy one of those grenades must have been. Maybe ten kilos, maybe twenty. It certainly could not have weighed more, I thought, because by March 1945, we, who were big-boned and tall, didn't weigh more than forty kilos ourselves, and it is takes superhuman effort to lift even half of your body weight in such a weak condition. I also tried to calculate how many grenades we must have carried during one shift.

I remember only that I had to muster all my physical and mental strength even to stand by the conveyor belt to be able to grab the grenade and drag it to the wheelbarrow or box, to run back and pick up the next grenade, when, as I carried the one before, I already felt that it would be the last I could pick up and carry, and when the third and fourth were already on the way.

Lili.

I couldn't have asked for a better partner than Lili. She was absolutely fair. The head of the grenade is slightly thinner than its bottom. After a certain number of grenades, we changed places. Lili was never tired. Lili was never in low spirits. Lili always came up with something that made life bearable.

It was much more difficult placing the grenades in the crates than atop the barrows. We held the grenade and, as we bent down to lower it into the crate, we had to be careful lest it slip and roll onto our hands or feet. We had to hold it back from rolling out of our grasp. I can still feel the lightning flash of pain in my spine every time we lowered a grenade into place.

If the city of Stadtallendorf had not extended an invitation to us in 1990, I probably still wouldn't have the answers to some of my questions. When they handed me the factory's records, this is what I read in the assessment for the year 1944 written by its board of directors:

> Our assessment re. the one thousand Hungarian Jewish women who began work in August [1944] is satisfactory. Thanks to the use of the Jewish female workforce, filling the nearly 50 kg, 15 cm large grenades was accomplished with the best possible results.

I also learned from the records that we packaged eight hundred grenades per shift, which meant that, with my "dance partner" Lili at one end and me at the other, we carried fifty-kilo grenades from the conveyer belt to the containers and then placed them inside, when we weighed a mere forty kilos ourselves. Where did we get the strength? Who knows? But then, a Fahídi does everything to the best of his or her ability. Bravo! I managed to win the acknowledgment of the German munitions industry.

By March 1945 all of us had lost about a third of our normal body weight. There is no getting used to hunger and thirst, except perhaps the way the proverbial donkey of the poor man did that died before he could get used to it. In Auschwitz, the thirst was perhaps the most unbearable thing. In Allendorf we didn't have to go thirsty, but we had other things to make up for it.

Starvation goes through several phases – some are horrible, others even more so. When a human being still resembles a human being and is very hungry, he keeps thinking of food. In Auschwitz, as well as in Allendorf, at first we constantly cooked. There was no recipe in the world we didn't recite to each other. Unfortunately, when you're hungry and keep thinking about food, you feel physical pain. During the next phase of starvation, we tried to go easy on ourselves and made up our minds that instead of cooking, we'd concentrate on culture, which proved to be one of the most effective of our efforts at self-preservation. We went to the theatre and the cinema, and we attended concerts. Someone would throw in the title of a film, and the rest of us would tell the story, until it all added up. We remembered the title of a play and put together the story. If we attended a concert, we sang whatever we wanted to hear – a bit of Beethoven, Schubert, or Mozart, or arias from various operas. Next, someone would mention the title of a book, and the rest of us would piece the story together. We also recited poetry. But after an hour or so, we were cooking again.

The third phase of starvation is the least painful because everything is muted, pale, without character. Almost imperceptibly, the world retreats. It becomes uncertain, as if seen through a glass darkly. But most striking of all, you no longer care. When I reached this phase, it scared me so much that I made up my mind that I would resist. I was afraid that I'd forget who I was. So each morning when the horrible shouts of *los! los!* – quickly! quickly! – woke us up (to this day, when I wake up, I wake up in the camp with my heart pounding), I repeated my name, my address, and searched for something in my head, a poem, a tune, anything I could remember, before I dragged myself out to the Appel.

Regardless of the weather, we had to be out on the Appelplatz by dawn. We were not allowed to wrap our blankets around ourselves. It was impossible to avoid thinking, What am I doing here? What have I done? And why me? Who is responsible? Standing there in my threadbare rags, in rain, snow, and freezing weather, among the other nine hundred and ninety-nine of my friends who were just as cold, just as hungry, and did work every bit as physically exhausting as mine, I felt as lonely as if I were at the bottom of the deepest well in the farthest circle of hell. And my nine hundred and ninety-nine fellow inmates felt the same way.

If physical suffering can be ranked, every one of us suffered the most from different things. Some from hunger. I suffered most from the cold. I always disliked the cold, even as a child, and never learned to ski. I never felt inclined. I had to learn to skate because they took me out to the skating rink and taught me, but I never liked it. No matter how warmly I was dressed, my hands and feet were soon as cold as icicles. They turned white and wanted to break off. The only thing that helped me was to run home and sit in a nice warm bath.

In August, when we were taken to Allendorf, we wore a simple grey linen dress and a kerchief on our shaved heads. We also had a pair of wooden clogs for our feet. The caring staff of our little camp wanted to make sure that we wouldn't waste our precious time on looking after our wardrobe. In the factory we wore overalls.

With the passage of time, summer gave way to fall, and fall to winter. Sometime around October the heads of our camp woke up and requisitioned warm clothing from Auschwitz, which we got. In place of warm winter underwear, warm clothes, and warm shoes, we were each given a coat. In line with the latest Häftling fashion, each coat had a stripe on the back cut out of another coat. After all, we were women and we liked to follow the latest fashion trends. In short, we were now as fashionable as could be, except that the coats were definitely not suitable for winter. Mine must have once belonged to a young adolescent who couldn't have been more than a hundred and fifty-five centimetres tall. She must have looked pretty in her green tweed spring coat. Green is also my favourite colour. Not so the red stripe running down the back, according to the Auschwitz fashion fad. By the way, I was twenty centimetres taller than my coat. The difference was made up by my bare arms and legs sticking out of it.

The winter of 1944–5 was just like every other winter – it was cold, and it didn't even have to be colder than average, the thermometer didn't have to drop below zero for me to feel it, seeing how I lacked the amenities of shoes, socks, warm underwear, warm clothes, a warm coat, hat and gloves, a scarf, and everything else that people use in civilized places to keep themselves warm. We walked precariously along the hard frozen path to the factory, there and back, twice a day in clogs but no socks, our feet blue from the cold, our bodies covered by a thin linen dress and a useless coat we sarcastically nicknamed "lipit'an'ka," the name of a Slovak folk garment we used back home metaphorically to indicate that someone was not dressed properly for the weather.

But more horrible than all the rest were the barrack and the night. Though there was a stove in the barrack, it served only for decoration, because there was no firewood and no coal. We had only our breath and our body heat to stave off the cold – not that it did us much good in the uninsulated wooden barrack, where there was no appreciable difference in temperature between the inside and the outside.

When your hands and feet approximate the above-mentioned icicle-like state and there is no tub of hot water anywhere, you want to sleep, because you're dropping from fatigue. You've spent the day carrying grenades, you've dragged yourself home along the frozen road, and the food you were given didn't have enough calories to warm you. And so, you start to shiver. You shiver from cold. You shiver from everything. You shiver from the inside out with no relief in sight, and the double bunk shivers along with you.

Anikó slept on the bottom of our double-decker bunk, and I slept on top, and when the irrepressible shivering came over me, I climbed down to Anikó, and she put her arms around me, rubbed me, and gently patted me on the back, trying to keep me warm and calm. Though we had our threadbare, filthy-smelling blankets to cover us, and I also had the warmth of Anikó's breath and body to keep me warm, it took time before she could calm me down and stop the shivering. I like to call Anikó my other half. When we were evacuated from the camp, we got separated and for many years I had no news of her, certainly not that she'd got married in America. So when I saw her married name on the list we used to organize the meeting at Allendorf for 1990, I didn't recognize it. Before the ceremonial opening, when three hundred and thirty of us met from all corners of the world, we suddenly found ourselves standing face to face. Our joy knew no bounds.

I should add that out out of the five Gärtner girls in our barrack, about whom I will tell more later, some worked in the

"Aussenkommando," or outdoor work site, and not in the factory. This meant that they swallowed less toxic material. On the other hand, they levelled the ground in the open, where either the rain or the snow or the sun would come beating down on them, and they had to pick-axe the frozen ground, carry heavy stones, and so on. But sometimes they managed to get their hands on some kindling or paper and even found matches. Thanks to them, the stove in our barrack sometimes gave off a bit of heat. But this was not at all the norm.

When you do not get enough calories, not even enough to keep your normal body weight up, and in the meantime you are forced to meet impossible physical demands, you suffer not only physical but emotional ills as well. It becomes next to impossible to remain who you are. Since you are suffering from top to toe, the little that remains of you is as heavy and burdensome as a black hole. You can barely drag it along with you.

Since we see each other so rarely, when we meet, Anikó and I spend a lot of time recalling our shared memories. There is one story in particular that we keep relating to each other. I remember perfectly well that on one horrible winter day when it was cold and dark and I was so tired and inert that I didn't want to get up and go stand on the Appelplatz, Anikó stood by my bunk and talked to me. She told me that the next day the war would be over and the day after that we'd be going home, and at home everything would be just as it was, with my parents and Gilike waiting for me, and that I must go out to the Appelplatz for their sake, if not my own, I couldn't stay behind, I couldn't do that to *them*. And she kept talking until I found myself standing outside. For her part, Anikó remembers perfectly well that, as she put it, I saved her life, since not going to the Appel was tantamount to suicide. According to Anikó, she was the one that didn't want to get up because she was so weak and inert that she couldn't move. But I kept talking until we were out on the Appelplatz, and so we lived through another day. What is the truth? Who knows. In *Penguin Island*, one of my favourite books, Anatole France writes that it requires a distance of two hundred years to know with any certainty what really happened, and he may be right, if what interests you can be found in the records. But what about our story? Probably, both versions are true.

Anikó in 1990.

Anikó and I have our own special Kaddish.[3] We recite it every time we meet. It consists of us saying out loud the names of the people we remember. We conjure up the streets of Debrecen and, going from house to house, we conjure up those who once lived there just as we remember them.

Part of our method of self-preservation was to keep up each other's hope that someday we'd amount to something. We talked to each other about what we'd study once we were free. We took it very seriously, and we believed in it, too.

It was extremely important that we could look to the future and forge plans for ourselves. Lili and of course Klári as well wanted to continue their studies. Klári dreamed of high school, while Lili was thinking of university education, and they both achieved the latter. Klári eventually became program director at the Hungarian State Radio, and Lili retired as chief consultant to the National Bureau of Statistics. If only we'd known back in Allendorf!

Anikó was talented in many areas and could have become anything, but she was most attracted to the fine arts. In Allendorf, she made things out of clay. She fashioned a piano for my birthday from the wick she stole from the mouth-cavity purse of a grenade. Later on, in civilian life, she became an outstanding sculptor. Her works are highly imaginative. In a public space in Huntington near New York, there's a menorah by her that is rooted in a tree with branches that light up. Her many students adore her. In 2004 she received a commission from the Hungarian Ministry of Culture to fashion a memorial for the twenty-fifth anniversary of Sándor Márai's[4] death, which I saw in San Francisco, where Márai died. I wanted to be a pianist, but by the time the opportunity presented itself, it turned out that I could no longer sit.

In Allendorf, we came up with the idea of putting on plays for our own entertainment. It was a good way to occupy ourselves. In Auschwitz there was an orchestra that played the "Circus March"

---

3 Kaddish: Here it refers to the Jewish mourning prayer to be recited for the dead.
4 Sándor Márai (1900–1989), Hungarian writer and memoirist, best known for his novel *Ambers*. He emigrated from Hungary in 1948 and lived for the rest of his life in San Diego.

by Fučik, who, judging by his name, was a Czech composer. Every morning and every evening, those going off to work or returning from work marched into their respective camps to this music, whose strains filtered into our camp as well. In Allendorf, we had to rely on our ingenuity and willingness to have fun, which luckily didn't abandon us entirely.

The first performance was organized by Erzsi Brodt and her team, not ours. Right at the beginning, when we still felt the closeness of Auschwitz (and so it has remained to this day), the Hauptscharführer announced a noble competition to lift our spirits. We were allowed to put on something cheerful.

Erzsi Brodt wore a white blouse with puffed sleeved improvised from paper she got from the Revier, while the players' handkerchiefs served as stomachers. They pulled threads out of their blankets and – a veritable miracle – they managed to beg or borrow a needle, and turned their towels into skirts decorated with densely sewn-on leaves. They pinned the small yellow flowers of the ubiquitous and indestructible dandelions on their chests and in what little hair they had, and they danced and danced. It was a joy to watch. They even sang a little folk ditty, and with this number they won the coveted prize of the camp commander, a pail of marmalade and ten servings of margarine.

Erzsi Brodt was also in another number. She did a grifter dance. She asked for cigarettes to go with it from the Hauptscharführer lording it over us in the first row. The cigarettes, which served as a prop, were later exchanged in the kitchen for extra bowls of soup.

Anikó and I took our chance to play theatre very seriously. The floor of the dining room served as the stage. We performed Shakespeare's *Antony and Cleopatra* rewritten for two players. We wore modern costumes made out of cement bags, coloured string, wire, and other similarly noble material. We also danced to Boccherini's Minuet, and a humming chorus was the orchestra. If Puccini could get away with it, so could we. We wore appropriate costumes for this production as well. I even organized my own folk song choir.

We also put on a performance of "Snow White and the Seven Dwarfs." The seven tallest girls were the seven dwarfs. Snow White was played by Gabi, whom everyone loved, and who was, to put it politely, a professional bar singer. As a matter of fact, she had a pleasant, deep, sultry voice, like Katalin Karády,[5] whom all singers tried to imitate at the time. She made our lives bearable again and again with her singing. As the seven dwarfs we recited short couplets slighting the Germans, so that everybody laughed fit to burst, except the Germans, of course. Our interpreter told them that we were using untranslatable puns.

These performances meant lots of work, which proved therapeutic. For one thing, we had to figure out what to put on, then we had to change the text, the number of characters, and what have you, to accord with our possibilities. The "expensive" costumes had to be designed, too, and what was no small feat, they had to be made. The plays had to be directed, a playbill prepared, and so on.

In a place like the camp, even women will resort to rough talk now and then. Having spent so much time on a farm, I knew what my grandfather wanted when he said someone should bring him a pizzle, and I knew exactly which part of the bull he was referring to. However, it was only in the camp that my four-letter-word vocabulary was greatly enhanced. I also learned some Yiddish to go along with it.

Gabi, Snow White, had a sort of authority, and was a true original. After all, she knew a thing or two about people.

Anikó, the five Gärtner sisters, and nine other girls and women were quartered in the smallest room, sixteen of us on eight double bunk beds. Gabi christened our room the room for young ladies. She did not mean it in a sarcastic way, though. In fact, she even acted as our patron. She tried to save us from the rough language around us, kept our spirits up, and watched over us like a mother hen, and we loved her for it. When the camp was liberated – for the cat will always come out of the bag – she opened, as she said, her "office" once again, but we continued to love her. So it was a great disappointment to us that after we came back to Hungary she wouldn't recognize any of us and refused to talk to us. All the same, I think of her lovingly and am sorry that she disappeared from my life.

---

5 Katalin Karády (1910–1990), Hungarian actress and singer, the leading movie star of the interwar period, often compared to Marlene Dietrich.

Three of the five Gärtner sisters are on the right, with the author in the middle of the back row. The photograph was taken at our reunion in Stadtallendorf in 1990 in front of Heini Kurz's house.

The Gärtner sisters were ideal roommates. There were five of them, and they formed their own line of five: Erzsike, Ica, Klári, Adél, and Kati. Two of the five, Erzsike and Ica, were already married. The Gärtner sisters were very close and never fought. They were a good example to the rest of us, and incredible as it may sound, the sixteen of us in that small room never had a fight either. In a women's camp this was a rarity. We were dependent on each other and tried very hard to get along.

The five of us – my row of five – loved and respected the Gärtner sisters because they were always willing to help. They were big girls in our eyes, and they knew about life. Each had a trade. They were all good seamstresses except for Ica, who was a photographer. I first heard about Zionism from them, since they were all enthusiastic Zionists. I also first heard the word "aliya"[6] from them. After the camp was liberated, four of them went to Israel, while Ica went to the US. They were my extended family, a feeling that has lasted to this day. After the camp was liberated, I lived with them in various places. They were unselfish and sewed clothes for the others, myself included.

After we left the camp, we first made clothes for ourselves from all sorts of scraps, including duvet covers that had seen better days and had on them, in Gothic lettering in the shape of a wreath, "Good Night, Good Night," but of course that didn't stop us from wearing the clothes made from them during the day.

Kati Gärtner remembers one funny incident when after our liberation we went to one of the nearby villages to buy material for clothes. The German merchant didn't want to serve us and called for a German policeman, who threw us out of the shop. Well, that was all we needed! We called a policeman ourselves, an American, who now proceeded to liberate the German merchant from half his stock, and before long we had pink blouses, blue skirts, and so on. The Gärtner girls made me a warm skirt out of an old brown striped blanket. It is now on display at the Documentation and Information Centre in Stadtallendorf, in its very own showcase!

Kati also remembers that, though our lodgings had a sign saying "Off Limits to American Soldiers," the sign acted more like a call to action than an interdiction. When the US Army couldn't get the better of its baser instincts, it went looking for adventure, and before long, it found us. This is how it came about that once, when a handful of American patriots showed up on our doorstep, we somehow managed to explain to them who we were and why we

---

6 Aliya (Hebrew): literally "ascent," it came to mean the immigration of Jews from the diaspora to Israel.

were there, and the following day they showed up with a gigantic package of food as a way of apologizing!

Ilon Katz from Debrecen was also a great help to us. She was a deeply religious woman with black hair, sparkling eyes, and a small, well-proportioned physique, like a brunette doll. In Auschwitz, when we came out of the baths and they threw a piece of rag at each of us to wear, when her turn came there was nothing left, and she stood there naked as the day she was born. I will never forget the grotesqueness of the situation, because in Auschwitz there was no human dignity, and we were made to walk up and down in front of the selection committee and the whole world as much as it pleased our captors. Yet the way Ilon stood there naked, she was the embodiment of human dignity.

Ilon was the best informed of all of us. She knew from a most reliable source that the war would end tomorrow, or if not tomorrow, then the day after. She had it on good authority. She also knew that the day after the day after tomorrow we would all be going home, where everything would be just as we'd left it before we were sent to the ghetto, and our families would be waiting for us with open arms. She kept us from despair, and we wanted desperately to believe her. Her words were our one hope.

Ilon was a Blockälteste, and since she was deeply and sincerely religious herself, the other deeply religious girls and women gathered around her. Ilon was closer to a Yiddishe mame[7] than a Blockälteste. She always protested that her team was given the hardest work, and she stood up to the Hauptscharführer – a real Yiddishe "azes ponem."[8] "Who do you think you are?" screamed the Hauptscharführer. "I'm putting up with you only as long as I need you, so shut your mouth!" And Ilon did, but not for long.

Ilon also had a gift for resolving situations. Once two very religious young girls were crying over their microscopic piece of meat when Ilon found them. As it turned out, they had multiple reasons for their tears: they didn't know what kind of meat it was, probably treif, but they couldn't resist and ate it, and to add insult

---

7 The stereotypical figure of the overly protective Jewish mother.
8 Azes ponem (Yiddish): impertinent, cheeky.

to injury, they even liked it, which was a great sin. But Ilon came to the rescue. "My dear girls," said Ilon. "You're doing very hard work. You must eat what they give you because you must keep your strength up. Treif or not, it's meat, so eat it without tears, and if that's a sin, I'll take it upon myself. So you go on eating."

The whip that Ilon was given when she was appointed Blockälteste, and which, needless to say, she never used, is now on display at the Documentation and Information Centre at Allendorf.

Hauptscharführer Adolf Wuttke, the camp commander, was transferred to our camp from Buchenwald. It was said that in Buchenwald he was just as cruel as the other SS men. He was of middle age, and, as we learned, was the father of three daughters. His deputy, Ernst Schulte, was young and handsome. We called him "Bel Ami" and hated him with all our hearts. He made our life miserable every chance he got.

What prompted Wuttke to act like a human being in certain situations is a mystery. Maybe there was some human feeling left in him. Or maybe he realized that Germany had lost the war and it was just a matter of time before he'd be called to account for his actions. Be that as it may, he didn't allow his men to beat us for no reason, on major Jewish holidays he gave the day off to those who were observant, and he didn't make our Klári do physical work at the munitions plant. Klári was made a Stubendienst instead, which literally means "room servant." At the munitions plant there was a small room next to the dressing rooms, where her job was to warm up and portion out the food we took along with us from camp. Theoretically she should have also carried the big pot or at least half of it, but considering her physical condition, even the ladle was too much for her. Day by day she grew more and more transparent. But there was always someone willing to carry the food for her.

When we reached the munitions plant, we changed into our overalls and left Klári alone. Though we appeared for lunch or dinner, still, Klári spent at least seven hours per shift all by herself, and at an appreciable distance from us and indeed from everything. She was not allowed to leave her place and come after us to the workshop. She spent her time being afraid, always afraid. Being in a constant state of fear took years off her life. At a time when her young body called for a diet rich in fruit, vegetables, vitamins, and

minerals to strengthen her bones, she didn't even get enough calories to keep her undernourished weight steady. She ate her cattle
turnip along with us, a veritable delicacy. When we were liberated,
she weighed less than thirty-five kilograms.

The upshot of what she'd gone through showed itself after our
liberation. In no time at all, she became prey to various illnesses.
But she lived a full life. She had responsible work, gave birth to
children, and became a beloved grandmother. When the world
began to pale around her, she looked death heroically in the eye.
She was the youngest among us and should have outlived us.

After suffering through a cold night, shivering on the Appelplatz at dawn, and trudging along the forest path in driving snow,
we arrived at the cold and draughty munitions plant. We were not
allowed to leave our station, and if we had to, we were accompanied by our ladies' companions, the SS Aufseherins.

To ensure the quality of work was the responsibility of German
overseers, who taught us the basic minimum we needed in order
to manufacture the products without harming ourselves, or
anything else, for that matter. My first overseer hardly reached
above my waist. He was supposed to be a clown by profession,
but I always doubted it because the clowns I knew were humorous, quick-witted, and kind. Not so my overseer. He lacked at
least thirty centimetres to make him happy. Of these I had at least
twenty, and he took the insult out on me. He considered my arms
and legs sticking out of my overalls highly amusing. "Why don't
you tie your legs into knots so they don't stick out?" came the guf-
fawing advice, whereas he'd have probably given half his kingdom if he could have turned out taller himself. As luck would have
it, he was replaced by Peter, our Peter.

Peter was as huge as a gorilla, but he had the expression of an
angel. His voice was strong enough to fill up a room, any room. He
took advantage of this phenomenon and he screamed and shouted
so we'd know he was approaching, because he was incapable of
forcing us to do inhuman labour, even though that was his job.
When we heard him shout, we pulled ourselves together and
worked hard so he wouldn't have to answer for us. Peter came,
screamed, shouted, looked around, and meanwhile, as if completely by accident, he dropped the sandwich that they'd packed

for him at home, or else a couple of minuscule, disconsolate green apples would fall out of his pocket. Apples that small and wasted are not even known in Hungary, but to us they were beautiful and helpful beyond measure.

In 1990, during our week-long meeting, I looked for Peter in vain. In 2004, in honour of the fiftieth anniversary of our liberation, the Documentation and Information Centre of Stadtallendorf published the German original of this book, which I first wrote in that language. I was invited to the book launch and was asked by the Centre to do a number of readings. On one such occasion, I read what I'd written about Peter, and a couple of days later his daughter looked me up. She told me that she was a little girl at the time, but she remembered how scared her mother was that Peter's kindness to us would be discovered. It would have had dire consequences for every member of his family.

As for me, I was always cold. Being cold is my prerogative, because ever since I can remember I was and continue to be always cold, and I catch cold easily. When I was small, this began with my mother taking a look at me and announcing, "The child is running a low fever." She placed a hand on my forehead, they stuck a thermometer under my armpit, and wouldn't you know, I did have a bit of fever. I hated it desperately, because they put me in bed, and no matter how long it took, they wouldn't let me get up until my temperature was down. Even if it took months.

It was the same when I was admitted to the "Luthy," the Lutheran elementary school in Debrecen, because that was closest to our house. Time passed, but not so my low-grade fever. Luckily, the school had an excellent principal, Uncle Sándor Elefánty. Ovidius Naso (Ovidius of the Big Nose) didn't have a more fitting name. When he stopped in the doorway, he filled it up completely. Anyway, taking his clue from the example of Mohammed and the mountain, instead of me going to school, Uncle Elefánty came every afternoon to me after school, huge of bulk and smiling. He sat by the side of my little bed and poured the knowledge for the day inside me.

When Uncle Elefánty settled in his chair – like a cloud on the mountain peak – the chair gave a painful cry and a loud creak. I watched with growing concern as the sound of the creaking became louder by the day. I even asked my mother what I should do if the chair collapsed under Uncle Elefánty's elephantine weight. "Don't be silly, the chair won't break. Besides, remember that a polite little girl like you does not laugh when someone gets into trouble but feels sorry for them and helps them," my mother instructed me.

Needless to say, the moment came when the chair couldn't resist any longer, gave a last sigh, and as its joints fell apart it breathed its last, while Uncle Elefánty lay by my bed with his legs, covered in colourful socks, sawing the air, clearly with the intent to amuse me as much as he could. In response, I obligingly laughed fit to burst. A good thing I didn't clap my hands! Luckily, no ill befell Uncle Elefánty, and being a teacher to the core, he didn't take offence.

Uncle Elefánty and the other teachers like him, men and women both, were in possession of a great treasure – a sense of vocation. Back then we learned to write by combining every sound with a movement. The sound we made, the gesture that accompanied it, and the sound-picture on the page were simultaneously stored in various recesses of our brain. Also, from the very beginning, we wrote and learned to read in syllables, so by the time we reached the end of the alphabet, we knew how to separate words. Back then there was no dyslexia, dysgraphia, or the like. On the other hand, there were determined teachers. If a student didn't understand something, the teachers would explain it until he did. If he couldn't quite get the hang of writing, they would stay with him after school.

Teachers of Uncle Elefánty's ilk would have given back their teacher's diplomas rather than fail to teach a child to read and write. Times are changing, and there is even a theory to serve as a rationale.

I can't emphasize enough that for me the time spent at the Allendorf work camp was a time of miracles, because, while all winter I felt that I would freeze to death, I didn't get my usual yearly cold with the accompanying low-grade fever that would not relent. Unbelievable as it may sound, I didn't even cough, not once. Something inside kept me from catching cold in a situation where there were no handkerchiefs.

I felt again and again that I must survive every ordeal because then it would all be over faster. As I've mentioned before (not that it can be mentioned enough), we were poisoned nearly every day, and we frequently suffered from "gastric poisoning," as we called our feelings of nausea. When we also grew dizzy, could hardly stand on our feet, the world spinning around with us, and didn't even feel hungry any more, we were taken to the Revier, the camp hospital.

When I was a child, the word "Revier" had a nice ring to it. I must have been around ten when I first read the word in a poem by Heine or Witzenmann – woodland, meadow, or what today we'd call a nature reserve, in short, some pleasant place with trees that evokes a pleasant, lyrical feeling. But in Auschwitz the place that went by the same name was the most destitute, bleak, and dismal place on the face of the earth.

The labour camp at Allendorf also had a Revier where two inmates, the nurses Manci Wiesel and Judit Fürst, attempted the impossible – to cure the sick without any medicine or medical equipment. But in this Revier at least we were not in danger of being flung on top of a heap of corpses and being burned while still alive, which is what happened in Auschwitz.

Being taken to the Revier was paradise itself. There was no medicine or medical treatment, but there was plenty of rest. Anikó ended up in the Revier when a shell fell on her big toe while she was working. It was a great relief that she didn't have to go out to the Appelplatz and stand for Appel. She got a chance to pull herself together a bit and get some rest. I enjoyed a week of this heavenly privilege myself.

I've known for a long time that we must pay for everything. Even a slap in the face comes with a price tag. You must work to earn it. Fate handed me the privilege of safeguarding the bread for my row of five. In the morning, when we got our bread, we immediately ate half of it, since we were starving. Still, we had enough presence of mind to save the other half of our portion. When we returned from work dead tired and our eyes were sunken from starvation, we desperately needed the comfort of a bit of bread. As conditions got worse and the one kilo of bread got smaller and smaller and as our rations in Allendorf went from one-third to one-fourth, and eventually to one-fifth of a loaf, our bit of saved bread started disappearing. So it was a veritable relief for our row of five that during the week that I was lying in the Revier, we didn't have to be afraid that our bread would disappear, because I could keep an eye on it.

Had I ever done something mean or despicable, had I killed a man, or stolen anything or cheated, the punishment couldn't have been harsher. While I was on the verge of starvation, the bread for my row was under my pillow. The others were working. They were nowhere near their bread. But I was. I just had to reach out for it. I couldn't touch it, of course, not even my own portion, because the ritual for passing it around could not be violated. If ever I had an enemy or wanted something very, very bad to happen to someone, I'd wish them to be in my shoes at that time. To this day, I don't know how I managed to stand it.

Our camp was not bombed. The only small-size incendiary bomb that hit us struck the SS barrack. Our first thoughts went to our saved bits of bread. We ran to our locker and wolfed down the next day's rations. If we must die, at least we'll die with our bread in our mouths! No point leaving it to anyone else. After that, when the air raid sounded, the SS came running to our barrack. They were convinced that the bomb had been aimed at the SS barrack on purpose, which later turned out not to be the case. But it felt good, seeing their fear.

The humiliation is not something one can ever get used to or forget, so I don't even try. A Häftling is only a number. She wears it on her clothes. She has no name. She came from nothing and is headed for the gas chamber. She has nothing she can call her own except her limited bit of time – no present, no past, no future. Anyone, an SS Aufseherin, a Wehrmacht soldier from the guard, a foreman from the munitions plant, practically any German, in fact, can slap or kick her, abuse, revile, or curse her with or without cause. He can set his dog on her, can force her to do work that is inhuman. In short, he can do with her as he or she likes. The Häftling is not a human being. On the other hand, the greater the outer pressure, the greater the inner resistance. Despite all odds, we did not lose our humanity. We held our heads high, held our cutlery as we did at home, washed every day, brushed our teeth, and talked to each other just as we had back home. In spite of the circumstances, we respected and trusted one another, and we trusted our future as well. This is why we survived the camp. This is why we made it back home.

Sheepfold. Until our reunion in 1990, when I saw Allendorf again, I thought that there was only one sheepfold on the road between Allendorf and Ziegenhain, "my" sheepfold, in which I was liberated. Then I learned that there are hundreds of sheepfolds, but I wouldn't give up till I found my own.

My Sheepfold

Just as Endre Ady's fall came sneaking into Paris,[1] so did numerous signs signalling the end of the war come sneaking into our camp, our munitions plant, the path through the woods, the Appelplatz, everywhere, near and far, in March 1945.

What we felt most acutely was the reduction in our portion of bread from one-quarter to one-fifth of a small loaf, whereas even the quarter wasn't enough for anything. At the same time, the potatoes and minuscule bits of meat – in short, everything with the exception of the cattle-turnip – disappeared from our menu. Our condition was also deteriorating as we were perilously approaching the Muselmann state, as it was called in Auschwitz, and whose last station was the crematorium. Had the advance of the Allied forces in Western Germany been delayed, we'd have saved the Third Reich the cost of the gas, because we'd have died of starvation. We didn't know then that the crematoria at Auschwitz had already been blown up in anticipation of the advancing Soviet troops. We also didn't know that in Buchenwald, just a couple of kilometres from us, the crematorium, which had been fashioned according to the same blueprint as the one in Auschwitz, was working overtime. It is still standing there, undamaged. You can go see it.

---

1 Endre Ady (1877–1919), the leading Hungarian Modernist poet of the early twentieth century. One of his famous poems begins with the line, "Fall came sneaking into Paris yesterday."

At least every other year I make a pilgrimage to Buchenwald, because in Buchenwald I re-experience the mood of Auschwitz. In Buchenwald, I relive everything that happened to me in 1944 in Auschwitz. In Buchenwald, every stone, every dilapidated barrack still cries out to me. I didn't make it to the crematorium back then, or I wouldn't be alive now. The chambers in front of the baths that I know so well, as well as the furnaces, were built by the same firm and according to the same blueprints as those in in Buchenwald. The firm's name was Topf & Söhne, Erfurt.

In the early 1950s there was a documentary film about the experiments with Zyklon B. The filmmakers illustrated the effect of the gas by using geese and showed how they suffered for minutes on end before they suffocated.

When I walk through the bleak rooms with their cement floors and walls in Buchenwald, I find myself in Auschwitz. I see my mother get undressed. I see my little sister as she holds my mother's hand. I see my cousin Boci as she presses her six-month-old baby boy Ferike to her breast. I hear the shouts of *los! los!* as they are driven to the baths. I imagine them waiting for the water after the unbearable ride in the cattle car. I see that at first they don't realize that it's not water that's coming from the showerheads. I see my mother's face as it hits her that they are being annihilated. I see them suffocating from the Zyklon B. I see my mother suffering through Gilike's death agony as well as her own. I see my mother hoisting Gilike up high because the poison, whose specific gravity is heavier than air, flows downward, and I see them cling to each other in their vain attempt to gasp for air. The tormenting image is not restricted to Buchenwald. I see it at other times as well.

As we quietly and steadily inched our way towards starvation in the spring of 1945, we followed events with a sense of satisfaction. They were worth hundreds of calories. For one thing, the munitions plant had run out of raw materials. It had happened gradually. One time there were no shells to fill, another time the wagon didn't come, or there were no crates to pack the shells. On the other hand, there was so much trinitro-toluol and saltpetre stacked outside that they were still battling the environmental damage in 2004, and the detoxification of the underground water in Stadtallendorf cost millions of marks.

There was no work, so we milled around the plant sweeping, cleaning up, putting things in order. Luckily, there was still hot water, one of the factors that contributed to our survival, because, while in other camps the lice spread typhoid fever and tens of thousands of prisoners died at the last moment because they could not wash, we could shower in hot water every day. We had no lice, and we had no infectious diseases. Then one morning we dragged ourselves to the plant, and in the workshop where I worked, high up, just under the ceiling, we spotted the following, written in huge letters: NOUS SOMMES FRANÇAISES, NOUS RESTERONS FRANÇAISES, ET NOUS TRIOMPHONS DES BOCHES![2]

This signalled the end.

There were French, Belgian, Dutch, and Italian "free" workers (Freiarbeiters) in the plant. They were classified as "free" because they hadn't been dragged to Germany; for them, working in Germany was simply compulsory. Also, they were free to move about within a thirty-kilometre area. We learned about what was really happening from them. Although it was strictly forbidden to talk to them, we always found a way.

Needless to say, it was also forbidden to talk to the Russian POWs, who were at the bottom of the hierarchy of prisoners, not to mention that they were treated in violation of the Geneva Convention. Whatever the Germans used to torment us was applied many times over to the Russians, whom they beat and humiliated without any rhyme or reason whatsoever. For their part, the Russians were a proud bunch. They never forgot that they were fighting for Stalin and the Homeland here as well. They had to place the wrapped shells on a conveyor belt, which kept breaking down. They had a hand in this, needless to say. They sabotaged it, even though they knew they'd be beaten within an inch of their lives. Because they were fighting for Stalin and the Homeland.

After the liberation, the camp where the Soviet soldiers were kept was emptied out first. How we envied them! In less than ten

---

2 "We are French, we shall remain French, and will vanquish the Krauts!"

days, they would be going home! They brought the packages they received from the Red Cross over to our camp. After all, they didn't need them. They were headed home to their mothers, fathers, brothers, sweethearts, and wives.

It wasn't until I read Alexander Solzhenitsyn's eye-opening *Gulag Archipelago* many years later that I learned that the Soviet POWs whom I loved, respected, and commiserated with were sent to prison camps upon their arrival in their beloved homeland. Those who had spent as much time in a capitalist country among capitalists as the unfortunate Soviet POWs, doing slave labour for the German munitions industry, were clearly contaminated by capitalist ideology, and such dangerous thoughts must be cleared out of their heads, lest they contaminate their highly ethical Soviet environment as well. So what if they should perish in the process? So much the better. The Soviet Union is a large country, with many inhabitants, and a country's foremost treasure is its people. And a principle is a principle.

Since January 1945 we'd been watching the small lightning flashes in the evening and at night that signalled the bombing of Kassel. As far as we could tell, the small lightning flashes were gradually approaching, which meant that they were dropping bombs not just on Kassel but in its vicinity as well. The hum and drone of the American Liberators – the loveliest sound to which one can lower one's head on a pillow – could be heard with increasing frequency, and lasted longer and longer into the night. I can tell the sound of a Liberator to this day. I can tell it apart from a thousand other planes. (By the way, towards the end of the war, the British and Americans worked in shifts: the Brits flew during the day, the Americans by night. The aerial photograph of our camp was taken from a British fighter plane.)

We were restless and we were expectant, and we were restless and expectant on March 27, 1945 as well. On that day, we were not taken to the plant. We tried to guess what was afoot. The sound of the war with the muted rumble of the cannons was approaching, and the Allied planes flew overhead with increasing frequency. Then we were called to the Appelplatz off schedule, and there the Hauptscharführer announced that we were all going to leave the camp. I later learned the word that they used to describe the proce-dure: evacuation. They handed out our bread rations, one-fifth of a loaf per person – two hundred grams that were going to have to last us four days, though at the time we didn't know this.

It had already grown dark when the main gate of the Münch-mühle camp at Allendorf was opened and everyone – the one thousand prisoners, the camp commanders, the SS Aufseherins, the Wehrmacht guards, even the dogs – left, and we took off, not knowing where.

I'd depleted my reserves of energy by then and could hardly drag myself along the short, pleasant stroll through the woods that used to take us to the munitions factory and back. My legs felt as heavy as lead. In that freezing night in March, moving my legs, step by step, was unbearably painful. The strain I felt was as great as if I had to push Gellért Hill into the Danube. Each step meant yet another wound, as the wooden clogs I wore without socks ate into my flesh, wherever they came into contact with my feet. But we kept marching. The cook, the SS Zugsführer,[3] was waving his revolver, threatening to shoot anyone who lagged behind. We continued marching on and on with no end in sight, since instead of walking along straight roads, we took side paths across the fields and meadows. But we marched on, barely dragging ourselves. Then we stopped at last, and I saw the open door of a sheepfold and smelled the familiar smell of sheep. What joy! That smell transported me back home to the farm. I collapsed on the hay in a near-faint. It was warm, and I snuggled into it.

On March 28, 1945, planes zapped over our heads all day long, fighting each other as we sat in the hay, trembling with fear. We didn't dare leave the sheepfold. But when it was completely dark outside, we heard the familiar shout of *los! los!* Hurry, line up. So we're moving on, we thought.

I couldn't get to my feet. I was so weak I could not stand or straighten up. I had used up my last reserves of willpower to sur-vive the march of the night before so I wouldn't lag behind. And

---

3 SS Zugsführer (German): roughly the equivalent of a platoon commander.

now I had reached the outer limits of my endurance. I couldn't even lift my little finger. When you reach that point, you have no more willpower. Nothing matters. The world is at a distance, and it is vague and unsteady. All you know is that you want to be left in peace. You do not want to move or even think. You wouldn't be capable of it, anyway. Nothing matters any more. You couldn't care less about anything. You don't even know any more who you are or who you once might have been.

Besides, I couldn't slip my feet inside the wooden clogs any-more because they were covered with untold wounds and blisters, so I couldn't have walked if I tried. And yet, I managed to pull myself free of the hay and the fold, but then, in all the shouting and commotion, I couldn't find my row of five, so I went and stood on the right of the last row. The guard and a dog stood next to me.

The sheepfold was in the middle of a field. When I took it in, the scene was idyllic. A small spring with thin little trees and shrubs on its bank trickled in front of the fold, so we had to cross a lovely little wooden bridge. The picture was like my *ex libris* from my childhood, which showed my name and a little girl crossing a wooden bridge in the moonlight.[4] But on this particular wooden bridge a row of five were supposed to pass at once, whereas it was too narrow to accommodate it. When the second row and the rows behind them reached the bridge, they created a bottleneck, and confusion ensued. The guard standing next to me noticed and went up to the front with his dog so he could reinstate order and organize a smooth passage across the bridge.

The couple of steps I had to take from the fold to the last row exhausted my final reserves. I had no energy left for anything. I knew that I couldn't take another step, not one, and that nothing in the world mattered. Nothing. There was only one thing I could still manage to do – to lie down and remain motionless.

I sat down on the grass.

The guard up front reinstated order and the column continued, but I just sat in the grass, waiting for the guard to come for me and

---

4 *Ex libris* is the name plate placed in one's books. "Wooden bridge" is the literal translation of the author's family name, Fahidi.

scream at me to force me to get up, but I didn't care about anything anymore. I felt that I had reached the end of my road.

I was still sitting in the grass when the others marched on. I didn't even hear them anymore.

I don't know how long I sat there, whether it was for a few seconds or a few minutes, but the guard did not come for me.

And then it suddenly dawned on me that I was sitting in the middle of a strange German field all alone with the full moon above, its white rays illuminating me.

The realization that I was free did not penetrate the recesses of my mind!

I felt neither joy nor fear. I felt only that I must snuggle into the nice warm hay, and crawled back to the fold. I progressed on all fours, not only because I didn't have enough strength to stand up, but also because, thanks to the full moon, I would have been a clear target. It wasn't until I was well hidden in the hay that I was overcome with fear. I heard my heart pounding as it tried to knock free of my chest, and I asked myself what I was doing in Germany in a sheepfold at the end of the war, in the midst of bombing, cannon fire, and aerial battles. Once the sun came up, strangers would arrive, I thought. But who? SS soldiers? And what will I say to them about who I am, where I came from, and what I was doing here? What will become of me? Will they kill me now that the war is almost over?

And just then, the hay stirred at the other end of the sheepfold. One of my fellow inmates hadn't gone outside to begin with.

We had a busy night. About twenty-five of my friends came back to the fold in small groups, including, luckily, the five Gärtner sisters, with whom I'd shared a room in the camp. The sound of battle was getting closer now, and as we sat in the hay, we feared for our lives. Small windows ran along the sides of the fold at eye level. We organized a watch for all four sides and took turns.

First thing next morning, the shepherd appeared. We were alarmed, but it soon turned out that he was not right in the head, so we told him that we were waiting for a truck to pick us up. We kept telling him the same story for four days, but luckily he didn't seem to mind our presence.

Two events of note took place. At sundown of the second day, two German soldiers came towards the fold. They were fully armed, with their boots hanging round their necks. They were so close that we could hear what they were saying. We sat in the hay too scared even to breathe.

"Let's not go in," one of them said, "it's not dark yet. We might as well go on." And they did.

On March 30, 1945, the third day, we were still sitting in the hay in the fold. The two hundred grams of bread we had been given on the 27th had long since been gone, and there was no water. We had all come from Auschwitz, so we were well trained in going thirsty. We also learned by the side of the marshland in Auschwitz not to drink from water we were not familiar with. Though the small stream was trickling near the fold, we knew that the nearby munitions plant had poisoned all the running water, so we didn't dare touch it.

I was on duty by one of the windows when a familiar face appeared on the other side of the fold. It was our Eidechser![5] A lanky young man from Holland, a free worker, drove the electric trundle in the plant. We called the trundle the lizard because it moved about so quickly with its load of small objects. He said that the war would end within minutes, but it would be safer for us to stay in the fold. He also said that he would bring us some potatoes.

On March 31, 1945, the fourth day, we were waiting for the potatoes, but we never got them. On the other hand, in the windows and on the rooftops of the houses in the surrounding villages, people began waving white sheets. We decided that as soon as it got dark, we would go to the nearest village, because we couldn't take the starvation and the thirst any more. Then at sundown, we saw tanks with five-pointed white stars. They were heading straight for the fold.

We quickly climbed out of the hay, and, afraid that they might fire at the fold thinking that it contained fleeing German soldiers, we went outside and lined up in front. The tanks continued approaching, but strangely enough, we were no longer afraid.

Then the tanks reached us. They were driven by black Americans, who were the advance guard. The white Americans arrived

5 Eidechser (German): lizard.

two days later, when the air was clear. American democracy, it seems, was just like the others. All people are equal, but the whites are more equal than the non-whites.

These soldiers had never seen a German concentration camp, or German prisoners, Häftlings. We stood in front of the fold in a line, swaying uncertainly on our feet, in rags, a group of living ghosts, with lemon-yellow skin, a couple of centimetres of purple hair, and, on our faces, clear indications of four days of thirst and starvation. The sight took the soldiers by surprise. They saw right away that they would not be needing their firearms.

It took a long time to make them understand that we were human beings just like them, even if we didn't look it. We were not convicted criminals, we hadn't stolen or cheated or killed anyone. They couldn't understand what crime we'd committed that got us into the state we were in, because anyone who has been punished as harshly as us must have been responsible for grave crimes against society.

Meanwhile, it had got dark, and the temperature dropped. I was shivering with cold. One of the soldiers took off his sweater and put it on me. I still have it as living proof of empathy and humanity.

We started in the direction of the village with the white sheets. We stopped at the first house and rang the bell. What a peacetime gesture! Could there still be a house with a fence and a bell by the gate that you can press and it actually rings? A frightened peasant woman came to open the gate. The American soldier who was heading our group let her know in no uncertain terms that she'd better take us in, feed us, and provide a roof over our heads.

When the gate opened, I ran inside the house like one demented. In the twinkling of an eye I was full of energy again. I was driven by hunger and thirst. The way I made straight for the kitchen, you'd think I was a regular visitor to the house, and the way I made straight for the kitchen window and grabbed the bowl of boiled potatoes sitting on the sill, probably to cool off, you'd think I was familiar with the customs of the lady of the house.

I can't put into words what came over me. My heart was beating wildly, and I was shaking with excitement. During the past nine months, if we unexpectedly came into possession of some

Heini Kurz, 1945.

food, we always put it aside and ate it *together*. Now a whole bowl of potatoes was in front of me, and I stuffed them into my mouth with both hands so that I nearly gagged. By the time the others reached the kitchen, I was wiping away my tears, because even my tears started flowing from the effort of gobbling down the potatoes. How many of my unfortunate fellow inmates died because they stuffed themselves to bursting, not with potatoes but with meat or other food that people normally eat every day? Our intestines, atrophied and unused to eating anything fit for human beings, could not bear such a burden and stopped functioning. Some inmates who had suffered and survived the camps and the forced labour ate themselves to death as soon as they were free. A horrible, horrible tragedy.

It wasn't until I regained my senses and felt the smell of cleanliness around me – the kitchen with signs of cooking and the rooms in which people lived in a manner fit for human beings – that

I understood my own situation, the dirty, filthy state I was in and the gossamer thread that tied me to the world of the living. But not until then. An hour before the American tanks had arrived, I couldn't have cared less if that gossamer thread were to snap. But with the potato in my stomach, I held on to that thread for dear life, and I felt that it was as strong as the strongest rope. But I also felt the abyss that divided me from a life of normalcy.

For the first time, I felt the deep uprootedness that had been with me ever since my deportation, when I was separated from my parents and family, a feeling of uprootedness that is still my constant companion and will remain so as long as I live. It is one of the trademarks of life after Auschwitz. You cannot live long enough to get over it. Not only did I lose nearly all of my relatives; they don't even have graves. There is nowhere I can place a piece of stone in their memory. There is no grave that is my mother's and my father's. I take my mother lilies of the valley for her birthday on March 10 only in spirit. My father always gave her lilies of the valley. They were her favourite flower. I also buy her primroses every August as long as they are available, because my parents were married on August 24, 1924, and my mother's bridal bouquet was composed of primroses. From then on, my father always gave my mother primroses in celebration of their wedding anniversary.

We learned that the house where we were staying and where we would continue to stay for a couple of weeks more after the war was located on Schulstrasse in Ziegenhain and belonged to the Kurz family. The head of the family had died in the war. The humble farm and the house were kept in exemplary order by Frau Kurz. Her son, Heini Kurz, who today owns the house, was sixteen at the time. He was clearly moved by our condition. His head had been stuffed with Nazi propaganda, and suddenly there we were, the tangible products of Nazism, and we were the way we were, and not the way they said we were.

In 1990, when I found "my" sheepfold on the occasion of that unforgettable reunion week, we went to visit Heini Kurz as well. Ziegenhain did not exist any more. The small village had metamorphosed into the neat little town of Schwalmstadt. But the Kurz house was still standing on Schulstrasse, beautifully renovated. As soon as the five Gärtner sisters and I walked into the house, Heini called us by our names. He remembered us. He had raised his children, had become a grandfather, and had worked for years in Africa.

In April and May of 1945, while we were regaining our physical strength, we did not notice the passing of time. Our energy was spent building muscle and fat tissue between our bones and skin. As it generally happened in such cases, after so much starvation, we grew excessively fat and bloated. At first we could not stop eating. The American troops felt it their duty to make sure that we were well taken care of, and supplied us with mounds of quality foodstuffs that we couldn't and wouldn't resist. We felt there was much we had to make up for when it came to eating, and very soon we had regained our former pre-war weight.

On the night of March 28, 1945, when I crawled back into my sheepfold, my row of five continued their wandering and so I lost them, but I made friends with Magda Perlstein, who'd been hiding in the hay. It must be true that your name is your destiny, because Magda was a real pearl. When I bade goodbye to the Kurzes, Magda and I went to live in a small attic room above a grocery store. The house is no longer there, not even the street, both having fallen victim to town development in Stadtallendorf. The owner didn't like us one bit, unlike the Kurzes. The Gärtner sisters, who could always be depended upon, lived across the street, so we were reunited.

Magda was given the pet name Bodri or Curly, not only because her black hair formed a crown of curls around her face, but because a curly-haired dog is faithful and dependable. For one thing, she knew an American address, an aunt's or uncle's, and she knew it so well that if you woke her in the middle of the night, she'd tell you without making a mistake. She was later sent an affidavit, or entry permit, from this address. The other thing that was enviable about Magda was the fact that she found out that her brother Miklós had also survived deportation, and they met up in Germany. Even one of two such gifts of fate is a great boon. Either one means safety, you have somewhere to go to, you have a family, you have someone to cling to.

Curly, Olga, and I, June, 1945.

Magda and Miklós decided that Miklós would go home to look around, and then they would go to America. And as good as his word, Miklós went back home, was caught and taken for malenky robot,[6] a stint that usually took four to five years, with side trips to Siberia and the Gulag – provided you survived, of course. Luckily, Miklós survived and came back. After various trials and tribulations, in the wake of the revolution of 1956, he too ended up in America.

While Magda waited in America, she applied herself to her studies and became a nurse. All her working life she had only one place of employment. She was the assistant of a Hungarian doctor. Her son and daughter made her a happy grandmother. The

6 Malenky robot: literally, "a little work" (Russian). The popular name for the many cases of the abduction of able-bodied young men and women by the Red Army for forced labour.

older grandchildren have already turned out to be very gifted. Her oldest granddaughter will become a journalist, and she is already being published.

Under socialism, when it was ill advised to receive letters sent from the US, I broke off all my foreign relationships with the exception of my Israeli relatives. I lost track of Curly, too. Sometime in the 1980s, during the more liberal times of Kádár's goulash socialism, Bodri visited Budapest. She searched for me everywhere. It took her a while until she found my telephone number and called me. It was around midnight.

"Where are you, Curly, dear? I'm coming to get you," I said, and haven't let go of her hand since. Every year I look forward to the end of summer when she and Miklós visit Hungary. Her hair is not black any more, and neither is it curly, but her heart, her love, her loyalty, are just like they were – unaltered and eternal.

Meanwhile, it was June and July of 1945, time to look facts in the face. Lists were being circulated of people who had survived the various camps. As we listened to the news and read the newspapers, the dream world we had created for ourselves about our distant homes, our innocent pre-ghetto childhood, collapsed like a house of cards. It was time to decide: will I go home, or stay abroad? No one of my family was on any of the lists.

How can you separate your intellect and your feelings? You can't.

By the end of the war, it didn't take much brains to realize that there was no third side in Auschwitz. There were only two. You joined one and you died; you joined the other and you had a slight chance for survival. Those who were not on the other side were nowhere: my father, my mother, my little sister. I could not believe that Gilike was nowhere.

When I was a little girl and they asked me what I would like for a present, I always said that I would like a living doll, meaning a little brother or sister. I waited for eight years. Then one day my mother said that my wish would soon come true, and before long, they packed my toothbrush, my hairbrush, comb, pyjamas, and slippers, and moved me four houses down the street to our nice neighbour, Aunt Rezsinke. They said I wouldn't have to sleep over for more than two nights and by the time I got home, I'd have my living doll. But I didn't even have to stay for two nights, because the next morning Aunt Rezsinke woke me with a wide smile on her face and said that I could have my beautiful living doll now if we went home. I didn't even ask her for breakfast, only that she should take me home right away.

My mother was lying in bed, and I had never seen her so beautiful. Her face was radiant with happiness. My father was standing by the foot of the bed looking very content. And next to my mother was a rocking cradle, and in that cradle a real live doll, chubby as a Murillo angel and pink as a ripe peach. On top of her head there was a big cockscomb of bright red hair. She was gorgeous beyond my wildest dreams. She was in a deep, peaceful slumber. You could tell that she was inordinately satisfied with her situation in life.

I pulled my father aside, though to be truthful, I actually dragged him into the bathroom. I had something very serious to ask him, and it was for his ears only. Until that morning, I had the field to myself, I was their only child, the apple of their eye. I wanted this living doll very much and was very happy that she had arrived at last after having waited so long for her. But I needed to clarify my status, because I now had to share my rule with her. So I turned to my father. "Will it be all right for the child to use the familiar form of address with me?" Because from then on she was "the child" to me, too, a way for me to emphasize that I was there first. My father understood the seriousness of the question, and said "yes" in a very serious way.

My little sister was entered in the registry of births on April 24, 1933, the day of St George, as Ágnes Terézia Faludi. On the farm, this day signifies the beginning of life. It is the day that the sheep are driven out to pasture and the cattle are herded out to the alkali flats by Csikókút. The animals stay there until fall. There is no omen as favourable as being born on this day.

We were all very happy, but I felt that no one was happier than I. I was allowed to take the baby in my arms and rock her, to talk to her, to sing to her, to help when she was given her bath and her diapers were changed, and when she was being nursed. I was the big girl who is clever and can help; my mother needs me very much;

Gilike at three and five years of age.

considering the number of her chores, she couldn't possibly do without me. We even pushed the baby carriage together, proud as can be.

"The child" started babbling and cooing, and we babbled and cooed back at her. Ágnes, Ágika, we said endearingly, and after a while, Ágili, Gili, Gilike. And that was the name that stuck. My one and only Gilike, my precious.

She was exactly like me, except, for the time being, in a smaller edition. But there was nothing you couldn't do with her. For one thing, you could teach her exercises. We held frequent demonstrations for the family, and Gilike was getting more adroit by the day. She could already ride the swing without having to be pushed. She could do anything on the rings that I did. They said that we

My first personal ID after my liberation from camp.

walked on our hands more than on our feet. Gilike wasn't even five yet, but she was already a good swimmer. She played tennis with a small racquet. I had the best life of anyone, because I always had a playmate. We played badminton and handball, and we built sand castles. Gilike gave me everything due to an older sister – the same love and admiration I felt for my cousin Boci, who was eight years my senior.

Gilike must have been around six weeks old when her governess, Erna Riess, came to us from Vienna via the same au pair agency through which my parents had found Ruth Stein for me in 1928. Just like Ruth, Erna was a product of the Waldorf School. She was not yet eighteen at the time and didn't step off the train in a beautiful coat like Ruth. She wore a threadbare winter overcoat and carried a very small suitcase and a guitar with many colour-ful ribbons swept by the wind. Her thick honey-coloured hair was arranged in two flat buns over her ears. Erna was timid and very sweet. She played the guitar and sang, and I was happy to sing along with her. In no time at all, my mother seemed to have three daughters instead of two. Gilike loved her, too, and let us know it in no uncertain terms. The first word she uttered was not "mama." The first word she uttered was "Erna."

Erna grew up along with us under my mother's gentle guid-ing hand. She learned a lot of things she didn't have the chance to learn at home. Erna came from a poor family. My mother taught her manners, how to manage a household, how to dress and be socially at ease. When in 1943 Erna had to go home because her mother had died, instead of the little duckling that had come wob-bling to our home, the woman who left us was a real lady. She wept when she took her leave of us and promised to keep in touch. She didn't know how difficult it would be for her to keep her promise, but let it be said to her credit, she kept it.

A lot of time passed between 1945 and the 1950s. I don't believe in coincidences. When Erna thought of looking for me at the Alli-ance Française, she must have been guided by the power of Freud-ian hunch. As I've already mentioned, when I was an unskilled labourer I used to go to the language school's Budapest affiliate to warm up and to fill my lungs with pre-war scents. It was at the Alliance Française that Erna's letter reached me. In 1968, when she felt that it was safe to do so, she came to Budapest with her husband to wrap me in her arms. She was Mme Auberger by then. She lived in Arles, and had about six children. Her husband, a civil engineer, was president of the chamber of commerce of Arles. When we met we didn't know if we should laugh or cry. I returned her visit in 1975. She spoiled me rotten. During my one-week stay, she wanted to give me back everything she'd got from my mother.

As the spring of 1945 gradually turned to summer, my hair grew out. I read the lists of those who had survived, recorded in Ger-many with trembling hands. There were no names from my family. I started to force myself to get used to the idea that I had no living relatives left in the world. I could not conceive of going home and

not finding anyone there, and yet I had to go, it was the only way
to verify the fact. But most of all, I could not imagine that Gilike
would not be there. On the contrary. I imagined that I would be the
first one home and would wait for her, and she would soon appear.

In the summer of 1945, the American military police in the Hessen district was under the command of a captain by the name of
Dawning. He signed the ID paper in which it said that my permanent address is K.Z. (concentration camp) Auschwitz, and my
occupation is "ex-Häftling," meaning ex-convict. Today it is hanging on the wall of the museum in Stadtallendorf for all to see. So
much for what some Americans thought about human dignity. As
a matter of fact, except for our food, which they made sure was
more than adequate, they treated us in keeping with this view.
Dawning would not allow us to go home to Hungary, insisting
that it was full of Russians, so we might as well stay in Germany.
Finally we threatened to burn down his headquarters if he didn't
find us a train to take us home.

In October 1945 we finally took leave of our friends who decided
to stay in Germany or move on to Israel,[7] America, and so on. I
cried when I said goodbye to the Gärtner sisters, who were headed
for Israel. I didn't think I would ever see them again.

I found myself sitting inside a cattle car again. The trip seemed
never-ending. The wheels clattered unceasingly under us, and we
were on the train for weeks, since they delayed us at every station. I
celebrated my twentieth birthday in the wagon, just me and myself.
No one else knew about it. Those who would have celebrated with
me, my parents, my family, were long since dead. I couldn't help
thinking about the twentieth-birthday celebration they would have
planned for me, and what had become of it. I wanted desperately
to reach home and I wanted just as desperately never to reach it,
because as long as I'm en route, I thought, there is reason for hope.
Yet deep down I knew perfectly well that sooner or later I'd find
myself in Debrecen, and be confronted with reality.

On November 4, 1945, the day I reached Debrecen, the same
dirty-grey tattered clouds hung from the sky as on March 19, 1944,

7 Correctly: Palestine, as the state of Israel was not established until May 1948.

Gilike with Mari Vágó, 1940. (Gilike is on the right.)

the day the Wehrmacht occupied Hungary. When I looked at the sky, I felt as if I'd never left. But I had to look down, too. There I stood, at the station in Debrecen, everything in ruins around me, with not a stone left in place. Everything seemed unfamiliar. I had the impression that I'd never seen it before. On the way home, I looked at my uncle Tóni's house in Barna Street and found a heap of ruins. My heart beating wildly, I quickened my steps.

I ran past our house without knowing it.

I had already reached our neighbour's familiar gate when I realized that I should turn back, because the unrecognizable house I'd just passed was mine. As soon as I stopped in front of the gate, I understood that I would find nothing there. There was nothing left of our front garden that had been my mother's pride and joy; the flower beds, the carefully clipped boxwoods, the grapevines trailing up the walls were all gone. The garden had been hit by a bomb. Its proof, a deep hole, disfigured a neglected corner.

With my hand shaking, I rang the bell.

A stranger came to open the front gate. I said that this was my house and I had come home. He said he didn't care. It's theirs now, and there are more than ten people living there who belong to various families. There's no room for me. Good riddance.

That instant all my hopes faded and the harsh reality that I was now alone in the world gripped me by the throat. I had no one. No one.

According to the rules of Greek tragedy, fate always wins out. But you must earn your fate. You must commit crimes against humanity, archetypal crimes that horrify everyone, and so the end of the story serves to teach a lesson. But standing there dumbfounded in front of my own house, I couldn't help asking myself, what had I done, in accordance with the rules of Greek tragedy, to deserve this?

What you know with your brain you don't know with your heart. I knew that I had lost my parents. I could not accept it, of course, not even today, when in accordance with the laws of nature, they would be long dead. But the horrible, unjust manner of their deaths? Gilike's death in the gas chamber has left both my mind and my heart stunned. I kept hoping she'd return. In November of 1945, soon after my own return to Debrecen, my mother's younger sister Hédi saw my name on a list, but only mine, which told her that only I had survived. She sent someone for me and gave me asylum in her home in Érsekújvár in Czechoslovakia. I lost count of the times I crossed over to Hungary from there, answering the sudden urge to hurry back to Debrecen because this time I would find Gilike there.

When the regime change of 1989 made it possible for me to have my private business, I was issued a permit to work in foreign trade. The permit was issued by the Municipal Council of Budapest's Fifth District and had the serial number twenty-six. Once in the 1990s I exported 16,600 embroidered pieces to Finland. The registered trademark was Gili, and the logo was a little dancing girl with braids. This way her name was kept alive. I still feel that

I should send more messages out into the world because Gilike is out there somewhere, except I don't know where. But one day she will ring my doorbell and say, "It's been a long time. Let's do a cartwheel!"

In 2004 I happened to be in Germany when an ad appeared in a Budapest newspaper with the following words: "I am looking for Gilike's older sister from Debrecen. I was Gilike's girlfriend," along with a name and an Australian telephone number. Since I was away, on my return I found several messages on my answering machine from people who had read the ad. The name was unfamiliar to me, but by calling the Australian number, I was able to trace the ad to Marika Vágó. She had been a gorgeous little girl, the youngest member of the wonderful Vágó family, and really Gilike's close friend. They loved playing under the piano or the table, where they spent hours whispering. It was thanks to them that the grown-ups of their respective families became friends, too.

Like so many decent families with good names and spotless reputations, the Vágós also became the victims of socialism. Marika's father was imprisoned on trumped-up charges. Her mother suffered a nervous breakdown. Marika's sister died tragically at a young age, leaving a little boy behind. Marika ended up in jail herself. Later, she moved as far away from Hungary, the scene of her suffering, as she could. She even changed her name. And I didn't even get to see her when she finally visited Budapest. It wasn't in the cards for me. There are no coincidences.

Magda Perlstein, Heini Kurz, and I. Reunion Week, Stadtallendorf, 1999.

The Unforgettable Reunion Week

In 1989 every major newspaper in Hungary published an advertisement asking all those who had worked in the Allendorf munitions plant during the Second World War to contact the magistrate of Stadtallendorf.

We in Hungary were trained to forget our own Holocaust, or, if we couldn't, we learned that we shouldn't talk about it, or, if we must, at least not in public. All totalitarian states have certain things in common. A crow will not scratch out the eyes of another crow, and we obeyed and said nothing. No wonder. We wanted to be left in peace.

For most of us, modern Germany continued to be just as it had been in 1945, when we had left it: a fascist state where they'd killed our relatives and where we got off by a hair's breadth, where they tortured and humiliated us, that we remember only in our worst nightmares. When I read the advertisement, I thought what my former fellow Häftlings must have been thinking: What do they want from us, *even now?*

Living in Hungary, we couldn't possibly imagine the changes that had by then taken place in Germany, where the people confronted their past, where they had the courage to draw certain conclusions from it and the strength to admit their crimes. Time and again, history levels the charge of collective guilt against a people or a state, something post-war Germany accepted. Still, this irritates me. There is no collective guilt. You are guilty only if you have committed a crime. For the same reason, I find unacceptable

Interpreting for Mayor Manfred Vollmert during Reunion Week, October 25, 1990.

When I caught my first glimpse of the camp, Allendorf, 1990.

any religion that upholds the idea of original sin. As far as I'm concerned, every human being is born good, beautiful, and innocent,
and starts life with a clean slate, and it is up to him what he will
write on it. The burden of responsibility is his alone. He cannot put
the blame on someone else.

During the Reunion Week in 1990, I found a new Germany.
The motto of the reunion was "REMEMBERING IS THE KEY TO
RECONCILIATION." It was a hand held out to us with humble
respect. We had to take it. A lot of time has passed since the war,
and today's twenty- or thirty-year-old Germans say, I hate to think
what my grandfather or grandmother might have done when they
were the same age as I am now. When will young people in Hungary ever say that?

On April 10, 2005, Germany celebrated the sixtieth anniversary of the liberation of all the German concentration camps. The
ceremonies were held in Buchenwald and Weimar. They invited
twelve hundred former Häftlings from the countries Germany had

occupied during the Second World War – from Poland, Belgium, the Netherlands, Denmark, Russia, Ukraine, Hungary, and so on. Representatives of the liberating Allied forces and the Soviet Red Army were also among the guests.

All groups delivered a speech in the theatre at Weimar. The motto of the commemoration was: "The Second World War, Auschwitz, mass annihilation, and racial discrimination are part of the identity of today's Germany." The other motto was: "The Soviet Red Army was also a liberator in its contribution to the defeat of Nazi Germany."

I love life and hope that I will live to see the day when the four anti-Jewish laws (1920, 1938, 1939, 1941), the Hungarian pre-Holocaust regime, meaning Kamen'yec-Podolsk (1941), and the Hungarian Holocaust (1944) that claimed six hundred thousand Hungarian lives and was perpetrated by Hungarians will all be similarly acknowledged as part of Hungary's identity.

When the original version of this book appeared in Germany in 2004, I was honestly surprised at its reception. Ever since it was first published I've been receiving requests to read from it, and I often meet with senior high-school students – young people seventeen and eighteen years of age. I am repeatedly touched by the way history is taught in Germany, as well as the preparation of the teachers. I consider these meetings my mission.

Whenever I am called, I go, and the young people send me thank-you letters. I can't help asking myself: When will they ever call me to speak in a Hungarian school? When will high-school seniors on the threshold of adulthood bombard me with questions and give voice to their feelings of sympathy?[1]

And yet for a long time now the question is not what happened sixty, seventy years ago. In those years, death marched through Europe in Wehrmacht boots, and half of the continent lived in constant fear and trembling. Fear flooded Europe. If the fears of my family, the Hungarian Jews, the Jews, non-Jews, Gypsies, and

---

1 Since the writing of these lines, Éva Fahidi has participated in similar events with teachers and students of all leading high schools in Budapest and Debrecen.

Memorial plaque in the camp, Allendorf, 1990.

other persecuted groups living under German occupation had merged into one, the world would have sunk under its weight.

We must talk about this, too. But today, *it will not suffice*. Suffering is always senseless. There is no suffering, especially suffering caused by history, of which we could say, "It made sense because ..." It is sad, but true: I can't talk about my own horrible experiences and have those who did not live through them understand. Only experience is convincing, and there is a danger that,

With Anikó and Lili, 1990.

The official unveiling of Anikó's statue in Mayor Manfred Vollmer's office, Standallendorf, October, 1992.

for lack of experience, anything could happen again, as indeed we see it happening in various parts of the world. We just have to look around us. As long as there is racial discrimination, whether out in the open or swept under the carpet, as long as there is room for hatred, contempt, and scorn, the danger of genocide remains real. And not only its danger, but its *fact*. Just think of the late twentieth century. Or think of today.

Germany takes the chance of the rebirth of fascism seriously, and is fighting against it in earnest.

But what about us?

As this writing indicates, I am hopelessly optimistic. There is no fear in the eyes of my grandchildren, and may there never be. Perhaps they, Marci, Zsófi, Mihály, and Luca, and the rest of their generation, will be able to create a better world than the one my own generation has built.

Appendix A

The Münchmühle Camp[1]

FRITZ BRINKMANN-FRISCH

The Münchmühle camp was named after the mill built over the Münchbach stream located in its immediate vicinity. It is located in Hessen province, on the highway connecting Kirchhain and Neustadt, two kilometres southwest of Allendorf.

The camp, which consisted of twenty-six barracks, was built in 1940 and was the property of the state-owned MONTAN (short for Verwertungsgesellschaft für Montanindustrie GmbH or Mining and Foundry Merchandising Co. Ltd). This company was also the owner of all the fixed assets of VERWERTCHEMIE (GmbH zur Verwertung chemischer Ergzeugnisse or Chemical Products Merchandising Co. Ltd). The VERWERTCHEMIE was a subsidiary of DYNAMIT AG (Dynamite Nobel Joint Stock Co.), which manufactured and filled explosives for every unit of the Wehrmacht at a number of locations all over the Third Reich. The rental for the fixed assets and the barracks were paid to MONTAN by the lessee, VERWERTCHEMIE.

At various times, the camp had a variety of inmates; civilian forced labourers, men and women – Polish, Dutch, French, Italian; prisoners of war – French, Serbian, Italian, as well as units of the Reich Labour Service. During the period between August 1944 and March 1945, the camp acted a satellite of Buchenwald and as a concentration camp. It was inhabited by a thousand Hungarian female Häftlings, most of them from Hungary, a minority from Slovakia.

---

1 This essay originally served as the Afterword to Éva Fahidi's book published in German.

In late March 1945 the camp was evacuated towards Ziegenhain. In the two years following the war it was used by the United Nations Relief and Rehabilitation Administration (UNRRA), mostly to house Polish internees. The camp was dismantled in 1947.

In May 1988 representatives of Marburg-Biedenkopf County unveiled the beautifully executed memorial on the cement blocks of the former washrooms.

The Allendorf Munitions Plant: The Use of Forced Labour, the Numbers and Structure of the Labour Force

As a result of the steadily increasing shortage of labour, the munitions industry began to use more and more civilian forced labourers and prisoners of both sexes, and after 1942, a growing number of concentration camp Häftlings. The managers of the various plants competed with each other for concentration camp prisoners, assigned to them by the SS to be used in the munitions industry. The VERWERTCHEMIE of Allendorf also applied for Häftlings in order to fill their orders. On June 6, 1944, camp commandant Piester of Buchenwald and Ringleb, the general manager of VERWERTCHEMIE, met in Allendorf. We know from the transcript of the minutes that they wished to employ female Häftlings for roadwork, for filling hand grenades and bombs, and for work in the laundry and the sewing workshop. In order to ensure that work would continue uninterrupted for twenty-four hours, they planned to have either three eight-hour or two twelve-hour shifts. They also planned to recruit SS Aufseherins from among the local women factory workers and to put up an electric fence around the camp. General Manager Ringleb insisted on getting male prisoners for all production and loading and shipping work. They agreed on 3 and 5 Reichsmark (RM) per labourer, depending on whether they were skilled or unskilled.[2] The SS finally billed the

2 According to the practice of the Third Reich, the state billed the factory owners for the use of forced labourers and prisoners.

factory 4 RM for the use of every Häftling, including unskilled labourers and women.

In addition to the minutes of the Allendorf meeting, there is another document that sheds light on the conflict between the SS and the plant managers. By September 1944, the plant was not able to recruit the number of female guards required by the WVHA, the Economic and Administrative Main Office of the SS. At the same time, they wanted to increase the number of Häftlings by 350 persons. Furthermore, Piester criticized the lack of co-operation shown by the plant managers and demanded more sympathy for the "work" of the SS, which, in the interest of the factory, facilitated the uninterrupted supply of labourers. Piester also found it unusual that he should be asked to sign a contract for lending Häftlings to the plant. "We were able to come to an agreement with many other companies that we supplied with Häftlings from the concentration camp at Buchenwald without a contract," he insisted. The profiteers did not need a signed agreement to reveal that both parties profited from trafficking in human lives. After the war, the industry insisted on maintaining the myth that the SS "forced" the Häftlings on them.

Häftlings: Division by Age and Fluctuation of Their Numbers

There are two separate lists at our disposal for determining the statistics on the age of the Häftlings. The list prepared in Auschwitz on August 13, 1944 contains the first and last name, the birth date, and place and profession of each prisoner. On the basis of this list, another was prepared on October 20, 1944 in Buchenwald, the headquarters for the Münchmühle camp. A comparison of the two lists indicates that there are three women who are on the Auschwitz list but are no longer on the Münchmühle list. They were replaced by three other Häftlings, probably still back in Auschwitz. Dated on October 12, 1944, the commandant of the Allendorf work camp sent the relevant corrections as well as the corrections in the spelling of the names along with one thousand index cards in its report

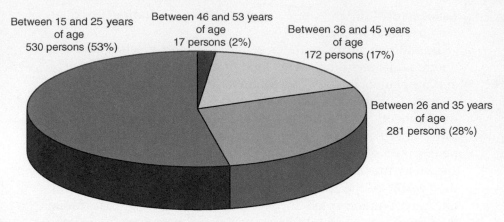

Between 15 and 25 years
of age
530 persons (53%)

Between 46 and 53 years
of age
17 persons (2%)

Between 36 and 45 years
of age
172 persons (17%)

Between 26 and 35 years
of age
281 persons (28%)

Total: 1,000 persons

Women working at Münchmühle divided by age.

to Buchenwald. It is only logical that the index cards compiled at the Allendorf office served as the basis for the Buchenwald list.

Figure 1 represents the evaluation of the Buchenwald list. According to the data, at the end of the war the average age of the women was twenty-seven and one-quarter years; the oldest woman was fifty-three, the youngest fifteen years of age, which means that more than half of the women were between the ages of fifteen and twenty-five.

There is a third version of the list that appends the Buchenwald list. It was compiled during the first few weeks after the war and provides information on the postwar placement of the women as well as the pregnant and deceased women during the war. On the basis of this list and other records, we can establish the following changes in the number of Häftlings: On October 27, 1944, five pregnant women were sent back to Auschwitz through the Mühlhausen work camp. On November 8, 1944, Jolán Hauer died. The cause of death on her death certificate is indicated as icterus haemolyticus, or toxic poisoning brought about by contact with toxic chemicals in the course of work. On December 23, 1944, the ATG of Leipzig sent a woman to Allendorf, and on January 26, 1945, two women were transferred to Allendorf from Bergen-Belsen. In sum, at the time the camp was evacuated, there were 993 Häftlings.

Work Conditions

The reports about how satisfied the Buchenwald work managers were with the work of the Häftlings were made on the spot on the basis of the daily reports. These tell us the number of workers the plant required every day. In the case of skilled workers, the loan charge was 6 RM per person, and in the case of unskilled labourers, it was 4 RM per person, which was multiplied by the number of workers engaged in each type of work. The women working in the Münchmühle camp were considered unskilled labourers. The sum total of the loan charges was billed to the munitions plants.

Daily work reports are available from August 17, 1944, the day after the arrival of the Allendorf transport. Though the daily reports show that during the month of August only a handful of women were assigned work in the plant itself, the Buchenwald base camp charged a fee for every Häftling, except for those who were lying in the Revier. The SS charged the Allendorf plant nearly 650,000 RM for the period stretching from August 1944 to February 1945. The Häftlings worked six days out of seven, in twelve- or eight-hour shifts. The women were assigned to various sections of the plant – the munitions-filling stations, the laundry and sewing workshops.

The report compiled by the managers of the plant for the year 1944 tell us that they were highly satisfied with the work of the women Häftlings. "Our experiences with the women Häftlings set to work in August 1944 are extremely positive. Thanks to putting the Jewish female Häftlings to work, even the filling of the 50 kg, 15 cm shells proceed to our utmost satisfaction."

The toughest workplaces were the filling stations, where the extremely hazardous working conditions also had to be taken into account. The Häftlings' skin, hair, and nails turned yellow. In his detailed report, a French liaison officer would later write about the work at the camp: "Work consisted of filling bombs and grenades with explosives. The grenades weighed over 40 kilos, and every Häftling had to lift at least 1000 grenades per day." Some of the women, first and foremost the youngest, were assigned work within the plant, but some were assigned agricultural labour. Here working conditions were generally more favourable, and so were the provisions. Women who worked in production are still suffering from the damage to their health caused by the heavy toxins they worked with.

The Guards

The camp was encircled by a fence. The women were guarded partly by males, and partly by female guards taken from the Allendorf plant. Shortly before the camp was disbanded, the camp guard consisted of forty-six male SS guards, forty-seven female guards, two Häftling doctors, and eight Häftling nurses. The camp commandant was Hauptscharführer (SS sergeant) Adolf Wuttke, whom the majority of the women considered humane, but his deputy, Ernst Schulte(r), was remembered as a brute.

The Evacuation

As the American troops approached, the camp was evacuated on March 27, 1945. There are no documents to indicate the intended goal of the evacuees' forced march. The column first headed east, in the direction of Ziegenhain, then northeast, towards Fritzlar. During the march, the Häftlings as well as the guards went on their way in smaller groups. As a result, the full column gradually evaporated.

In the 1970s, when the Public Prosecutor's office searched for information, they found no indication of any death occurring during the evacuation march, and in 1971 the proceedings were closed. Once liberated, the women were looked after by the American troops and UNRRA, and were quartered with families or in public buildings. The American army and UNRRA also arranged for their return home or their travel to other countries.

Sentences against Guards and Members of the Camp Administration

The records of the Public Prosecutor include the names of forty-five Aufseherin. Of these, eighteen ended up in various postwar internment camps. The Oberaufseherin (commander of the female guards) and two other guards were sentenced in the Darmstadt camp trial to several years' imprisonment to be spent in a work camp. However, all women who had been sentenced were set free within eighteen to forty-two months.

Adolf Wuttke, commandant of the Münchmühle camp, was the only male member of the administration who was sentenced. He received four and a half years for physically abusing the inmates of Buchenwald. The fate of his deputy, Ernst Schulte(r), continues to be unknown.

The statue is at the Documentation and Information Centre of Stadtallendorf.
It was made by Anikó Veres, the author's "other half," who was a sculptor in
Huntington, New York.

Appendix B

The List of the One Thousand Women Taken from Auschwitz to Allendorf, August 13, 1944

1	23001	Abelsberg	Kraus Julia	1901.03.24.	Szarajevo
2	23003	Abraham	Sara	1921.09.23.	Halmi
3	23002	Abraham	Sarolta	1921.09.23.	Vamosatya
4	23004	Acs	Katalin	1914.10.20.	Munkacs
5	23013	Adler	Stern Aranka	1905.08.31.	Dioszeg
6	23012	Adler	Edit	1926.11.03.	Pozsony
7	23009	Adler	Fried Ella	1908.02.10.	Csenyete
8	23011	Adler	Gertrud	1929.04.20.	Pozsony
9	23005	Adler	Ida	1926.04.07.	Berezna
10	23010	Adler	Julianna	1926.09.07.	Ersekujvar
11	23007	Adler	Margit	1925.11.23.	Berezna
12	23006	Adler	Regina	1925.03.23.	Berezna
13	23008	Adler	Sarolta	1915.06.12.	Ersekujvar
14	23015	Ajlender	Ilona	1928.02.10.	Dombo
15	23014	Alexander	Edit	1919.01.06.	Miskolc
16	23016	Angyal	Terez	1912.03.03.	Gadoros
17	23019	Armuth	Eva	1923.11.07.	Nagykanizsa
18	23017	Aron	Alice	1923.01.04.	Derecske
19	23023	Balassa	Magdolna	1923.03.05.	Baja
20	23021	Balazs	Braunne Iren Iren	1905.12.11.	Mezőkovesd
21	23028	Balla	Livia	1926.10.18.	Debrecen
22	23020	Banyasz	Ilona	1910.05.19.	Derecske
23	23022	Baradlai	Jozsa	1919.01.31.	Budapest
24	23026	Basch	Ibolya	1921.11.22.	Miskolc
25	23025	Basch	Ilona	1920.09.18.	Miskolc

(Continued)

26	23024	Bauer	Silberer Erzsebet	1918.07.07.	Szeged
27	23027	Bauer	Julia	1923.04.13.	Somogyszil
28	23039	Becski	Katalin	1920.02.28.	Miskolc
29	23038	Becski	Fedorne Olga	1917.11.15.	Kisszeben
30	23029	Benedek	Judit	1922.03.02.	Budapest
31	23032	Berger	Pragerne Edit	1919.10.24.	Keszthely
32	23035	Bergerne	Weisz Erzsebet	1913.08.01.	Debrecen
33	23034	Berger	Ilona	1919.03.21.	Debrecen
34	23030	Berger	Klein Iren	1916.09.10.	Putnok
35	23033	Berger	Katalin	1925.03.02.	Debrecen
36	23031	Berger	Schlesinger Rozsi	1896.10.28.	Nagykanizsa
37	23080	Berkovics	Gyongyi	1925.07.15.	Hajduhadhaz
38	23081	Berkovics	Olga	1924.01.24.	Hajduhadhaz
39	23040	Berkovics	Horvai Zsuzsanna	1921.06.23.	Miskolc
40	23037	Berliner	Piroska	1918.10.10.	Kassa
41	23036	Birnbaum	Roza	1921.05.09.	Tornalja
42	23043	Biro	Frank Borbala	1902.10.19.	Kaposvar
43	23042	Biro	Katalin	1927.06.05.	Kaposvar
44	23041	Biro	Magdolna	1922.05.07.	Nagykanizsa
45	23047	Blau	Frieda	1921.12.12.	Tet
46	23045	Blau	Lukacs Ilona	1906.05.01.	Szombathely
47	23048	Blau	Marta	1926.03.07.	Tet
48	23046	Blau	Marta	1926.03.29.	Szombathely
49	23049	Blaustein	Weisz Ilona	1909.04.05.	Liszkatolcsva
50	23050	Blechner	Barbara	1919.09.26.	
51	23051	Blechner	Ferber Erzsebet	1914.08.28.	
52	23085	Bleier	Weisz Aniko	1925.10.16.	Debrecen
53	23054	Bleier	Magdolna	1923.09.27.	Ocsod
54	23089	Blum	Fischmann Edit	1923.08.08.	Pecs
55	23077	Boczan	Terez	1909.05.11.	Debrecen
56	23086	Bokor	Epstein Piroska	1918.02.04.	Pomaz
57	23087	Bokor	Zsuzsanna	1922.01.18.	Pecs
58	23083	Bondi	Anna	1911.12.25.	Pincehely
59	23082	Bondi	Olga	1903.03.02.	Pincehely
60	23076	Bonyhai	Leer Maria	1914.10.03.	Becs
61	23079	Bozoky	Berger Aliz	1907.01.23.	Debrecen
62	23078	Bohm	Zsuzsanna	1921.03.01.	

63	23071	Braun	Gyorgyi	1919.07.06.	Domoszlo
64	23072	Braun	Jolan	1921.08.	Vecs
65	23069	Braun	Klara	1922.10.15.	Mezőkeresztes
66	23073	Braun	Breier Rozsi	1921.12.12.	Domoszlo
67	23070	Braun	Spitzer Sari	1915.01.23.	Kaposvar
68	23053	Breier	Meier Ilona	1907.04.04.	
69	23065	Breszlauer	Julia	1925.06.25.	Szabadka
70	23066	Breszlauer	Jelinek Olga	1895.12.12.	Budapest
71	23055	Breuer	Majorovics Magdolna	1921.06.03.	Tiszaluc
72	23068	Bricht	Margit	1906.02.	Sumeg
73	23067	Brichta	Menczel Rozsi	1902.05.15.	Vagsellye
74	23074	Brieger	Aliz	1925.03.19.	Tibolddaroc
75	23052	Brieger	Spitzer A.	1907.02.04.	Marianosztra
76	23064	Brill	Rozsi	1909.12.23.	Nemeskolta
77	24000	Britz	Judit	1928.11.19.	Nyiregyhaza
78	23057	Brodi	Agnes	1926.05.29.	Debrecen
79	23056	Brodt	Erzsebet	1927.06.22.	Kaposvar
80	23062	Bruck	Erika	1927.03.31.	Galanta
81	23060	Bruck	Erna	1926.04.30.	Galanta
82	23063	Bruck		1922.07.25.	Pozsony
83	23061	Bruck	Sari	1923.06.14.	Galanta
84	23084	Brummer	Braun Jolan	1896.03.24.	Vasarosnameny
85	23058	Brull	Eva	1928.02.13.	Dombovar
86	23059	Brull	Ibolya	1924.04.14.	Budapest
87	23075	Bruller	Iren	1910.10.11.	Kecskemet
88	23044	Bugler	Kupfer Sari	1912.11.12.	Debrecen
89	23090	Csak	Kemeny Erzsebet	1908.04.05.	Budapest
90	23092	Czeisler	Kato	1924.01.29.	Onod
91	23091	Czeisler	Magdolna	1923.05.16.	Onod
92	23094	Cslllag	Eva	1919.12.26.	Kapuvar
93	23093	Czinner	Reisz Klara	1915.12.21.	Hodmezővasarhely
94	23095	Csizmazia	Reisz Etel	1919.11.29.	Kaposvar
95	23096	Csizmazia	Braun Lilli	1918.02.21.	Kaposvar
96	23996	Csizler	Margit	1909.03.11.	Miskolc
97	23103	Daniel	Klein Margit	1912.10.06.	Tortel
98	23097	David	Schwarz Hajnal	1908.05.30.	Torokszentmiklos
99	23098	David	Kato	1928.05.11.	Puspokladany

(Continued)

100	23099	David	Urlsfeld Margit	1905.08.13.	Puspokladany
101	23102	Davidovics	Blanka	1926.11.06.	
102	23101	Davidovics	Eva	1924.08.07.	Bodrogkeresztur
103	23100	Davidovics	Friedmann Ida	1910.04.26.	Aknaszlatina
104	23107	Dagos	Edit	1925.10.23.	Ersekujvar
105	23108	Degen	Magda	1925.12.01.	Ersekujvar
106	23118	Demeter	Friedmann Matild	1910.08.19.	Jolsva
107	23117	Demeter	Rozalia	1926.07.17.	Jolsva
108	23106	Desser	Eva	1926.02.23.	Pecel
109	23105	Desser	Maria	1924.06.25.	Pecel
110	23104	Desser	Auschpitz Rozsi	1907.11.13.	Salgotarjan
111	23109	Deutsch	Edit	1926.08.26.	Miskolc
112	23116	Deutsch	Eva	1927.11.07.	Tet
113	23113	Deutsch	Ilona	1920.03.05.	Jolsva
114	23114	Deutsch	Ilona	1926.02.26.	Tet
115	23112	Deutsch	Lili	1924.05.01.	Nagybozsva
116	23110	Deutsch	Magdolna	1925.03.06.	Miskolc
117	23111	Deutsch	Magdolna	1925.12.25.	Nagybozsva
118	23115	Deutsch	Weinberger Sari	1907.05.25.	Zilah
119	23018	Dicker	Jolan	1914.10.06.	Debrecen
120	23123	Dobo	Julia	1921.02.08.	Baja
121	23119	Dohany	Eva	1912.08.29.	Szabadka
122	23121	Domany	Weitzenfeld Olga	1910.12.16.	Miskolc
123	23120	Domany	Zsuzsanna	1926.10.18.	Miskolc
124	23124	Donath	Schwartz Cecilia	1910.11.17.	Jaszfalu
125	23122	Duxlor	Eva	1923.08.27.	Ersekujvar
126	23150	Eckstein	Bella	1926.07.14.	Pozsony
127	23149	Eckstein	Emma	1924.09.21.	Elek
128	23148	Eckstein	Olga	1923.08.07.	Elek
129	23144	Ehrenfeld	Karola	1912.08.30.	Korostopa
130	23145	Ehrenfeld	Katalin	1924.03.09.	Sarand
131	23147	Ehrenfeld	Klari	1907.07.28.	Almosd
132	23146	Ehrenfeld	Klein Sara	1918.10.30.	Debrecen
133	23143	Ehrenfeld	Guttmann Sari	1908.03.23.	Lupeny
134	23139	Eichler	Gabriella	1920.06.07.	Budapest
135	23135	Eilender	Rozsi	1928.01.28.	Dombo
136	23140	Eisnitz	Czetter Anna	1904.02.08.	Cegled

137	23126	Elek	Lanz Ersebet	1910.02.12.	Miskolc
138	23125	Elek	Eva	1926.08.16.	Miskolc
139	23130	Ellenbogen	Alice	1924.05.15.	Ersekujvar
140	23128	Ellenbogen	Anna	1923.09.28.	Ersekujvar
141	23131	Ellenbogen	Lőwy Erzsebet	1921.05.21.	Kalkapolna
142	23129	Ellenbogen	Klara	1926.04.15.	Ersekujvar
143	23127	Ellenbogen	Vera	1927.10.27.	Ersekujvar
144	23141	Emerich	Frankel Sara	1912.10.19.	Debrecen
145	23134	Engel	Agnes	1904.04.24.	Nagykorű
146	23133	Engel	Zsuzsanna	1919.08.20.	Vep
147	23132	Engler	Wolheimer Magdolna	1912.06.24.	
148	23142	Erczi	Grosz Eva	1914.07.21.	Izsak
149	23138	Erdős	Fischer Eva	1925.05.15.	Budapest
150	23136	Erdős	Judit	1921.02.27.	Debrecen
151	23137	Erdős	Katalin	1926.05.17.	Ozora
152	23151	Fahidi	Eva	1925.10.22.	Debrecen
153	23152	Falus	Leier Rozsi	1904.02.26.	Galszecs
154	23156	Farkas	Iren	1913.11.12.	Zsaka
155	23155	Farkas	Juliska	1914.07.24.	Vancs
156	23153	Farkas	Sari	1923.06.22.	Berezna
157	23154	Farkas	Zsuzsanna	1925.10.11.	Berezna
158	23157	Feig	Frieda	1924.05.13.	Tiszakaracsonyfalva
159	23158	Feig	Sari	1928.01.01.	Tiszakaracsonyfalva
160	23159	Feher	Magda	1919.06.19.	Miskolc
161	23162	Feldmann	Alice	1923.11.27.	Hajduszoboszlo
162	23161	Feldmann	Iren	1922.04.11.	Puspokladany
163	23165	Feldmann	Iren	1923.03.17.	Ujfeherto
164	23164	Feldmann	Lili	1922.05.27.	Hajduszoboszlo
165	23163	Feldmann	Magdolna	1921.02.21.	Hajduszoboszlo
166	23166	Fenyves	Magdolna	1925.11.20.	Pozsony
167	23160	Feldmar	Fekete Erzsebet	1910.02.25.	Hajduboszormeny
168	23168	Fenyves	Hedvig	1927.02.17.	Munkacs
169	23167	Fenyves	Donath Sari	1900.03.04.	Ersekujvar
170	23195	Feurer	Rozsa	1892.10.01.	Leva
171	23169	Fisch	Erzsebet	1918.08.10.	Debrecen
172	23170	Fisch	Maria	1919.01.01.	Debrecen
173	23179	Fischer	Etel	1904.01.21.	

(Continued)

174	23176	Fischer	Flora	1902.07.22.	Szombathely
175	23177	Fischer	Helen	1926.07.02.	Nagymegyer
176	23175	Fischer	Ilona	1909.02.15.	Szombathely
177	23172	Fischer	Stern Olga	1914.11.01.	Miskolc
178	23173	Fischer	Bella	1926.11.07.	Zenta
179	23174	Fischer	Hanna	1923.01.17.	Szombathely
180	23178	Fischer	Rozsi	1915.05.04.	Zombor
181	23171	Fischmann	Grete	1927.08.25.	Pozsony
182	23184	Fleischmann	Ella	1920.12.15.	Galanta
183	23183	Fleischmann	Eva	1910.01.18.	Becs
184	23186	Fleischmann	Iren	1918.12.08.	Galanta
185	23182	Fleischmann	Magdolna	1921.02.03.	Kaposvar
186	23185	Fleischmann	Magdolna	1924.05.11.	Galanta
187	23180	Flesch	Edit	1924.12.15.	Baja
188	23181	Flesch	Magdolna	1923.03.23.	Baja
189	23235	Flohr	Erzsebet	1918.07.18.	Onga
190	23233	Fodor	Veronika	1922.02.19.	Miskolc
191	23234	Fogel	Ilona	1919.12.08.	Miskolc
192	23232	Forbath	Marianna	1925.11.20.	Debrecen
193	23187	Frank	Eva	1912.06.10.	Szabadka
194	23188	Frank	Tarhi Flora	1912.10.20.	Aszod
195	23189	Frank	Vera	1924.06.27.	Debrecen
196	23223	Frankl	Eszter	1913.03.29.	Vagsellye
197	23222	Frankl	Frieda	1912.11.04.	Vagsellye
198	23224	Frankl	Malvin	1906.04.11.	Vagsellye
199	23191	Frankfurt	Schwartz Rozsi	1907.08.25.	Ozd
200	23192	Frankel	Gabriella	1915.03.06.	Hajdusamson
201	23194	Frankel	Szeren	1927.04.12.	Beled
202	23193	Frankel	Salamon Szidonia	1912.11.28.	Szakallasdombo
203	23226	Frei	Ronai Ilona	1916.11.15.	Miskolc
204	23196	Freud	Rozman Erzsebet	1921.10.27.	Debrecen
205	23197	Fried	Alice	1927.05.31.	Verebely
206	23198	Fried	Rosenzweig Hilda	1908.08.30.	Nagybossany
207	23199	Fried	Maria	1903.10.01.	Hacs
208	23221	Friedenthal	Erzsebet	1922.06.08.	Kaposvar
209	23220	Friedenthal	Maria	1919.12.31.	Balvanyos

210	23202	Friedmann	Anna	1926.03.28.	Nagykőros
211	23214	Friedmann	Erzsebet	1916.11.12.	Dunaszerdahely
212	23216	Friedmann	Erzsebet	1919.04.22.	Munkacs
213	23211	Friedmann	Frida	1922.05.05.	Beregszasz
214	23218	Friedmann	Gyongyi	1923.12.19.	Munkacs
215	23217	Friedmann	Hedvig	1921.12.27.	Munkacs
216	23215	Friedmann	Herta	1924.06.27.	Ersekujvar
217	23204	Friedmann	Geisz Iren	1925.01.22.	Miskolc
218	23212	Friedmann	Irma	1920.07.17.	Ersekujvar
219	23207	Friedmann	Julia	1923.10.25.	Debrecen
220	23208	Friedmann	Katalin	1928.01.02.	Debrecen
221	23209	Friedmann	Kato	1926.10.16.	Miskolc
222	23201	Friedmann	Kramer Klara	1905.02.14.	Miskolc
223	23213	Friedmann	Klara	1922.01.05.	Ersekujvar
224	23205	Friedmann	Lili	1921.01.16.	Miskolc
225	23203	Friedmann	Magdolna	1914.10.23.	Miskolc
226	23210	Friedmann	Magdolna	1925.11.20.	Miskolc
227	23206	Friedmann	Schafer Margit	1909.04.16.	Miskolc
228	23200	Friedmann	Rozsi	1928.06.18.	Bodrogolaszi
229	23225	Frimm	Neumann Melanie	1906.02.01.	Graz
230	23227	Fruchter	Ilona	1902.02.18.	Barcanfalva
231	23219	Fuchs	Frieda	1914.05.20.	Csorna
232	23229	Fuchs	Klara	1912.01.18.	Csorna
233	23231	Futo	Eva	1922.06.01.	Debrecen
234	23230	Futo	Ibolya	1919.10.03.	Debrecen
235	23228	Furth	Judit	1922.03.20.	Miskolc
236	23244	Gabor	Lili	1923.12.27.	Cegled
237	23243	Gabor	Terez	1925.04.25.	Cegled
238	23242	Gacs	Ibolya	1923.02.07.	Debrecen
239	23241	Gacs	Iren	1925.03.21.	Debrecen
240	23240	Gacs	Maria	1927.12.07.	Debrecen
241	23297	Galambos	Klara	1923.12.05.	Budapest
242	23239	Ganz	Berkovics Helen	1913.01.03.	Kiskőros
243	23238	Garai	Gizella	1924.08.12.	Tolna
244	23236	Garai	Ilona	1923.02.05.	Tolna
245	23237	Garai	Rozsi	1921.07.22.	Tolna
246	23247	Gartner	Adel	1922.02.18.	Szalonna

(Continued)

247	23250	Gartner	Erzsebet	1918.06.28.	Miskolc
248	23245	Gartner	Ilona	1917.06.15.	Szatmarokorito
249	23248	Gartner	Kati	1924.01.20.	Szalonna
250	23249	Gartner	Klari	1920.04.01.	
251	23246	Gartner	Sari	1920.06.15.	Szatmarokorito
252	23263	Geiszler	Fellner Erzsebet	1904.04.14.	Ostffyasszonyfa
253	23262	Geiszler	Eva	1926.11.12	
254	23264	Geiszler	Magda	1925.01.29.	Ostffyasszonyfa
255	23269	Gelb	Ella	1912.12.19.	Mezőkovesd
256	23260	Gerő	Blanka	1906.04.16.	Feketebalog
257	23261	Gerő	Valeria	1913.03.23.	Selmecbanya
258	23266	Gestettner	Rozsi	1925.06.28.	Győr
259	23265	Gestettner	Sari	1926.01.28.	Győr
260	23341	Gewurtz	Frieda	1922.08.22.	Tet
261	23270	Gewurtz	Renee	1916.04.08.	Kolozsvar
262	23342	Gewurtz	Sara	1919.06.21.	Tet
263	23259	Glied	Margit	1921.07.23.	Bereg
264	23254	Gluck	Erzsebet	1904.05.10.	Bacsalmas
265	23255	Gluck	Ilona	1928.01.25.	Alsosag
266	23257	Gluck	Klara	1915.09.19.	Alsosag
267	23252	Gluck	Klari	1926.11.03.	Miskolc
268	23253	Gluck	Lili	1924.12.19.	Miskolc
269	23256	Gluck	Magda	1923.04.08.	Alsosag
270	23258	Gluckmann	Erzsebet	1916.03.03.	Pusztadobos
271	23271	Goldberger	Sarolta	1925.12.25.	Papa
272	23273	Goldmann	Anna	1925.10.08.	Csokva
273	23272	Goldmann	Eva	1925.09.09.	Csokva
274	23296	Goldschmied	Erzsebet	1927.03.18.	Kapuvar
275	23274	Goldstein	Anna	1920.11.08.	Nyircsaholy
276	23326	Goldstein	Borbala	1928.01.09.	Diosgyőr
277	23324	Goldstein	Edit	1919.07.19.	Diosgyőr
278	23466	Goldstein	Ella	1914.03.12.	Agcsernyő
279	23325	Goldstein	Klara	1921.08.29.	Diosgyőr
280	23276	Goldstein	Magdolna	1927.04.01.	Galanta
281	23275	Goldstein	Olga	1922.05.25.	Nyircsaholy
282	23338	Gottlieb	Anna	1927.09.15.	Debrecen
283	23339	Gottlieb	Balkanyi Edit	1907.06.08.	Debrecen
284	23336	Gottlieb	Erzsebet	1927.02.26.	Sarospatak

285	23337	Gottlieb	Zsuzsanna	1924.03.17.	Nyirbator
286	23267	Gotzl	Marta	1927.06.15.	Szombathely
287	23268	Gotzl	Spielmann Rozsa	1904.10.12.	Kőszegpaty
288	23277	Grossmann	Grosz Julia	1906.03.13.	Debrecen
289	23278	Grossmann	Klari	1926.12.31.	Debrecen
290	23315	Grosz	Agnes	1918.03.19.	Szarvas
291	23312	Grosz	Anna	1925.05.16.	Deaki
292	23303	Grosz	Friedmann Aranka	1909.09.26.	Eperjes
293	23302	Grosz	Erika	1927.04.19.	Miskolc
294	23310	Grosz	Erzsebet	1905.04.01.	Kisjenő
295	23306	Grosz	Erzsebet	1913.11.18.	Debrecen
296	23305	Grosz	Eva	1925.11.30.	Debrecen
297	23311	Grosz	Ilona	1926.04.08.	Tecső
298	23304	Grosz	Julia	1922.02.14.	Ujpest
299	23318	Grosz	Julia	1923.02.18.	Hajduhadhaz
300	23313	Grosz	Julia	1924.02.09.	Debrecen
301	23317	Grosz	Katalin	1927.05.28.	Hajduboszormeny
302	23309	Grosz	Magdolna	1924.12.11.	Okany
303	23307	Grosz	Marta	1922.01.08.	Mezőkovesd
304	23316	Grosz	Rozsi	1923.11.14.	Hajduszoboszlo
305	23308	Grosz	Sari	1914.03.20.	Putnok
306	23314	Grosz	Weisz Szeren	1908.06.04.	Pilis
307	23319	Groszmann	Ibolya	1922.01.17.	Miskolc
308	23322	Groszmann	Klara	1923.12.15.	Szihalom
309	23321	Groszmann	Klein Lili	1926.07.05.	Debrecen
310	23323	Groszmann	Magdolna	1924.04.01.	Miskolc
311	23320	Groszmann	Fuchs Margit	1919.03.25.	Debrecen
312	23346	Grun	Ibolya	1925.07.11.	Hajduboszormeny
313	23290	Grunbaum	Ilona	1903.03.19.	Győr
314	23291	Grunberger	Edit	1925.09.14.	Miskolc
315	23293	Grunberger	Erzsebet	1921.03.26.	Kaposvar
316	23292	Grunberger	Regina	1918.07.06.	Hajdusamson
317	23283	Grunblatt	Knopfler Ilona	1915.03.15.	Debrecen
318	23340	Gruner	Ibolya	1826.06.18.	Hajduboszormeny
319	23285	Grunfeld	Edit	1910.01.19.	Szombathely
320	23286	Grunfeld	Erzsebet	1908.03.20.	Szombathely
321	23284	Grunfeld	Pfeifer Ilona	1909.07.18.	Jaszkarajenő

(Continued)

322	23288	Grunfeld	Ilona	1922.04.20.	Hajduszoboszlo
323	23287	Grunfeld	Sari	1916.10.03.	Tornyosnemeti
324	23289	Grunhut	Julia	1911.11.07.	Zalaegerszeg
325	23295	Grunmann	Ella	1914.11.14.	Debrecen
326	23294	Grunmann	Iren	1913.11.28.	Debrecen
327	23279	Grunwald	Schreiber Elza	1918.06.20.	Hejőcsaba
328	23280	Grunwald	Katalin	1925.08.17.	Rozsnyo
329	23282	Grunwald	Lili	1924.08.26.	Ersekujvar
330	23281	Grunwald	Fodor Terez	1905.03.01.	Rozsnyo
331	23301	Grunzweig	Ibolya	1924.06.24.	Szedres
332	23300	Grunzweig	Julia	1921.01.01.	Szedres
333	23299	Grunzweig	Piroska	1926.06.09.	Szedres
334	23298	Grunzweig	Sara	1917.06.10.	Csenger
335	23088	Gubics	Alice	1926.09.22.	Ersekujvar
336	23345	Gubics	Edit	1925.05.04.	Ersekujvar
337	23343	Gulyas	Livia	1923.05.24.	Pincehely
338	23329	Guttmann	Klar Emma	1919.08.01.	Karcag
339	23328	Guttmann	Helen	1919.03.29.	Szolyva
340	23327	Guttmann	Hermina	1926.06.21.	Szolyva
341	23335	Guttmann	Ibolya	1922.10.10.	Satoraljaujhely
342	23332	Gutmann	Kramer Jolan	1906.05.01.	Tolna
343	23334	Gutmann	Lidia	1926.09.27.	Des
344	23330	Guttmann	Magdolna	1926.10.12.	Miskolc
345	23333	Gutmann	Marta	1928.04.14.	Des
346	23331	Guttmann	Erdős Mari	1909.01.17.	Keresztespuspoki
347	23344	Gyemant	Reiling Maria	1903.01.14.	Szolnok
348	23350	Haas	Margit	1908.04.21.	Zalaegerszeg
349	23384	Haber	Ilona	1909.06.09.	Tatabanya
350	23383	Haber	Maria	1910.12.24.	Tatabanya
351	23382	Hajdu	Vera	1923.12.27.	Pely
352	23349	Hajnal	Karacsonyi Erzsebet	1905.04.01.	Budapest
353	23386	Halasz	Livia	1921.08.25.	Szombathely
354	23388	Halmos	Judit	1924.03.06.	Budapest
355	23357	Halpert	Ligeti Klara	1917.07.05.	Kapolcs
356	23347	Handler	Eva	1926.09.24.	Szilagysomlyo
357	23385	Handler	Lusztig Iren	1906.03.10.	Tiszacsege
358	23348	Handler	Vera	1925.03.22.	Pecs

359	23359	Hans	Ilona	1910.03.15.	Harsany
360	23358	Hans	Jolan	1917.07.15.	Harsany
361	23387	Hartmann	Erzsebet	1915.01.27.	Onod
362	23356	Hartmann	Lili	1926.03.08.	Hangacs
363	23355	Hartmann	Deszberg Szeren	1900.09.03.	Hangacs
364	23381	Hartstein	Klein Marta	1921.08.26.	Eger
365	23351	Hauer	Agnes	1929.03.19.	Miskolc
366	23352	Hauer	Roth Jolan	1898.10.17.	Tokaj
367	23353	Havas	Kaiser Edit	1897.04.16.	Debrecen
368	23354	Havas	Heimann Hajnal	1915.01.16.	Sarvar
369	23367	Heimann	Etel	1911.12.30.	Berlin
370	23393	Heimann	Lili	1917.06.02.	Debrecen
371	23365	Heimann	Rozsi	1908.10.09.	Bori
372	23366	Heimann	Szerafina	1920.02.02.	Sarvar
373	23368	Heimlich	Anna	1926.06.08.	Debrecen
374	23398	Heimlich	Marta	1926.10.11.	Tarcal
375	23371	Heisler	Anna	1915.04.07.	Cegled
376	23369	Heisler	Auschpitz Eva	1911.03.12.	Szabadka
377	23370	Heisler	Zopf Rozsi	1909.08.30.	Eszek
378	23372	Hejduska	Strausz Terez	1912.12.26.	Szabadka
379	23364	Herskovics	Agnes	1924.09.03.	Debrecen
380	23362	Herskovics	Ibolya	1922.05.10.	Hajduboszormeny
381	23363	Herskovics	Schwarz Ilona	1915.07.13.	Debrecen
382	23360	Herskovics	Ilona	1922.04.25.	Debrecen
383	23361	Herskovics	Spitzer Magdolna	1915.04.27.	Hajduboszormeny
384	23374	Herz	Anna	1923.06.16.	Ersekujvar
385	23373	Herz	Ilona	1922.02.01.	Ersekujvar
386	23392	Herzog	Fisch Bella	1916.01.01.	Magyar sor
387	23394	Hiller	Rozsi	1919.09.20.	Tapolca
388	23397	Hirschfeld	Lenke	1922.10.07.	Vac
389	23396	Hirschl	Roth Ella	1900.09.09.	Szabadka
390	23407	Hirschl	Heyek Irma	1905.12.16.	Becs
391	23406	Hirschler	Jolan	1903.04.15.	Gutahaza
392	23375	Hoch	Krakkauer Erzsebet	1904.02.18.	Janoshalma
393	23376	Hoffmann	Agnes	1928.05.08.	Ersekujvar
394	23378	Holczer	Magdolna	1923.07.02.	Szombathely

(Continued)

395	23377	Holczer	Klein Szidonia	1906.09.09.	Egyhazasradoc
396	23400	Hollander	Alice	1925.11.21.	Szombathely
397	23401	Hollander	Zimmermann Edit	1922.05.02.	Szombathely
398	23399	Hollander	Eva	1926.11.08.	Szombathely
399	23395	Hollander	Frieda	1910.07.14.	Piszke
400	23402	Hollander	Klara	1924.12.08.	Szombathely
401	23379	Hollos	Friedmann Anna	1894.08.22.	Satoraljaujhely
402	23391	Holzmann	Blau Hermin	1910.06.22.	Nagykorű
403	23380	Horn	Grosz Regina	1905.09.25.	Alsoszőlős
404	23405	Horn	Vera	1923.10.08.	Nyiregyhaza
405	23390	Horovitz	Judit	1928.12.03.	Dedes
406	23389	Horovitz	Neufeld Szeren	1906.09.05.	Torna
407	23404	Hoflich	Aranka	1920.04.18.	Bakonytamasi
408	23403	Honig	Ibolya	1922.02.10.	Rohod
409	23411	Israel	Erzsebet	1909.12.30.	Egyek
410	23410	Israel	Malvin	1910.03.15.	Szuhakallo
411	23408	Israel	Rozsi	1914.08.08.	Egyek
412	23409	Israel	Rozsi	1917.08.06.	Kaposvar
413	23412	Jellinek	Olga	1915.04.01.	Kaposvar
414	23413	Jozsef	Blanka	1921.02.09.	
415	23414	Junger	Edit	1927.10.05.	Miskolc
416	23416	Junger	Erzsebet	1925.09.11.	Miskolc
417	23415	Junger	Gizella	1922.10.03.	Miskolc
418	23473	Kaiser	Lili	1905.04.24.	Tapolca
419	23427	Kaiser	Magda	1914.02.15.	Debrecen
420	23542	Kallai	Singer Julianna	1900.04.13.	
421	23540	Kammer	Margit	1908.01.12.	Nagymacsed
422	23541	Kammer	Szidonia	1909.06.26.	Nagymacsed
423	23533	Kardos	Spitzer Iren	1914.06.19.	Zalaszentmihalyfa
424	23531	Kaszas	Varadi Zsuzsanna	1920.12.16.	Győr
425	23538	Katz	Rona Gyorgyi	1918.06.17.	Kaposvar
426	23417	Katz	Husz Ilona	1915.02.05.	Bonyhad
427	23418	Katz	Beregi Julianna	1906.01.19.	Kiskunfelegyhaza
428	23419	Katz	Katalin	1921.09.09.	Kecskemet
429	23539	Katz	Margit	1925.03.25.	Ermihalyfalva
430	23420	Katz	Vera	1924.12.09.	Kecskemet

431	23546	Kaufmann	Adler Erzsebet	1910.05.05.	Miskolc
432	23545	Kaufmann	Valeria	1920.01.14.	Jolsva
433	23543	Kazar	Livia	1926.04.22.	Tornalja
434	23544	Kazar	Schon Vilma	1906.04.03.	
435	23488	Keller	Goldberger Magdolna	1910.12.18.	Mikepercs
436	23481	Kemeny	Fodor Erzsebet	1903.11.21.	Kormend
437	23479	Kemeny	Klara	1913.04.07.	Turkeve
438	23484	Kende	Kovacs Eva	1924.09.10.	Debrecen
439	23483	Kende	Fleischer Gizella	1914.11.20.	Ujfeherto
440	23482	Kender	Fleischer Rozsi	1921.12.28.	Feherto
441	23537	Kepes	Livia	1913.10.20.	Nagyatad
442	23480	Kerekes	Edit	1927.03.03.	Budapest
443	23470	Kern	Ilona	1925.02.01.	Balmazujvaros
444	23532	Kerenyi	Julia	1916.07.10.	Cegled
445	23471	Kertesz	Erzsebet	1917.06.03.	Miskolc
446	23485	Kertesz	Szabo Ilona	1904.12.04.	Hencida
447	23486	Kertesz	Kato	1925.11.02.	Hencida
448	23487	Kertesz	Magdolna	1923.09.08.	Hencida
449	23478	Keszler	Bella	1928.06.16.	Borgoprund
450	23477	Keszler	Ella	1925.01.15.	Debrecen
451	23489	Keszler	Lampel Ilona	1909.05.19.	Dombovar
452	23526	Keszler	Katalin	1926.03.08.	Miskolc
453	23527	Keszler	Fulop Magdolna	1914.12.09.	Debrecen
454	23475	Keszler	Magdolna	1923.07.05.	Debrecen
455	23525	Keszler	Treitel Magdolna	1923.07.21.	Miskolc
456	23474	Keszler	Ottilia	1926.06.26.	Debrecen
457	23476	Keszler	Rozsi	1926.11.23.	Debrecen
458	23530	Kiraly	Maria	1920.10.17.	Tapolca
459	23524	Kitaier	Spitzer Irma	1909.01.18.	Debrecen
460	23500	Klinenberg	Olga	1912.05.20.	Peterreve
461	23535	Klinger	Iren	1912.11.19.	Budapest
462	23496	Klinger	Lili	1913.01.31.	Vagsellye
463	23561	Klein	Reich Aranka	1911.07.18.	Ocsa
464	23438	Klein	Edit	1924.02.04.	Onod
465	23431	Klein	Edit	1925.05.12.	Jolsva
466	23564	Klein	Edit	1927.03.19.	
467	23430	Klein	Hofmann Ella	1923.05.24.	Jolsva

(Continued)

468	23425	Klein	Elza	1911.03.11.	Tiszacsege
469	23549	Klein	Erzsebet	1908.04.07.	Biharnagybajom
470	23433	Klein	Gabrierlla	1922.03.24.	Hajdudorog
471	23428	Klein	Rothne Hermin	1906.09.18.	Szabolcs
472	23426	Klein	Kupfersteinne Ilona	1904.08.08.	Nagyrabe
473	23422	Klein	Siegelbaumne Ilona	1903.11.01.	Miskolc
474	23435	Klein	Ilona	1925.04.19.	Miskolc
475	23441	Klein	Ilona	1927.07.27.	Tiszadada
476	23421	Klein	Iren	1921.03.19.	Hajdunanas
477	23555	Klein	Iren	1927.12.27.	Szenc
478	23552	Klein	Katalin	1919.01.21.	Debrecen
479	23548	Klein	Klara	1908.07.14.	Budapest
480	23553	Klein	Klara	1922.05.11.	Csaszartoltes
481	23442	Klein	Grunbaumne Klara	1924.01.24.	Eger
482	23432	Klein	Klara	1924.02.21.	Tiszadada
483	23558	Klein	Leonora	1926.01.08.	Győr
484	23423	Klein	Livia	1914.09.07.	Tiszacsege
485	23560	Klein	Magdolna	1920.09.15.	Karcag
486	23547	Klein	Magdolna	1921.12.10.	Nagyleta
487	23437	Klein	Magdolna	1922.03.12.	Onod
488	23424	Klein	Magdolna	1923.08.12.	Debrecen
489	23444	Klein	Magdolna	1924.11.26.	Csorna
490	23556	Klein	Magdolna	1926.06.22.	Stomfa
491	23563	Klein	Weiszne Malvin	1906.10.16.	Mezőkeresztes
492	23559	Klein	Maria	1923.05.26.	Győr
493	23550	Klein	Maria	1923.08.18.	Debrecen
494	23434	Klein	Margit	1919.11.11.	Hajdudorog
495	23436	Klein	Margit	1926.11.13.	Onod
496	23429	Klein	Marta	1926.10.09.	Budapest
497	23440	Klein	Marta	1927.07.15.	Tiszadada
498	23443	Klein	Piroska	1921.10.25.	Csorna
499	23551	Klein	Piroska	1924.10.27.	Debrecen
500	23562	Klein	Roza	1918.06.21.	Mezőkeresztes
501	23557	Klein	Roza	1927.03.20.	Csorna
502	23554	Klein	Sarolta	1921.06.07.	Hajdusamson

503	23445	Klein	Terez	1920.05.05.	Csorna
504	23439	Klein	Veronika	1927.08.28.	Onod
505	23497	Klopot	Anna	1916.01.22.	Hajduszoboszlo
506	23498	Klopot	Gitta	1923.10.31.	Hajduszoboszlo
507	23513	Klor	Erzsebet	1922.03.15.	Nagyleta
508	23512	Klor	Katalin	1923.08.16.	Nagyleta
509	23521	Kluger	Goldberger Margit	1899.10.25.	Miskolc
510	23494	Knopfler	Irma	1912.04.12.	Debrecen
511	23495	Knopfler	Heimler Zsuzsanna	1918.09.03.	Szombathely
512	23462	Kohn	Blanka	1918.07.14.	Valkhaz
513	23449	Kohn	Blanka	1920.05.31.	Pozsony
514	23456	Kohn	Cecilia	1923.08.24.	Dunaszerdahely
515	23448	Kohn	Felbermann Edit	1920.07.01.	Sopron
516	23454	Kohn	Erzsebet	1925.10.30.	Bekescsaba
517	23455	Kohn	Erzsebet	1925.10.27.	Debrecen
518	23458	Kohn	Eta	1916.06.17.	Kaposvar
519	23459	Kohn	Komlos Eva	1911.03.07.	Baja
520	23450	Kohn	Hedvig	1923.01.07.	Balassagyarmat
521	23465	Kohn	Iren	1927.03.18.	Miskolc
522	23461	Kohn	Jolan	1920.11.18.	Valkhaz
523	23460	Kohn	Julia	1923.05.05.	Sellye
524	23457	Kohn	Kato	1918.05.05.	Keleviz
525	23452	Kohn	Lenke	1924.04.25.	Bekescsaba
526	23464	Kohn	Magdolna	1926.03.03.	Miskolc
527	23446	Kohn	Margit	1909.01.08.	Mad
528	23451	Kohn	Margit	1923.02.10.	Bekescsaba
529	23447	Kohn	Leichtmann Rozsi	1909.12.21.	Debrecen
530	23453	Kohn	Szeren	1921.10.29.	Bekescsaba
531	23463	Kohn	Szeren	1922.01.07.	Sajobabony
532	23536	Kolb	Eva	1923.03.06.	Puspokladany
533	23493	Kolisch	Erzsebet	1910.09.17.	Galanta
534	23589	Kolisch	Klein Ilona	1916.01.19.	Gyongyospata
535	23499	Koranyi	Eva	1923.11.30.	Budapest
536	23515	Kornhauser	Horovitz Gizella	1917.07.29.	Ujfeherto
537	23514	Kornhauser	Hedvig	1926.02.10.	Debrecen

(Continued)

538	23528	Kostolitz	Edit	1915.08.24.	Celldomolk
539	23529	Kostolitz	Eva	1924.06.16.	Celldomolk
540	23503	Kovacs	Anna	1922.05.18.	Miskolc
541	23502	Kovacs	Klein Erzsebet	1920.03.19.	Abaujbakta
542	23506	Kovacs	Kalman Iren	1904.11.29.	Tapolca
543	23504	Kovacs	Julia	1924.03.22.	Hosszupalyi
544	23505	Kovacs	Hoffmann Magdolna	1924.04.06.	Cegled
545	23501	Kovacs	Vera	1924.08.15.	Miskolc
546	23534	Kőnig	Taub Szeren	1902.10.16.	Vargede
547	23490	Krakauer	Eszter	1925.03.15.	Tet
548	23491	Krakauer	Neuschloss Margit	1919.12.11.	Tet
549	23508	Kratz	Olga	1921.09.01.	Hajduboszormeny
550	23518	Krausz	Blanka	1921.04.08.	Szőny
551	23516	Krausz	Etel	1923.05.19.	Parad
552	23511	Krausz	Fruchter Lili	1912.10.25.	Felsőviso
553	23519	Krausz	Livia	1923.06.15.	Miskolc
554	23509	Krausz	Lowy Magdolna	1906.04.14.	Ujpest
555	23520	Krausz	Margit	1922.04.05.	Miskolc
556	23517	Krausz	Piroska	1918.09.09.	Kaposvar
557	23510	Krausz	Valeria	1906.02.17.	Gyonk
558	23472	Kreiszler	Lili	1914.01.03.	Berettyoujfalu
559	23507	Kropf	Herskovics Sari	1914.02.14.	Karad
560	23469	Kuhn	Agnes	1925.12.19.	Debrecen
561	23467	Kun	Ilona	1921.09.27.	Kisterenye
562	23468	Kun	Feld Olga	1921.10.07.	Jolsva
563	23492	Kun	Schwarz Rozalia	1900.08.28.	Eger
564	23522	Kupfer	Anna	1919.10.03.	Debrecen
565	23523	Kupfer	Rizmovics Dora	1912.11.17.	Tarackoz
566	23575	Ladanyi	Ilona	1916.01.15.	Puspokladany
567	23574	Landsmann	Cecilia	1927.05.17.	Miskolc
568	23569	Langer	Rozsa Klara	1920.04.18.	Kaposvar
569	23573	Latzer	Eva	1923.10.20.	Szombathely
570	23570	Lax	Mandel Jolan	1919.11.20.	Ozd
571	23571	Lax	Klara	1917.02.22.	Ozd
572	23572	Lax	Mandel Maria	1915.07.28.	Ozd
573	23567	Lazar	Polner Anna	1903.03.19.	Eger

574	23566	Lazar	Judit	1927.09.13.	Sarkadkeresztur
575	23568	Lazar	Julia	1925.08.22.	Papa
576	23565	Lazar	Olga	1926.07.07.	Szegi
577	23606	Leb	Piroska	1918.06.01.	Nagyvarad
578	23602	Lebovics	Ilona	1911.03.25.	Debrecen
579	23577	Lederer	Jellinek Malvin	1895.01.15.	Magocs
580	23576	Lederer	Rozsi	1918.08.15.	Oszivac
581	23601	Lefkovics	Lili	1926.02.05.	Miskolc
582	23578	Lemberger	Klara	1920.01.15.	Mezőkovesd
583	23607	Lencz	Gottessmann Szeren	1900.08.28.	Polocz
584	23608	Lezer	Schreiber Rozsi	1923.06.08.	Kassa
585	23600	Lichtner	Hedvig	1916.02.29.	Galanta
586	23599	Lichtner	Bruck Terez	1919.04.08.	Galanta
587	23598	Liszauer	Julia	1925.02.19.	Tornalja
588	23605	Lok	Ilona	1922.06.17.	Bagamer
589	23604	Lok	Margit	1926.06.21.	Bagamer
590	23603	Lovasi	Gelberger Magdolna	1925.08.24.	Vamospercs
591	23597	Lobl	Judit	1928.01.26.	Szekszard
592	23596	Loffler	Baum Edit	1922.02.10.	Ersekujvar
593	23593	Loffler	Eszter	1925.08.15.	Ersekujvar
594	23595	Loffler	Judit	1923.05.24.	Ersekujvar
595	23591	Loffler	Lili	1922.07.14.	Ersekujvar
596	23592	Loffler	Maritta	1926.09.18.	Ersekujvar
597	23594	Loffler	Mira	1924.06.18.	Ersekujvar
598	23590	Lowensohn	Spielmann Katarina	1905.08.05.	Kőszegpaty
599	23588	Lowenstein	Sarolta	1925.07.06.	Beled
600	23587	Lowinger	Iren	1926.02.28.	Vagfarkasd
601	23586	Lowinger	Lili	1927.11.26.	Vagfarkasd
602	23579	Lowinger	Margit	1917.06.13.	Galanta
603	23581	Lowy	Korvai Ella	1906.06.07.	Miskolc
604	23584	Lowy	Almasi Etelka	1922.01.03.	Cegled
605	23582	Lowy	Ibolya	1922.01.17.	Miskolc
606	23580	Lowy	Jolan	1920.03.30.	Miskolc
607	23583	Lowy	Fried Klara	1914.12.20.	Csenyete
608	23585	Lowy	Varadi Magdolna	1910.01.01.	Alsokubin

(Continued)

609	23609	Lukacs	Reisz Ilona	1918.06.23.	Balassagyarmat
610	23610	Lukacs	Judit	1923.01.05.	Szombathely
611	23628	Maly	Hoffer Franciska	1897.06.19.	Budapest
612	23625	Mandel	Anna	1923.02.28.	Debrecen
613	23626	Mandel	Erzsebet	1924.09.24.	Debrecen
614	23621	Mandelbaum	Erzsebet	1923.01.14.	Berettyoujfalu
615	23622	Mandelbaum	Eva	1924.12.12.	Berettyoujfalu
616	23623	Mandelbaum	Ilona	1919.11.03.	Berettyoujfalu
617	23624	Mandelbaum	Magdolna	1921.08.29.	Berettyoujfalu
618	23619	Mandler	Zobel Judit	1908.02.04.	Ersekujvar
619	23620	Mandler	Hoffmann Rozsa	1910.10.08.	Ersekujvar
620	23612	Mannheim	Neuhaus Magdolna	1917.07.16.	Torokbecse
621	23618	Markovits	Erzsebet	1924.06.19.	Tallya
622	23627	Markovits	Magdolna	1915.10.29.	Miskolc
623	23611	Markus	Ilona	1922.08.11.	Harsany
624	23757	Markus	Sugar Magdolna	1920.05.07.	Budapest
625	23615	Marmor	Erzsebet	1921.08.04.	Tornalja
626	23614	Marmor	Sarolta	1920.01.21.	Tornalja
627	23613	Marton	Lili	1911.04.04.	Tapolca
628	23617	Matyas	Kato	1922.12.21.	Debrecen
629	23616	Max	Blanka	1903.03.14.	Sopron
630	23631	Mendelevics	Ilona	1927.02.16.	Harsany
631	23630	Mermelstein	Trankovics Blanka	1925.06.03.	Egerag
632	23629	Mermelstein	Rozsi	1924.06.29.	Debrecen
633	23632	Meszaros	Kiraly Zsuzsanna	1919.10.04.	Pecs
634	23636	Mindszenti	Marmorstein Rozsi	1910.08.25.	Szatmarnemeti
635	23635	Molnar	Ilona	1911.06.10.	Tarcal
636	23633	Moser	Groszfeld Szilvia	1896.03.17.	Gyulahaza
637	23634	Mozes	Marta	1926.07.14.	Debrecen
638	23641	Muller	Lina	1923.01.19.	Tarackoz
639	23639	Muller	Edit	1925.12.20.	Miskolc
640	23643	Muller	Erna	1925.01.23.	Galanta
641	23638	Muller	Ibolya	1924.05.19.	Miskolc
642	23642	Muller	Klara	1925.12.17.	Alsoszeli

643	23637	Munster	Singer Magdolna	1919.04.30.	Baja
644	23640	Muller	Magdolna	1926.06.10.	Miskolc
645	23646	Nagel	Hermin	1905.03.20.	Szadalmas
646	23647	Nagel	Margit	1906.09.05.	Pelyvas
647	23645	Nagy	Gartner Ilona	1920.02.13.	Diosgyőr
648	23644	Nagy	Lili	1914.09.13.	Budapest
649	23659	Nebenzahl	Eva	1924.07.05.	Hajdusamson
650	23660	Nenicska	Weisz Izabella	1900.10.16.	Tiszaszederkeny
651	23661	Nenicska	Magdolna	1924.01.11.	Miskolc
652	23648	Neufeld	Zsuzsanna	1923.07.05.	Szabadka
653	23652	Neubart	Katalin	1923.09.11.	Puspokladany
654	23651	Neuhaus	Iren	1920.01.19.	Nagyfodemes
655	23650	Neuhaus	Margit	1924.11.02.	Saly
656	23654	Neumann	Edit	1923.08.03.	
657	23653	Neumann	Erzsebet	1912.06.25.	Debrecen
658	23655	Neumann	Iren	1908.10.19.	Palfa
659	23649	Neuschloss	Hermina	1918.07.19.	Paks
660	23657	Neuwalder	Eva	1926.11.04.	Miskolc
661	23656	Neuwalder	Magdolna	1925.07.16.	Miskolc
662	23658	Nothi	Goldstein Anna	1914.04.03.	Tiszaszentmarton
663	23662	Nyitrai	Berkovics Erzsebet	1905.12.21.	Kunszentmarton
664	23663	Nyitrai	Kohn Klari	1904.08.18.	Szekesfehervar
665	23664	Oberlander	Weisz Magda	1916.07.29.	Miskolc
666	23666	Ohrenstein	Sugar Jolan	1915.05.31.	Kolozsvar
667	23665	Ohlbaum	Terka	1923.10.16.	Puspokladany
668	23669	Pal	Anna	1924.03.19.	Budapest
669	23668	Pal	Hartmann Ella	1907.10.28.	Cegled
670	23667	Partos	Steiner Margit	1916.09.10.	Szeged
671	23670	Pauner	Richter Eva	1922.09.16.	Kaposvar
672	23672	Perl	Erzsebet	1923.09.04.	Maramarossziget
673	23671	Perl	Schwarz Grete	1910.07.05.	Pozsony
674	23673	Perlstein	Magda	1922.06.11.	Miskolc
675	23685	Peter	Balazs Anna	1914.02.08.	Poroszlo
676	23698	Peter	Eva	1927.02.20.	Budapest
677	23686	Peter	Magdolna	1927.11.07.	Abafalva
678	23692	Pfeffer	Friedmann Aranka	1914.01.04.	Pusztaradvany

(Continued)

679	23688	Pick	Klara	1919.08.31.	Szabadka
680	23687	Pick	Reich Margit	1920.06.21.	Szabadka
681	23695	Platzer	Walder Anna	1902.03.16.	
682	23696	Platzer	Schnitzer Iren	1920.08.20.	Puspokladany
683	23682	Polacsek	Terez	1917.02.08.	Debrecen
684	23680	Pollak	Blum Bozsi	1913.11.09.	Debrecen
685	23679	Pollak	Francsics Lujza	1903.06.20.	Kőszeg
686	23681	Pollak	Goldstein Margit	1908.02.13.	Debrecen
687	23689	Politzer	Lanc Aranka	1905.07.04.	Miskolc
688	23683	Popper	Edit	1924.02.28.	Kecskemet
689	23684	Popper	Weiner Hilda	1910.10.06.	Nogradpatak
690	23690	Potok	Edit	1927.06.10.	Balassagyarmat
691	23691	Potok	Iren	1928.05.06.	Balassagyarmat
692	23697	Prager	Spitz Erzsebet	1909.04.07.	Derecske
693	23676	Preisz	Aliz	1922.09.16.	Miskolc
694	23674	Preisz	Edit	1925.06.08.	Miskolc
695	23675	Preisz	Iren	1921.01.27.	Miskolc
696	23677	Preisz	Judit	1924.03.12.	Miskolc
697	23678	Preisz	Olga	1926.06.16.	Miskolc
698	23693	Princz	Justitz Ilona	1908.07.12.	Miskolc
699	23694	Princz	Spielmann Janka	1909.03.22.	Budapest
700	23702	Racz	Iren	1908.10.16.	Miskolc
701	23701	Rauchwerger	Sarkadi Erzsebet	1904.11.28.	Nagyleta
702	23710	Rechnitzer	Weinberger Gizella	1902.08.06.	Zalaegerszeg
703	23716	Rechnitzer	Irma	1904.10.15.	Tapolca
704	23708	Rehberger	Lea	1927.03.03.	Győr
705	23711	Reich	Gardos Judit	1923.09.11.	Debrecen
706	23712	Reich	Balkany Rozsi	1906.05.01.	Satoraljaujhely
707	23709	Reimann	Kertesz Judit	1924.05.14.	Kaposvar
708	23700	Reiner	Marosi Ibolya	1917.07.04.	Budapest
709	23699	Reiner	Valeria	1898.08.12.	Feltot
710	23704	Reinherz	Berta	1924.09.04.	Zsolna
711	23705	Reinherz	Zita	1921.03.21.	Okormező
712	23713	Reinitz	Gizella	1912.10.13.	Forro-Encs
713	23714	Reinitz	Magdolna	1927.07.19.	Miskolc
714	23706	Reisinger	Schreiber Ella	1906.06.08.	Kapuvar
715	23749	Reisinger	Remenyi Ibolya	1916.09.14.	Szilagycseh

716	23707	Reisinger	Nora	1922.03.31.	Becs
717	23715	Retek	Ibolya	1926.11.21.	Miskolc
718	23745	Reti	Hermann Rozsi	1909.02.08.	Mezőtur
719	23748	Riesz	Grunberg Olga	1896.01.31.	Miskolc
720	23719	Ripp	Spitzer Frieda	1912.09.18.	Kemenessomjen
721	23721	Ripp	Muller Olga	1907.08.28.	Nagykikinda
722	23747	Ritscher	Hirsch Piroska	1900.08.01.	Tapolca
723	23717	Robert	Lang Anna	1919.09.14.	Papa
724	23725	Rosenbaum	Federer Margit	1899.10.09.	Janoshaza
725	23737	Rosenberg	Erzseber	1912.03.26.	Kunhegyes
726	23733	Rosenberg	Katalin	1924.07.13.	Miskolc
727	23720	Rosenberg	Lili	1925.12.06.	Ozd
728	23734	Rosenberg	Muller Roza	1899.12.25.	Diosgyőr
729	23724	Rosenberger	Ilona	1925.01.28.	Tapiobicske
730	23735	Rosenberger	Krausz Jolan	1912.09.12.	Lenti
731	23736	Rosenberger	Margit	1909.02.18.	Igal
732	23739	Rosenfeld	Anna	1916.10.01.	Debrecen
733	23728	Rosenfeld	Eva	1925.11.02.	Becs
734	23731	Rosenfeld	Iren	1924.12.04.	Kaba
735	23730	Rosenfeld	Judit	1926.06.28.	Győr
736	23732	Rosenfeld	Magdolna	1923.03.26.	Debrecen
737	23729	Rosenfeld	Loffler Rozsi	1905.12.22.	
738	23726	Rosenheim	Klara	1926.01.15.	Nagykanizsa
739	23746	Rosenstein	Erzsebet	1911.07.24.	Tuzser
740	23738	Rosenthal	Weisz Margit	1900.10.25.	Miskolc
741	23727	Rosenwasser	Rozsi	1923.09.15.	Nagyrakos
742	23722	Rosenzweig	Lili	1917.08.10.	Szabadka
743	23723	Rosenzweig	Weisz Margit	1906.09.01.	Nyircsavoly
744	23740	Rosmann	Edit	1922.08.27.	Miskolc
745	23753	Roth	Emma	1914.10.01.	Artand
746	23754	Roth	Klara	1913.05.19.	Kecskemet
747	23718	Roth	Rosenfeld Rozsi	1902.09.05.	Paks
748	23703	Rothschild	Judit	1925.04.14.	Sumeg
749	23743	Rozsa	Edit	1927.12.18.	Galanta
750	23744	Rozsa	Szidonia	1921.05.19.	Pincehely
751	23742	Rozsahegyi	Ilona	1926.09.08.	Debrecen
752	23741	Rozsahegyi	Magdolna	1927.11.28.	Debrecen
753	23755	Rubinstein	Sara	1922.02.17.	Maramarossziget

(Continued)

754	23751	Rude	Dora	1914.05.20.	Rozsnyo
755	23750	Rude	Elza	1916.06.02.	Maramarossziget
756	23752	Russ	Zsuzsanna	1923.07.01.	Ersekujvar
757	23850	Stein	Abraham Roza	1910.02.23.	Oszivac
758	23852	Stein	Szidonia	1926.02.26.	
759	23851	Stein	Vera	1923.03.21.	Ersekujvar
760	23880	Steinberger	Vera	1921.03.21.	Tolna
761	23887	Steiner	Dora	1915.10.10.	Koka
762	23885	Steiner	Erzsebet	1911.08.14.	Szombathely
763	23889	Steiner	Katarina	1924.02.12.	Parad
764	23886	Steiner	Magda	1925.10.09.	Ersekujvar
765	23888	Steiner	Szabo Margit	1914.04.03.	Budapest
766	23910	Steinfeld	Jasz Borbala	1902.10.10.	Zolyom
767	23909	Steinfeld	Erzsebet	1921.06.13.	Cegled
768	23840	Stern	Lowy Boske	1902.08.24.	Nagyteteny
769	23838	Stern	Ella	1918.11.18.	Dombovar
770	23848	Stern	Klein Erzsebet	1908.12.12.	Eger
771	23836	Stern	Scwartz Eva	1922.07.24.	Kassa
772	23839	Stern	Berta	1926.03.28.	Nemeskosut
773	23844	Stern	Eisler Ibolya	1917.08.25.	Mezőkovesd
774	23843	Stern	Magdolna	1919.05.29.	Mezőkovesd
775	23837	Stern	Lebkovics Maria	1923.07.01.	Miskolc
776	23849	Stern	Landler Irma	1902.03.14.	Nagyszakacsi
777	23847	Stern	Lenke	1925.10.20.	Szombathely
778	23841	Stern	Sari	1926.10.27.	Beled
779	23842	Stern	Wertheimer Borcsa	1915.03.19.	Mezőkovesd
780	23845	Stern	Bruck Valeria	1903.03.24.	Felsőoszko
781	23846	Stern	Zsuzsanna	1925.02.09.	Szombathely
782	23834	Strausz	Weisz Borbala	1908.10.21.	Torokszentmiklos
783	23832	Strausz	Eva	1922.02.15.	Pozsony
784	23833	Strausz	Lea	1923.12.15.	Pozsony
785	23835	Strausz	Lenke	1914.11.14.	Hőgyesz
786	23884	Strauszmann	Ilona	1924.03.16.	Debrecen
787	23882	Strauszmann	Katalin	1922.10.11.	Debrecen
788	23883	Strauszmann	Magdolna	1925.11.06.	Debrecen
789	23878	Struch	Hamburger Eleonora	1906.10.23.	Alsopahok

790	23822	Safrany	Friedlander Hedvig	1921.10.22.	Miskolc
791	23821	Safrany	Steiner Maria	1919.03.28.	Kispest
792	23820	Safrany	Rozsi	1914.09.01.	Miskolc
793	23756	Saphir	Katalin	1923.10.09.	Tarcal
794	23759	Sauber	Amalia	1917.12.20.	Sztropko
795	23913	Sauber	Romer Helen	1912.03.17.	
796	23758	Sauber	Rozsi	1915.05.16.	Sztropko
797	23908	Seidler	Eszter	1927.04.02.	Pozsony
798	23881	Siklosi	Fleischer Sari	1914.04.15.	Szekszard
799	23867	Silber	Schwartz Margit	1903.08.24.	
800	23868	Silberer	Rozsa	1923.05.18.	Debrecen
801	23873	Silberstein	Weisz Lujza	1912.05.14.	Ujvidek
802	23760	Simon	Anna	1925.07.29.	Szekesfehervar
803	23855	Singer	Schiller Erzsebet	1926.05.10.	Pincehely
804	23857	Singer	Bauer Etelka	1909.10.18.	Peterreve
805	23858	Singer	Ilona	1906.11.11.	Vagfarkasd
806	23854	Singer	Haas Jolan	1903.09.23.	Zalaegerszeg
807	23856	Singer	Klara	1911.08.12.	Munkacs
808	23853	Singer	Lili	1928.05.01.	Csaktornya
809	23859	Singer	Rozsa	1918.11.19.	Mezőcsokonya
810	23870	Sipos	Brett Anna	1911.12.30.	Kecskemet
811	23871	Sipos	Vera	1924.05.12.	Debrecen
812	23872	Sipos	Vadas Zsuzsanna	1921.08.14.	Debrecen
813	23875	Solti	Eva	1923.10.18.	Szolnok
814	23874	Solti	Livia	1921.01.02.	Szolnok
815	23784	Sommer	Eva	1926.07.14.	Szekszard
816	23999	Sommer	Szeren	1918.11.16.	Galanta
817	23783	Sonnenberg	Julia	1926.08.29	Szabadka
818	23775	Spiegel	Laszlo Marianna	1919.05.17.	Budapest
819	23776	Spielmann	Grosz Ella	1918.08.07.	Gyulakeszi
820	23865	Spitzer	Hajnal	1927.05.04.	Miskolc
821	23864	Spitzer	Kaufmann Judit	1905.04.06.	Szabadka
822	23866	Spitzer	Margit	1920.08.03.	Magyaratad
823	23863	Spitzer	Eisenberger Margit	1913.03.20.	Ujfeherto
824	23860	Spitzer	Margit	1916.01.01.	Miskolc
825	23862	Spitzer	Klein Maria	1907.07.12.	Debrecen

(Continued)

826	23861	Spitzer	Sarolta	1907.10.18.	Debrecen
827	23869	Sugar	Neumann Roza	1914.11.	Debrecen
828	23768	Sved	Maniner Julia	1912.01.12.	Hajduboszormeny
829	23830	Szabadi	Magdolna	1918.09.30.	Cegled
830	23831	Szalai	Sara	1924.07.05.	Pecs
831	23898	Szandel	Gitta	1914.06.29.	Tiszabogdany
832	23892	Szasz	Szilagyi Aranka	1903.04.28.	Kalocsa
833	23891	Szasz	Vielwahr Margit	1911.01.30.	Sumeg
834	23251	Szatmari	Ilona	1919.01.17.	Losoncapatfalva
835	23765	Szedő	Magda	1925.07.25.	Szarvas
836	23879	Szekely	Maria	1922.01.07.	Budapest
837	23911	Szemere	Kraj Anna	1909.12.10.	Megyaszo
838	23762	Szofer	Olga	1927.02.09.	Zenta
839	23761	Szofer	Terez	1920.05.24.	Tet
840	23763	Szőlősi	Rosenzweig Kato	1914.10.10.	Szabadka
841	23769	Schaffer	Eckstein Eta	1916.04.17.	Debrecen
842	23771	Schaffer	Klara	1926.06.16.	Szabadka
843	23770	Schaffer	Singer Viktoria	1906.08.03.	Peterreve
844	23890	Scheer	Edit	1919.12.16.	Szeged
845	23907	Scheiber	Lenke	1913.10.19.	Kemenesmagasi
846	23899	Schiller	Back Lili	1910.04.09.	Nyitra
847	23772	Schillinger	Eva	1923.09.13.	Szeged
848	23766	Schlesinger	Grumberger Ilona	1913.09.12.	Celldomolk
849	23767	Schlesinger	Zsuzsanna	1922.07.09.	Kecskemet
850	23773	Schliesser	Klar Piroska	1915.05.01.	Hajdudorog
851	23827	Schlussler	Mezei Rozsi	1905.03.30.	Marosvasarhely
852	23829	Schnitzler	Margit	1896.03.03.	Abadszalok
853	23912	Schochmann	Maria	1925.08.20.	Nagycsongova
854	23897	Schon	Rosenbaum Berta	1914.03.03.	Debrecen
855	23896	Schon	Erzsebet	1914.01.02.	Debrecen
856	23894	Schon	Lefkovics Ilona	1910.07.16.	Debrecen
857	23893	Schon	Magda	1914.05.10.	Kaposvar
858	23895	Schon	Margit	1916.01.24.	Miskolc
859	23826	Schonbaum	Frida	1920.05.12.	Vagvecse
860	23824	Schonbaum	Margit	1905.06.17.	Vagvecse
861	23823	Schonbaum	Rozsi	1915.03.18.	Vagvecse

862	23825	Schonbaum	Zsuzsanna	1925.08.11.	Vagvecse
863	23777	Schonberger	Magda	1924.08.30.	Miskolc
864	23900	Schonberger	Noemi	1922.09.23.	Szeged
865	23774	Schontag	Lukacs Kamilla	1905.12.31.	Szombathely
866	23901	Schreiber	Adrienne	1922.03.08.	Hejőcsaba
867	23905	Schreiber	Blanka	1917.03.01.	Jolsva
868	23904	Schreiber	Edit	1920.09.23.	Jolsva
869	23906	Schreiber	Erzsebet	1915.02.14.	Jolsva
870	23903	Schreiber	Hajnal	1915.10.18.	Ungvar
871	23902	Schreiber	Rozsi	1920.10.22.	Hejőcsaba
872	23780	Schultz	Etel	1912.10.24.	Galanta
873	23782	Schultz	Hilda	1926.06.17.	Galanta
874	23779	Schultz	Magda	1926.10.29.	Tornalja
875	23778	Schultz	Sara	1924.01.09.	Tornalja
876	23781	Schultz	Sari	1912.10.20.	Galanta
877	23828	Schwalb	Eva	1926.06.29.	Eger
878	23877	Schwalb	Fanni	1923.06.24.	Kunhegyes
879	23876	Schwalb	Gizella	1924.06.24.	Kunhegyes
880	23789	Schwartz	Aranka	1925.07.24.	Szentistvan
881	23788	Schwartz	Borbala	1923.10.23.	Szentistvan
882	23816	Schwartz	Strikker Eliza	1912.11.09.	Szombathely
883	23806	Schwartz	Erzsebet	1917.01.15.	Debrecen
884	23791	Schwartz	Erzsebet	1921.05.05.	Tornalja
885	23797	Schwartz	Erzsebet	1921.10.01.	Deaki
886	23798	Schwartz	Ezsebet	1925.01.05.	Nyitraujlak
887	23814	Schwartz	Eva	1925.06.22.	Foldes
888	23794	Schwartz	Eva	1926.05.22.	Pecel
889	23800	Scnwartz	Helen	1906.05.06.	Kisdobsza
890	23805	Schwartz	Ilona	1909.01.26.	Nyirbokony
891	23793	Schwartz	Ilona	1916.05.11.	Debrecen
892	23809	Schwartz	Julianna	1922.03.23.	Miskolc
893	23817	Schwartz	Klara	1926.12.26.	Szekszard
894	23795	Schwartz	Livia	1927.09.29.	Kecskemet
895	23785	Schwartz	Klein Margit	1902.02.17.	Tiszadada
896	23813	Schwartz	Margit	1922.06.25.	Szarvas
897	23792	Schwartz	Margit	1923.04.16.	Tornalja
898	23811	Schwartz	Maria	1904.02.16.	Diosgyőr
899	23787	Schwartz	Marta	1926.11.20.	Miskolc

(Continued)

900	23808	Schwartz	Klein Olga	1920.05.05.	Debrecen
901	23801	Schwartz	Rozsi	1903.05.24.	Diosgyőr
902	23812	Schwartz	Rozsi	1905.08.19.	Abrany
903	23786	Schwartz	Rozsi	1916.08.31.	Miskolc
904	23807	Schwartz	Rozsi	1918.01.30.	Debrecen
905	23796	Schwartz	Rozsi	1922.05.01.	Tecső
906	23804	Schwartz	Jozsef Sari	1907.11.12.	
907	23810	Schwartz	Sarolta	1919.10.09.	Putnok
908	23802	Schwartz	Sarolta	1921.01.02.	
909	23799	Schwartz	Valeria	1926.03.16.	Nyitraujlak
910	23790	Schwarz	Berta	1901.12.09.	Nagyleta
911	23815	Schwarz	Weisz Klara	1916.03.24.	Szekszard
912	23803	Schwarz	Gluck Rozsi	1914.09.05.	Tarna
913	23818	Schwartzenfeld	Weisz Maria	1900.01.15.	Diosgyőr
914	23819	Schwartzkopf	Eva	1925.10.28.	Debrecen
915	23916	Tichler	Erzsebet	1919.12.16.	Ersekujvar
916	23190	Trankovics	Ibolya	1925.10.02.	Pecs
917	23914	Tuppler	Gottlieb Erzsebet	1904.08.10.	Satoraljaujhely
918	23915	Tuppler	Zsuzsanna	1922.09.25.	Ungvar
919	23917	Ungar	Schonberger Erzsebet	1905.06.22.	Fertőszentmiklos
920	23918	Unger	Berta	1926.08.29.	Kapuvar
921	23919	Ungerleider	Kovacs Elza	1909.05.15.	Debrecen
922	23985	Vajda	Lőbl Ada	1920.08.15.	Selmecbanya
923	23995	Vass	Schon Rozsi	1910.07.07.	Nyiregyhaza
924	23994	Veszpremi	Etelka	1896.12.09.	Győr
925	23992	Vilmos	Frischmann Zsuzsanna	1922.01.21.	Miskolc
926	23991	Virag	Breslauer Livia	1919.11.05.	Szabadka
927	23990	Vogel	Cecilia	1917.09.10.	Szolyva
928	23988	Vogel	Blobstein Fanni	1914.08.29.	Tornalja
929	23989	Vogel	Maria	1917.09.10.	Szolyva
930	23959	Wachs	Helen	1927.03.16.	Felsővizso
931	23960	Wachs	Pick Maria	1900.03.05.	Abony
932	23976	Wachs	Terez	1912.07.10.	Cegled
933	23963	Wahl	Eisler Maria	1907.03.15.	Csepreg
934	23964	Wahl	Roth Rozalia	1922.11.08.	Szatmarnemeti
935	23981	Walder	Ilona	1905.12.01.	Somogyszil

936	23978	Walfisch	Klara	1916.05.30.	Szarvas
937	23979	Wachter	Ibolya	1925.11.07.	Mezőnagymihaly
938	23987	Weichselbaum	Edit	1925.02.07.	Miskolc
939	23952	Weinberger	Lowingen Agnes	1922.12.09.	Miskolc
940	23951	Weinberger	Malvin	1922.11.13.	Miskolc
941	23953	Weinberger	Margit	1921.11.28.	Miskolc
942	23974	Weissenstein	Erzsebet	1904.02.10.	Felsőabrany
943	23975	Weissenstein	Iren	1902.03.16.	Felsőabrany
944	23933	Weisz	Berger Anna	1920.10.20.	Pozsony
945	23938	Weisz	Adel	1916.09.16.	Debrecen
946	23993	Weisz	Bella	1922.02.18.	Galanta
947	23926	Weisz	Edit	1922.03.22.	Ersekujvar
948	23929	Weisz	Edit	1926.08.04.	Eger
949	23936	Weisz	Ella	1914.09.18.	Kunhegyes
950	23932	Weisz	Ella	1921.06.20.	Kanyahaza
951	23928	Weisz	Elza	1923.11.04.	Borogszasz
952	23931	Weisz	Klein Erzsebet	1912.11.25.	Miskolc
953	23949	Weisz	Kostelitz Eszter	1907.10.10.	Bonyhad
954	23935	Weisz	Eszter	1922.05.31.	Debrecen
955	23945	Weisz	Eva	1921.03.12.	Vagsellye
956	23940	Weisz	Eva	1923.07.18.	Derecske
957	23946	Weisz	Kato	1923.12.06.	Debrecen
958	23941	Weisz	Gluck Lili	1918.05.28.	Dombovar
959	23920	Weisz	Schwartz Lujza	1908.10.01.	Sajoszentpeter
960	23948	Weisz	Magdolna	1920.12.25.	Kisujszallas
961	23939	Weisz	Magdolna	1923.03.15.	Derecske
962	23923	Weisz	Margit	1912.12.06.	Onod
963	23924	Weisz	Margit	1919.04.01.	Mikepercs
964	23930	Weisz	Margit	1920.05.17.	Jolsva
965	23921	Weisz	Margit	1922.01.22.	Debrecen
966	23937	Weisz	Klein Maria	1901.12.07.	Torna
967	23925	Weisz	Maria	1915.11.09.	Budapest
968	23927	Weisz	Maria	1922.05.03.	Beregszasz
969	23944	Weisz	Maria	1927.01.07.	Galanta
970	23942	Weisz	Pollak Matild	1900.05.16.	Ocsod
971	23947	Weisz	Schwartz Rozsi	1905.05.29.	Gyoma
972	23950	Weisz	Sari	1917.09.23.	Pozsony
973	23922	Weisz	Szeren	1909.07.21.	Onod

(Continued)

974	23943	Weisz	Vera	1926.06.04.	Nyitra
975	23968	Weiszberger	Elza	1922.05.02.	Miskolc
976	23969	Weiszberger	Eta	1924.02.19.	Meszes
977	23934	Weisz	Halasz Reich Erzsebet	1908.10.29.	Pecs
978	23982	Weitzenfeld	Terez	1917.05.15.	Miskolc
979	23954	Weltlinger	Erzsebet	1925.07.28.	Egyhazasradoc
980	23955	Weltlinger	Magdolna	1923.12.29.	Egyhazasradoc
981	23983	Wertheimer	Margit	1917.05.08.	Hajdusamson
982	23980	Wichter	Rozsi	1925.10.03.	Csorna
983	23958	Wieder	Edit	1930.03.27.	Debrecen
984	23957	Wieder	Ibolya	1929.01.15.	Debrecen
985	23956	Wieder	Iren	1924.03.04.	Felsőzsolca
986	23962	Wiener	Edit	1924.05.18.	Tiszacsege
987	23961	Wiener	Pollak Grete	1916.03.20.	Tiszacsege
988	23984	Wiesel	Maria	1922.09.01.	Miskolc
989	23977	Wiesner	Gizella	1920.05.17.	Teglas
990	23967	Wilhelm	Edit	1926.12.21.	Szombathely
991	23965	Wilhelm	Margit	1914.08.30.	Szombathely
992	23966	Wilhelm	Rozsi	1920.05.03.	Szombathely
993	23970	Winkler	Ilona	1913.06.20.	Sopron
994	23971	Winkler	Katalin	1919.08.27.	Szombathely
995	23986	Wohlfeiler	Erzsebet	1929.04.16.	Szepesvaralja
996	23972	Wollstein	Eva	1925.01.26.	Beled
997	23973	Wollstein	Valeria	1926.02.18.	Beled
998	23764	Zafern	Sarolta	1926.08.21.	Nagykaroly
999	23997	Zollner	Heimler Eszter	1902.01.24.	Csanig
1000	23998	Zollschan	Margit	1910.08.04.	Volcsej